Reinterpreting
social
democracy

MANCHESTER
1824

Manchester University Press

Critical Labour Movement Studies
Series editors
John Callaghan
Steve Fielding
Steve Ludlam

Already published in the series

John Callaghan, Steven Fielding and Steve Ludlam (eds), *Interpreting the Labour Party: approaches to Labour politics and history*

Dianne Hayter, *Labour's traditional right in the 1970s and 1980s*

Reinterpreting social democracy

A history of stability in the British Labour Party and Swedish Social Democratic Party

Jonas Hinnfors

Manchester University Press

Manchester and New York

distributed exclusively in the USA by Palgrave

Published by Manchester University Press
Oxford Road, Manchester M13 9NR, UK
and Room 400, 175 Fifth Avenue, New York, NY 10010, USA
www.manchesteruniversitypress.co.uk

Distributed exclusively in the USA by
Palgrave, 175 Fifth Avenue, New York,
NY 10010, USA

Distributed exclusively in Canada by
UBC Press, University of British Columbia, 2029 West Mall,
Vancouver, BC, Canada V6T 1Z2

British Library Cataloguing-in-Publication Data
A catalogue record for this book is available from the British Library

Library of Congress Cataloging-in-Publication Data applied for

ISBN   0 7190 7362 6 *hardback*
EAN   978 0 7190 7362 5

First published 2006

15 14 13 12 11 10 09 08 07 06   10 9 8 7 6 5 4 3 2 1

Typeset
by Northern Phototypesetting Co. Ltd., Bolton, Lancs.
Printed in Great Britain
by CPI, Bath

To James Cronin with
best wishes from the author

Contents

Series editors' foreword

The start of the twenty-first century is superficially an inauspicious time to study labour movements. Political parties once associated with the working class have seemingly embraced capitalism. The trade unions with which these parties were once linked have suffered near-fatal reverses. The industrial proletariat looks both divided and in rapid decline. The development of multi-level governance, prompted by 'globalisation' has furthermore apparently destroyed the institutional context for advancing the labour 'interest'. Many consequently now look on terms such as 'the working class', 'socialism' and the 'labour movement' as politically and historically redundant.

The purpose of this series is to give a platform to those students of labour movements who challenge, or develop, established ways of thinking and so demonstrate the continued vitality of the subject and the work of those interested in it. For despite appearances, many social democratic parties remain important competitors for national office and proffer distinctive programmes. Unions still impede the free flow of 'market forces'. If workers are a more diverse body and have exchanged blue collars for white, insecurity remains an everyday problem. The new institutional and global context is moreover as much of an opportunity as a threat. Yet, it cannot be doubted that compared with the immediate post-1945 period, at the beginning of the new millennium, what many still refer to as the 'labour movement' is much less influential. Whether this should be considered a time of retreat or reconfiguration is unclear – and a question the series aims to clarify.

The series will not only give a voice to studies of particular national bodies but will also promote comparative works that contrast experiences across time and geography. This entails taking due account of the political, economic and cultural settings in which labour movements have operated. In particular this involves taking the past seriously as a way of understanding the present as well as utilising sympathetic approaches drawn from sociology, economics and elsewhere.

John Callaghan
Steve Fielding
Steve Ludlam

List of boxes and tables

Boxes

Tables

Preface and acknowledgements

Much as the New Labour Party, I sometimes wish my academic life was all about entirely novel and creative things. In the end it seems I am drawn back to what my research always tried to accomplish: Some sort of understanding of political parties' ideological life. This book is no exception, but its focus is new, after all. The idea of comparing the Swedish Social Democratic Party and the Labour Party has been in the back of my mind far too long. When I finally got on with it I enjoyed every bit of the work. It was originally inspired by my old PhD supervisor, Bo Särlvik. His untimely death some years ago was a great loss and I should have liked to have his sharp and insightful comments. At least I have been fortunate to have access to Bo's excellent collection of works on British politics, now in the Political Science Department at the Gothenburg University.

The work took me on several trips to the Politics Department at the University of Stirling, Scotland. My talks there with Eric Shaw on social democracy have been extremely useful for this book. Behind the piles of paper, greenery, tea mugs etc. in his office there is also an astonishing amount of data on the Labour Party, which proved very helpful to me. Graham Timmins, Head of Department, has contributed with invaluable help by inviting me as guest lecturer to the Department on very generous terms. The hospitality Eric and his wife Sue, Graham and his wife Sabine have shown me is overwhelming. You are true friends! I am also very grateful to the rest of the staff at the Politics Department who really have done everything to make my visits there wonderful experiences.

In the Gothenburg University Political Science Department I am lucky to have a host of talented colleagues. Together they contribute to a truly creative academic atmosphere, which I am proud of being part of. Special thanks to Lennart J. Lundqvist who always encourages me, to Marie Demker, whose down-to-earth hard work is an example I have tried (often in vain) to follow, and to Ulf Bjereld who is not only a wonderful friend, but on top of all his academic merits provides me with all the gossip I need.

I also want to thank Jon Pierre for his generosity when he, in a disturbingly distant past, let me do my own thing in our, until then, joint research project, to which the last stone is now put through this book. The first part of the project was generously sponsored by the Bank of Sweden Tercentenary Foundation.

Much later, at a Stockholm conference on the future of the labour movement, I was encouraged by Stefan Berger, Glamorgan University, Wales, to consider a publisher. I am very indebted to him and, subsequently, to the professional approach to their work shown by the Manchester University Press staff.

Towards the end, Ed Page, now at Birmingham University, gave me wise advice on language style. Thanks a lot Ed, I have tried to cut down the metaphors by at least 90 per cent.

Gunilla, Siri and Maj have lovingly accepted my occasional ramblings to the other side of the North Sea. I can't promise they are completely over but at least this book project is now finished.

Gothenburg

Part I
Foundations

1

A challenge

Unless we ourselves take a hand now, they'll foist a republic on us. If we want things to stay as they are, things will have to change. D'you understand? (Giuseppe di Lampedusa, *The Leopard*)

Social democracy at the crossroads?

It appears to be common knowledge, that the combined effects of globalising world capitalism and a sudden availability of new economic ideas have made twenty-first-century social democracy abandon its central tenets in favour of neoliberalism. Purportedly, even some of the most traditionalist members of the social democratic *famille spirituelle*, the British Labour Party and the Swedish Social Democratic Party (SAP) have succumbed to the new ideas. According to this view, 'neoliberalism continues apace . . . despite so-called social democratic parties being in power'[1] (McGann Blyth 1999: Chapter 11). The new views on the economy are not necessarily loved by the social democrats. However, according to Jonathon Moses (1995a: 422): 'As exchange controls have become increasingly difficult to maintain, and traditional policy weapons have become increasingly unwieldy and ineffective, regional and global integration has effectively imposed upon states an iron law of policy.'

Allegedly, Labour's 'contemporary stance reflects the neo-liberal belief that the notion of an interventionist State imposing collective decisions upon an economic system of market exchange is outmoded and irrelevant' (Hay 2002: 460; see also Hay 1999: 42ff.; Heffernan 2000: viii; Panitch and Leys 1997: 237ff.; Thomson 2000: 7; Wilde 1994) whereas SAP has fallen 'victim to the ascendancy of neo-liberal economic thought' and begun the demise of the strong State (Lindvall and Rothstein 2004: 2; see also Garrett 1993; Geyer 1997: 96; Moses 1994; Moses 2000; Rothstein 1992).

Obviously, political parties sometimes make dramatic policy changes. How else could they survive in a changing world? They adjust, they adapt and they reinterpret as part of their normal lives. The world is perpetually changing. But even as some policies change, others are kept stable. Whereas changing means is the order of the day it does not preclude stability in overarching goals. This book will question the validity of the view about a triumphant neo-liberalism but at the same time suggest a challenging view about stability. Acceptance of the market economy in combination with a wide array of market-correcting measures is, and has been, at the core of social democracy, at least since the 'Golden Age' in the 1960s.

Change?

Consider some speeches by leading representatives of two of the world's strongest and most traditionalist social democratic parties:

> I will never let the [budget] deficit get out of control. . . . We will not spend money we have not earned. . . . Let us be honest with ourselves: we must never again become a Party that is seen as anti-success, anti-competition, anti-profit, anti-markets. (Gordon Brown, the UK Chancellor, addressing the Labour Party conference, 27 September 1999).

> It took us four years to re-balance the budget. It was the toughest budget strengthening programme by any country at any time. It is not social democracy to place the public sector in debt (Göran Persson, the Swedish Prime Minister, addressing the Labour Party conference, 30 September 1999).

Whatever theoretical tool you might use, these politicians do not appear to fight on the socialist barricades. Evidently, their statements are a distance away from fundamental tenets of socialism in either its Keynesian or more planning-oriented version. Budget balance was not a top priority in the old shibboleth. Nor was praise for free markets, profits, budget cutting and competition. Maybe there is something in the ideology-change thesis after all. Perhaps neo-liberalism has indeed crept into the very core of these parties, including their leaderships. Granted the brevity of these quotes, SAP and the Labour Party seem to stand close in their new ideological approach to the relationship between State and market. Indeed, in his comparison of Swedish and American policy change during the last century, Mark McGann Blyth (1999: 492; for other Labour/SAP comparisons, see Kitschelt 1994: 267–72) claims that:

> In fact, the SAP have been following a dual strategy since their return to power, a strategy very similar to that pursued by 'New Labour' in the UK. That strategy is on the one hand to dampen expectations as much as possible while anticipating the reactions and accommodating the preferences of business. On the other hand, the strategy towards the public is to maintain that the 'welfare state is safe' while nonetheless accepting the same reformist agenda as the Conservatives.

This is a view of something like a Trojan horse, silently slipping inside the party headquarters. Citizens, party members and voters are led to believe there is nothing to worry about and that everything is in good order but suddenly the beast will show its real and lethal character. Business interests will brush aside solidarity and spirits of community. Whether by force or at their own will, the leaders of social democracy are said to have abandoned social democratic ideology.

As has been proved elsewhere, both parties have made distinct economic policy changes lately. Several scholars regard the policy turns as in tandem with a near-perfect international consensus on the merits of neo-liberalism, emerging after the collapse of the Bretton Woods system 1968–73, and in the wake of globalisation and economic shocks like the 1992 currency crisis which severely hit both the UK and Sweden.

In common terminology, traditional democratic socialism and neo-liberalism would correspond to 'interventionism' and 'non-interventionism' or 'laissez faire' respectively. The terms would imply that neo-liberalism rejects political interference in the economy in favour of letting market forces run free.

Although it would be a mistake to claim that neo-liberalism will never support state-intervention of any kind (Notermans 2000: 35) its brief version claims the fight against inflation, not unemployment, to be a first priority. Taxes should be cut and the welfare state slimmed down to a minimum (Kitschelt 1994; Löwdin 1998; McGann Blyth 1999; McNamara 1998; Peck 2001; Rhodes 1998. For an account of the wide array of Labour's various interventionist policies during the 1960s – all firmly embedded in the context of the market economy, see Middlemas 1990; Stewart 1977). Given that Labour and the SAP are both extremely traditionalist social democratic parties, such a change is almost hard to believe and would indeed give us scope to discuss the history of social democracy. But is the change-thesis really valid?

Stability?

In the midst of change, stability seems to reign. Look at what Tony Blair, the British Prime Minister, and his Swedish colleague, Mr Persson, had to say at the 1999 Labour Party conference on their goals for the future:

> More than 1 million still unemployed. . . . [O]ur attack on youth unemployment is the route to social justice. . . . I can tell you today we will continue to get more money into schools and hospitals in a way we can sustain year on year on year . . . economic efficiency and social justice are finally working together . . . it is possible to cut poverty and run the economy well. (Tony Blair, the UK Prime Minister, addressing the Labour Party conference, 28 September 1999)

> And how many people would not lose hope and turn their backs on democracy if those of us who have jobs were to abandon the struggle to reduce unemployment? . . . The Right claim that our options are different; that we must choose between development and equality, between growth and solidarity. They claim that equality and solidarity are a hindrance to growth and development. We know that the opposite is true. We want development and equality. (Göran Persson, the Swedish Prime Minister, addressing the Labour Party conference, 30 September 1999)

Members of the academic world need to be professionally cautious. Party conferences have a tendency to be well rehearsed. Most probably, the two leaders desired to communicate the same fundamental worldview. Showing unity is part and parcel of smooth political communication. However, as will be shown later, these speeches were no exceptional cases. No one would deny the strategic exigencies facing Labour and the SAP. Nor would anyone reject claims that the parties have introduced private partnership solutions in the public sector or indeed sold out parts of that sector. But here, as well as in a multitude of party documents, Messrs Blair and Persson still seemed to regard themselves to be free to work in the direction of the fulfilment of surprisingly stable deep-rooted ideological values.

Of course, many party leaders might see strategic advantages in adhering to the good old times. A heroic history can spread glory to latter-day politicians as well. But the values Blair and Persson focussed on, concerned the need to correct the unfair outcomes of the international capitalist market economy, and they spoke with an amount of fervour.

Behind the self-praising rhetoric there was sufficient emphasis on keywords such as 'reduce unemployment', 'cut poverty', 'social justice', 'solidarity' and 'equality', to venture a tentative conclusion about far more continuity with the past than mere strategic necessity or outright deceit would have us believe (see Driver and Martell 1998). Moreover, statements like 'we will continue to get more money into schools and hospitals' and 'we want development and equality' would hardly dampen voters' expectations. So why open their flank to demands from voters, members and the media if the real intention was clear-cut neo-liberalism?

Consequently, the opposite conclusion – a distinct element of ideological stability – is also credible, which is somewhat surprising given the fashionable belief that neo-liberal ideas should have conquered the parties entirely (Hall 1992; Herman 1999; McGann Blyth 1999; Moses 1994; Moses 1995).

Policy change?

One of the major means of correcting the outcomes of the international capitalist market economy rests with the welfare state. Sweden's position as the 'image' of a Golden-Age social democracy is well documented but several scholars seem to be turning a blind eye to the shortcomings and insufficient funding of the welfare state during the Golden Age. This is especially true of the family policy sector. From a feminist interpretation this peculiar blind eye would be rather shocking, and this is the more stunning as several scholars actually include something like equality for the sexes in their more general discussions about the core elements of social democracy (more on this below). The fact that much research underestimates the family sector is no new or limited phenomenon. Gösta Esping-Andersen's (1990) and others' mainstream research has been criticised for its inability to account for the differences welfare-state variations make for women (Sainsbury 1996). The neglect appears to affect also views about the character of social democracy.

Since 1975 – leaving the Golden Age – an immense expansion of day-care establishments has been implemented. In 1965 there existed about 10,000 day-care places catering almost exclusively for the needs of lone mothers. In 2000 the number had surged to over 500,000 places. The percentage of children one to six years old enrolled in the system has gone from 17 per cent in 1975 to 85 per cent in 2002 (2002: one to five years, with nearly 100 per cent for six year olds; Skolverket 2004b). At the same time the number of paid parental leave months has been increased from six to thirteen, the latest addition of months having taken place in 2002. Is this really neo-liberalism?

When the day-care programme was originally launched in 1975, the expansion was by all means impressive but still proved to fall far below the Social Democrats' repeatedly expressed targets to meet the demand for day-care places in five years' time. The expansion was also a long way from fulfilling parents' expectations. In any single year from 1975 to 1995, the number of children waiting for day-care places was close to 100,000. The pressure upon parents who had to leave their children unattended or who had to give up jobs because there was no child-care available was immense. The random way in which the few available places were actually distributed was nothing short of a bureaucratic failure (Schlytter 1993). As Schlytter proves, the shortage of day-care places led to severe problems with how to allocate the places to parents. Several legal paragraphs, based on partially con-flicting ideological goals, regulated the distribution of places. One paragraph focussed on the advantages accrued to the particular child. Another paragraph was set to allow the social authorities to decide on the basis of a general assessment of the case in question. As it happened, the general assessment almost always turned out to deal with the economic consequences for the particular family for receiving or not receiving a day-care place. Without a place one of the parents (mothers usually) would have to leave his/her job with dire economic consequences for the family. During the 1980s four out of five children in day-care received their places on the basis of paragraph 6 (the general assessment). Consequently, the system seldom prioritised the needs of the children. Moreover, it turned out that middle-class families who were strong in many respects (economic resources, education, ability to understand the legal-bureaucratic system) received places in dispropor-tionate numbers. Middle-class skills proved to be highly useful in order to under-stand how the system worked and make the best of it (Schlytter 1993: 164ff.). The outcome is ironical and paradoxical, given the Social Democrats' working-class backing and original aim at designing the day-care system so as to secure income security for working-class families through the realisation of the two-income family.

Towards the end of the 1960s/early 1970s a number of Swedish Royal Parlia-mentary Investigation Committees presented results revealing severe economic problems in families with more than two children (SOU 1967, No. 52:, 70ff.). More than every fourth family with children and with only one parent gainfully employed fell below the officially set poverty line (SOU 1972, No. 34: 153, 219; SOU 1983, No. 14: 324f.) and for families with children generally the period between 1975 and 1981 provided no economic improvements whatsoever (SOU 1983, No. 14: 324f.).

The party leadership by no means always covered up the rather embarrassing shortcomings. In a keynote speech at the 1968 Party conference, Alva Myrdal, who entered the cabinet a few years later and became the 1982 Nobel Peace Prize Laureate, issued this bitter criticism against the state of the Swedish welfare state:

In truth today's conditions are by no means satisfactory not even in our rich country and even after all reforms. The revelation of new facts – for instance as has already been made official by the Royal Parliamentary Investigation Committee on low incomes – and as elucidated by the great number of new contributions critical of society . . . reveal severe shortcomings. To a large extent these shortcomings are relics from the old society of social class and estates, of which their dogged tenacity should shock us more than they do. (Myrdal 1968: 190)[2]

Indeed, those conditions were nothing to write home about as examples of a solid welfare state record. The general problem for the Social Democrats has been that their preferred social-policy ideology is so expensive. In the 1970s and 1980s, the Party made substantial efforts to extend day-care facilities as well as to extend the length of parental leave. Although the economy grew substantially in the 1980s the Government budget seemed unable to cope with such an enormous task, neither goal was accomplished satisfactorily until much later. During the 1990s, in contrast, in spite of severe economic problems, the expansion accelerated. In 1997 the number of places finally met with parents' demand. Further improvements were implemented around the year 2000.

Targets and plans were indeed impressive in this field during the Golden Age of Social Democracy but the final economic effort to put action behind the rhetoric never materialised, or came about at a much later stage. Of course, dissenting views about the ability of the current Swedish welfare state to survive in a globalising world also exist (see Gould 1993, 1996). Others support the view that '[o]verall, it appears to be the case that Scandinavian governments have generally made policy changes so as to preserve basic principles of universalism, generosity and equality; certainly, privatisations, markets and means-testing have made inroads, but these incursions have been limited in most cases' (Swank 2000: 114).

A strong welfare state has been considered to form the core of social democratic thinking. '[T]he most important criterion of Social Democratic achievement was the nature and extent of welfare state reforms' (Castles 1978: 57). A critique about welfare-state retrenchment would then concern a very sensitive area for social democracy and there is indeed no shortage of claims about welfare retrenchment. Several authors raise warning fingers about what they see as scaled-down public sector mechanisms in the 1990s (Geyer et al. 1999; Scholte 2000). But, empirical facts indicate a different picture even during the darkest moments of 1990s recession. In fact, the SAP and Labour show surprising social policy continuity with the past. The universal welfare state was far from being abandoned in Sweden, despite obvious shocks to the system. There has also been a tendency to 'over-estimate the radicalism of Labour in the past' (Smith 1994: 709, quoted in Coates 2001: 298) and to under-estimate today's radicalism. In the UK there are clear signs of strengthening the universal elements, though universalism never seems to have been a particularly dominating part of Labour's ideology. As for the period before 1992 these observations square well with Pete Alcock's (1992: 140) conclusion that 'these pressures [for the continued legacy of the welfare state], despite the caution of the leadership's recent limited promises on welfare, are unlikely to be excluded for long from the agenda of any Labour Government in the 1990s which maintains a commitment to the development of state welfare' and Martin Smith's (1992: 220) 'Labour continues to distinguish itself from the other parties by its commitment to equality and the universal provision of welfare.'

As proof of the continuity one may point to a number of fiercely contested (from the right-wing parties) SAP policy decisions, which have followed in the wake of improving economic conditions. Benefit levels in major income-related social-insurance programmes were restored in 1996 and billions of *kronor* have been earmarked to sustain the health-care sector. Since then, families have received benefit improvements on a scale clearly reminiscent of earlier days. Child allowances have been raised substantially; generous fee ceilings in the day-care establishments were decided on in 2001 and implemented 2002, as was parental leave extension from twelve to thirteen months (at 80 per cent of ordinary salary, taxable). Finally the family support sector has been lodged firmly into the universal Swedish welfare state after decades of (in practice) means-tested allocation. This has been a major step away from any interpretation of neo-liberalism in Sweden's welfare regime.

Perhaps even more to the core of social democracy, is the case of income protection against wage losses due to sickness. In terms of Esping-Andersen's notion that de-commodification was socialism's strategic response to capitalism's commodification of labour power, sickness benefits would count as a prime example of such a strategy. 'To socialism the commodification of labour is an integral element in the process of alienation and class' (Esping-Andersen 1990: 44) and sickness benefits provide protection to the worker from the crude outcomes of market forces.

By being able to keep up one's pay during times of sickness the worker is protected. By applying the same logic the introduction of waiting days in the sickness benefit system will crudely expose the worker to the market forces to the extent that even the health is jeopardised. Therefore, when the Swedish 1991–94 non-socialist Government reintroduced a waiting day in the sick-leave insurance and reduced compensation levels from 100 per cent to 65 per cent (of pre-tax salary) for the first three compensated days, to 80 per cent as of the fourth day and to 90 per cent as of the ninety-first day, these measures were felt to deal a blow to the working-class. When the ensuing SAP Government kept the alterations, the blow was felt to be even heavier.

However, even though a single waiting day is still operative the compensation levels were improved in 1996. Even supposing the old levels may never come back; the present level is at 80 per cent of pre-tax salary for the entire period of sickness (except the single waiting day). While the degree of commodification certainly was kept higher than compared to pre-1991 standards, the system improved significantly in comparison with the 1991–96 regulations.

There is a fair case to hold that by slightly increasing the degree of commodification the SAP actually managed to save the whole system from collapsing, which would have meant drastic cutbacks and probably radically increased commodification levels (Winberg 1997). Even though ideas rather than actual measures are utilised in this study to underpin arguments about social democratic market ideologies, we are probably on safe ground to claim that the history of the sickness benefits provides us with an indication of the SAP's willingness to keep the system as intact as possible. A related problematic – though outside the immediate scope of this book – is the fact that by supporting the 1991 cutbacks the SAP actually contributed in the act of damaging a clearly visible and powerful, well organised, voting group (more or less the entire workforce but particularly its own core blue-collar groups who had limited means to use private insurances to reduce the negative effects of the benefit cutbacks). According to Pierson (1994), that kind of easily detected and punished policy behaviour is less likely to take place in a modern democracy. There will always mobilise strong resistance from voters and affected organisations. The reason the SAP took this dangerous path – they were actually targeting key social democratic voter groups for immediately noticeable and painful cutbacks – could of course have been caused by a radically changed ideological position. However, the later improvements rather point in the direction that the SAP felt there was no escape route if the system was to be saved in the long run.

There is no denying that the social security systems have been under economic strain but, in spite of tremendous economic pressure, the Swedish welfare state escaped the 1990s more or less unscathed. Although such a stance is somewhat disputed, there is sufficient evidence to agree with Stephens et al. (1999: 181) that 'by international standards, [Scandinavian welfare states] are still and continue to be very generous welfare states. Despite the introduction of waiting days and . . . cuts of replacement rates in unemployment, work injury, sick pay, and parental leave from 90 to 100 per cent to about 75 per cent . . . they still fit the institutional model.' Since then several substantial improvements have been introduced to the system. 'Although cuts were made in the 1990s, they have not changed the basic character of the Swedish welfare state' (Lindbom 2001: 187; see Svensson 2001).

Perhaps surprisingly Pennings (1999) defines Swedish Social Democracy as more in favour of market solutions than the British Labour Party. However, whether Pennings' indicators of ideological distances correspond to absolute or relative levels of neo-liberalism is less clear. According to Pennings, 'high levels of tax-supported spending levels correspond with relatively strong pledges in favour of retrenchment. Where the levels of spending are low, this emphasis on retrenchment is not so strong or even absent.' Pennings concludes (1999: 751f.) that

> Social democratic socio-economic policy-making is aimed at keeping or restoring the balance between state and market. Most social democratic parties are in favour of retrenchment in countries where the level of welfare statism is traditionally high. . . . In this way, both a growth and a decline of the public sector may be favoured by one and the same actor under different conditions and both may be interpreted as a sign of rational behaviour (i.e. optimising electoral support by favouring a balance between social and economic welfare).

The UK is indeed less of a clear-cut case. The welfare state was never as diverse and far-reaching as in Sweden and eighteen years under the Conservatives contributed to some severe public sector under spending. In the UK, lone mothers were indeed deprived of some allowances post-1997 by the Labour Government and private partnership solutions have no doubt changed the outlook of the public sector.

But, at the same time, the present Labour Government has restored some labour union rights (though they are still surprisingly shaky), introduced minimum wage levels (albeit at low levels), raised child allowance levels, increased parental leave and is at present allocating substantial new resources to the NHS as well as to the school system. To some extent necessary financial backing via the tax system is provided by the government (Glyn and Wood 2001; McKay 2001). All in all, there is a case to claim that in spite of tremendous economic pressure, the welfare states escaped the 1990s more or less untouched. Annesley and Gamble (2004: 157) even claim that: 'The UK is not yet Sweden, but it appears to be moving in a new social democratic direction than towards the USA's ways of dealing with contemporary social risk.' This is not to deny that several unions – and Labour backbenchers – have been fiercely opposed to some of the plans to reform the public sector, e.g. introducing university student top-up fees, foundation hospitals etc.

A leading authority on social policy has concluded that the Blair administration 'has a commendable and effective policy of redistribution to the lower income working poor and their children. . . . The attack on inequality may still look small in comparison to the powerful economic forces at work but it does move in the opposite direction to nearly two decades of budget policy' (Glennerster 2001: 402). A number of other policies, over urban renewal, neighbourhood regeneration and the 'Sure Start' scheme to compensate for educational disadvantage, indicate that the Government has embarked on a serious drive to end social exclusion. At the same time, increased reliance on means-testing – with an emphasis on work and a reluctance to increase non-work benefit rates – has become one of the main features of New Labour's welfare state agenda (Brewer et al. 2002). The approach has been described as 'selective universalism' (Glennerster 2001) that is a combination of universal public services (NHS and State education) coupled with an increasing reliance on means-testing for the provision of welfare payments (see also Hinnfors and Shaw 2004).

Thus, while some programmes have indeed been slimmed down or even scrapped others have been introduced or improved (or restored). When looking back, we must not confine our search to actual reforms and reform proposals only. When judging the present, we must not limit our investigation only to those programmes, which have suffered cutbacks. Shortcomings during the Golden Age should be included as well as progress today. Neglect of public sector funding today (for instance, as regards UK railways) has to be compared with neglect of public sector funding decades earlier (for instance, as regards UK railways). Given a nuanced analysis the policy scales appear to be in balance rather than tilting in any neo-liberal direction.

A brief comment on the role of labour unions is called for. While Swedish unions have increased their memberships to extremely high levels (roughly 80 per cent of the workforce unionised, see Kjellberg 2002: 2) rather than losing members, UK unions have waged a losing battle against dwindling membership. In 2000 a mere 29 per cent of the workforce was unionised (mostly in the public sector), down from 52 per cent in 1980 (Kjellberg 2002: 2). In many respects, the 'Labour Party movement' has cut off its organisational backbone. Moreover, union affiliation has become a public sector, white-collar matter rather than a blue-collar affair.

On the other hand, the new UK labour relations reforms laid out in 1998 were greeted by the TUC as 'the biggest advance in workers' rights for a generation' (Taylor 2001a: 252). However, a number of exceptions and limitations in the legislation leaves the question open, whether the Labour Party really championed the unions' 'legitimate rights' based on 'fairness, not favours' or whether the Government wanted the status quo of 'the existing balance of bargaining power, which favours the employer' (Shaw 2002: 13). In conclusion, Labour's measures appear after all to represent 'an increase in employee representation (in respect of grievances, collective redundancies, transfer of undertaking and through union recognition), marginally enhanced job security (action on unfair dismissal and parental leave) and extended information and consultation' (Undy 1999: 332).

As proof of the relentless force of market ideas within social democracy generally, Martin Rhodes (1998: 113) stresses 'a common shift from flat-rate to earnings-related benefits' in welfare programmes. However, Rhodes runs into trouble when we take the very epitome of the social democratic Golden Age, Sweden, into account. The foundations of the modern Swedish welfare state, sickness benefit (introduced 1955) superannuated pensions (1960), parental leave (1973) were all earnings-related and introduced long before the recent alleged pressures for change from new ideas and economic developments. Whatever reason behind this trend, there was at least a distinctly strategic element, captured in Tage Erlander's (the legendary 1945–69 Swedish Prime Minister) open-minded opinion that, 'superannuated pensions, when implemented, will contribute to social democracy's prospects of governing in this country, because superannuated pensions as such are something of a battering-ram to capture positions within the middle class' (*Riksdag* minutes AK 1962 32: 32, Erlander). If there is any trend since the 1950s it might even be fair to claim that the earnings-related element is a touch less obvious in 2004 compared with the Golden-Age era – though hardly to the extent that earnings-related benefits have lost their importance.

With categorisations like Rhodes' there was either no Golden Age at all, or the Golden Age was indeed reconcilable with acceptance of market forces. In spite of being logically sound, the first view still becomes untenable in the sense that the very object of our studies, social democracy itself, vanishes into thin air. The second interpretation accepts the view that social democracy has indeed existed and this more optimistic view is reconcilable with the thesis put forward in this book: Social democracy has seldom strayed very far from accepting the liberal market economy. Of course a view that real social democracy in practice was contradictory to a theoretically derived ideal type of social democracy would not in itself have been remarkable or untenable.

If neo-liberalism had the upper hand, why then would the SAP bother to raise the levels of compensation for parental leave and sick leave once they had been reduced? Why would the Labour Party favour increased parental leave, an improved NHS etc.? Wouldn't a neo-liberal do everything to keeping the levels low! A pragmatic social democrat, on the other hand, would reduce the level of compensation when there were no other means available to keeping national finances in order (always a top priority) and then raise the level again when resources allowed so. By doing so the pragmatist would try and save the fundamentals of the overarching system as far as possible.

Presently we will look into the ideological fundament behind day-to-day policy decisions like increasing or decreasing social support levels. In order to claim anything about ideological stability or volatility we need data on ideology rather than on day-to-day policy standpoints. The following study will provide such data.

The age of the Golden Age?

The concept of a Golden Age of Social Democracy is an elusive one but some consensus appears to exist that social democracy as a major political force began its first phase of golden years with the Swedish 'red-green' Social Democrat-Farmers' Party crisis agreements in the 1930s. A couple of decades later the Golden Era peaked not only in Sweden but also for social democracy in general. There is no final arbiter around to decide for us but as the apex of the Golden Age of Social Democracy it might be reasonable to suggest 1965 (Karvonen and Sundberg 1991: 6).

Someone might object that 1965 is a poorly chosen starting point. As Labour was in government in 1966 the Party might have felt an urge to behave more modestly than in 1964 when the Party approached the general elections from the opposition benches. The same problem applies for the SAP, only here the methodological dilemma is even worse. Being continuously in office position between 1936 and 1976 (if we discount the three-month-long June–September 1936 Farmers' Party Government – the so-called 'Summer Cabinet' – the SAP were in office even from 1932), the SAP must then have been forced into modesty for the better part of Swedish modern political history. The entire Golden Age period in Sweden saw social democrats at the helm of government affairs. Thus there is no way we can validate ideological similarities or differences between government and opposition periods. We have to live with this shortcoming. As for later periods though, the SAP have been in and out of office to such an extent that any policy variations will appear in the documents.

In the British case we can in fact validate the chosen time point by a preliminary look into the data. A close inspection of the 1964 manifesto ('The New Britain') gives us no cause to draw any new conclusions as regards the suitability of 1965 as a starting point. While the manifesto was full of references to 'socialist planning' and rife with criticism of 'economic free-for-all' politics an assessment of the rhetoric reveals that the socialist planning intended by the Labour Party in opposition was not entirely revolutionary. Labour wanted to 'encourage industries', 'improving facilities', 'providing better terms of credit' (but only when business 'justifies' it; and we may quietly wonder whether business will ever provide better terms than those set by the market) in order to reach a long-term satisfactory trade-balance. What we find is an array of market carrots rather than planning or socialist sticks. 'A third way' in different words. Or, if we were less understanding, not a third way at all but rather a full recognition of the way the capitalist economy functions supplemented by earnest ideas about how to deal with the less agreeable results of the market economy. Some authors would argue that this combination of policies – market economy plus some corrections – would constitute a third way more based on communitarianism than socialism (Berman 2003: 142).

As regards the public sector, the Party wanted to loosen up on restrictions so that nationalised industries would be able to operate more freely on international markets. The only 'socialist' element was the labelling of these measures, not the content as such (Labour 1964). As will become clear in Chapter 3, the 1964 policies as they appeared in the 1964 manifesto were very close to those in the 1966 equivalent.

In a reversal of the Swedish situation where the SAP was in office for decades, the methodological problem concerning the Labour Party rather concerns the extremely long 1979–97 period out of office. For the latter part of the 1965–2002 period we have Labour data from office as well as out-of-office years but the 1980s was out-of-office only. We have to make do with what we have.

So when is a party's ideology best reflected: In government or in opposition? There can be made a case for both stances. In opposition the Party leadership may feel free to really elaborate on the Party's true ideological foundations without any strings attached. Since our interest here is focussed on ideology before strategic considerations enter the parties' proposals we might – from this point of view – want to emphasise opposition years.

On the other hand, one can equally well argue that the party's true ideology is only put to the test when the party is really forced to give priority to certain issues over others. Such priorities are only made in government position. Only then is the party forced to take responsibility for its actions and we might – from this opposite point of view – want to emphasise government years (see Shaw 1996: 212).

In the present study we will be open-minded and use data from both government and opposition years without making any analytical distinction between them *per se*. However, the more stable our empirical results will be, the more we will be able to be at ease with the validity of the results. In the event of surprising ideological shifts we will have analyse the data carefully to decide whether change in office could provide a plausible explanation.

Puzzles

Two puzzles confront us. First, if neo-liberalism reigned supreme, with both neo-liberal ideas available for a long time and with a number of upsetting currency crises behind them, why would parties like Labour and the SAP still be so concerned about unemployment? Why would the parties continue allocating vast resources to the welfare state, especially given that the parties have actually been more and more successful in bringing in the votes from market-strong middle-class voters? ('Higher service' voting for Labour 1997: 34 per cent (Evans et al. in Evans and Norris 1999: 90); 'Higher service' voting for SAP 2002: 25 per cent

(Holmberg and Oscarsson 2004: 62); Social security and health expenditure as a percentage of GDP 1980, UK: 21.3 per cent, 1990: 22.3 per cent; Sweden 1980: 32.4 per cent, 1990: 33.1 per cent (Esping-Andersen 1996: 11); Health expenditure as percentage of GDP 2000, UK: 7.7 per cent, Sweden 8.5 per cent; public sector share of health expenditure 2000, UK: 83 per cent, Sweden: 85 per cent (UK National Statistics 2005)).

Second, if social democratic acceptance of liberal market principles were an effect of a wave of neo-liberal ideas in the international debate from the 1980s and 1990s, why would the SAP and Labour politicians be so concerned with inflation, budget balance and earnings-related programmes already in the 1960s and 1970s at the very apex of what many authors label the Golden Age of Social Democracy (Esping-Andersen 1996)?

Stability is a much under-emphasised aspect in dealing with social democracy. Although the Labour Party was one of the very first social democratic parties to embark on the road away from Keynesianism and the SAP one of the last, it appears leaders from both parties have taken a rather matter-of-fact attitude towards the means of achieving sufficient resources to realise the kind of welfare state they envisage. We may also conclude – albeit tentatively – that many 'new' policies are neither very new nor do they present very far-reaching threats to the parties' fundamental ideologies.

Third, it is of course still a fact that on the face of it, economic policy (i.e. on a level below the overarching ideology – see Chapter 2, the section on Bringing ideology back in) appears to have changed rather dramatically in the sense that both countries have deregulated their money markets, joined the European common market, rendered their central banks independent from direct political interference, abandoned the fixed currency exchange rates etc. At the same time, welfare policies are left roughly unscathed. There have been clear elements of privatisations in the social services sector (Blomqvist and Rothstein 2000; Driver and Martell 1998; Svensson 2001) but the SAP and Labour still back very extensive welfare state policies (see Hinnfors and Shaw 2004). How was this combination of policies ideologically possible?

Suffice it here to say that there is indeed scope for conclusions about important elements of social democratic value stability. As will be seen later, this stability takes on a two-pronged character. At an overarching ideological level on the relationship between State and market, distinct acceptance of the market economy can be shown on the one hand to have existed in SAP/Labour ideology long before the so-called 'Black Wednesday' in September 1992, when – in the wake of heavy currency speculation – the British pound was left to float in September 1992. The Swedish *krona* followed suit shortly afterwards after unprecedented interest rate increases and financial turmoil (Hinnfors and Pierre 1998). In this sense some of the steps towards market-conforming policies (free central banks etc.) would be less puzzling because they would have been carried out against a backdrop of deep-rooted and well-established overarching market acceptance.

On the other hand, as was mentioned earlier, the claim made here is that the core aim of social democracy – protecting market-weak groups in society and doing so inside the liberal market economy – has remained the same for a long time. This would be rather natural given that the view on the role of the market economy has included large-scale arrangements for checking the effects of the market economy and these arrangements have remained untouched by the various changes in economic policy (indicated above) as such. Thus, the following reinterpretation of social democracy is based on the presumption that neither were the SAP and Labour as market-economy hostile at the height of the Golden Age nor are they as market-economy friendly forty years later as has been claimed elsewhere.

A causal framework

Without in any way making too bold claims about explanatory modelling I would still suggest the following causal framework for my study. Behind day-to-day policies like child care benefit levels, NHS public funding support etc., we expect some kind of overall ideological position to be influential. It would be a mistake to assume a perfect relationship between ideology and actual policies but the notion that, in the end, ideology plays an important role in explaining parties' behaviour is not very controversial as such.

With the data based on qualitative elaborations and with the research object being the complex world of human activity one should be cautious about the possibility of making too precise projections in the social sciences. However, within acceptable limits, it might be reasonable to claim that the present study is based on the hypothesis that if overarching ideology remains stable over time, then over the long run day-to-day policies – such as welfare state spending and character – will also remain stable. Over shorter time periods strategic deliberations and a host of unpredictable factors might influence policy and create rather unstable results. In the longer run these influences will even out.

Since we have clear indications that day-to-day policies for counterbalancing the outcomes of the market economy have indeed remained rather stable, we have reason to believe that overarching ideology too has remained fairly stable. The day-to-day policies in question are within the welfare state sector, i.e. the market-correcting sector. The ideology at the centre of attention here will be beliefs about the market economy in general and about the international capitalist market economy in particular.

While the present work focuses on the degree of stability within the social democratic ideological project, it is fair to remember that several other changes in the social democratic movement are clearly visible over the last decades. It has to be emphasised that stability in this particular ideological field by no means precludes the possibility of change in other, related fields. To some extent the unions' influence over the parties' policies have been reduced and the relationship between elite and mass has been altered. For instance, it has been claimed (Howell 2000; see Panitch and Leys 1997: 237ff.) that 'ending the association, in the minds of voters and business, between the Labour Party and organised labour . . . is the defining core of the modernisation project. It is seen as central to the ability to appeal to more affluent swing voters, and to win the confidence of employers and financial interests.' True as this observation may be, the confidence of employers and finan-cial interests certainly was no unimportant element in the old days either.

The Swedish corporative State was founded on the explicit assumption that the unions as well as employers' associations should feel confident towards the government. One could almost say it was one of the cornerstones of social demo-cratic policy to keep up extremely good relations with the leading Swedish indus-trial giants (Blyth 2002: 113; Öberg 1994). Therefore to hold that New Labour's effort to gain the confidence of the business establishment is a sign that nothing is left of social democracy is perhaps a touch myopic. On the other hand, the Swedish model has been built on very friendly relations with the unions as well. On this account the Labour Party perhaps fares less well, although this phenomenon is not altogether new.

Other differences in the way the social democratic movement has developed concern the relationship between the leadership and the voters and members. With mass membership declining rapidly the legitimacy of the rank-and-file members deteriorates gradually in favour of the party leader and, perhaps, the voters. While the elite–mass question is important earlier research yields no definitive answer as to the nature of how the relationship has developed over the last decades. Mem-bership has declined but criticism of leader indifference to the wishes of the rank and file is a tune at least as old as party studies themselves. From the advent of modern mass parties, scholars, the most prominent of them Robert Michels, have claimed, that organised internal democracy has deteriorated from an idyllic past comfortably put at about thirty-forty years earlier (Michels 1925; Pierre 1986).

On a more ideological level the old so-called clause IV of the Labour Party's con-stitution has been revised. The old version, which had been contested for a long time spoke of 'the common ownership of the means of production, distribution and exchange, and the best obtainable system of popular administration and con-trol of each industry and service'. The new version tells instead of 'common endeavour', 'a dynamic economy', 'a just society', 'an open democracy' and 'a healthy environment'. No doubt the symbolic change this revision entailed was substantial even though the new views had taken root within the Labour leadership long ago (Peele 1997: 91).

Whether these other changes should be included in a study of social democratic ideology is an interesting point for discussion. The social democratic movement as such is of course well worth studying and could be observed from a multitude of angles and approaches (see, for instance, Cronin's impressive work on New Labour; Cronin 2004). However, one does not necessarily have to perform all these laudable tasks in the same piece of work. The problematic presented in this study is not concerned with all the interesting nuances of social democracy as a whole but confined to the question of market ideology. One could very well imagine a situation where most aspects of the general movement were stable whereas the market ideology changed considerably. Or, one could imagine a reverse situation with stable market ideology within a changing general movement context. It would be highly interesting to combine the development of ideology with that of, say, the development of mass–elite relationship. However, to pull the pieces together we need a firm understanding of the pieces themselves. This book is about providing some such firm knowledge of one of the key pieces, ideological views about the international capitalist market system.

Within the social democratic family of parties, the SAP and Labour represent widely differing histories of development as regards organisation, time of tenure etc. In that respect the choice of the SAP and Labour in this study would come within reach of a most-different-case method.

The concept of change

Innocuous as they may appear, the terms change and stability are far from unequivocal. When is a 'change' a change? When is something 'stable?' How can one empirically distinguish the nature of these phenomena as regards the parties' ideologies? Given the scope of this study: To discuss whether claims about social democratic change from socialism to neo-liberalism hold any truth one needs to elaborate on the meaning of change. Unfortunately, the terms change and stability invite analytical complications. Nevertheless, the difficulties must be faced. These matters are discussed in this chapter. Chapters 8–10 will resume the discussion and elaborate on the position of social democracy in a market economy.

At least two general forms of change can be considered. First, change may be the sum total of several extremely small changes which, taken individually, would not have been regarded as any change at all. Together they work in a way as drops of water hollowing out a rock. Second, abstaining from formal change (e.g. refraining to compensate for inflation) may in the long, or even medium, run lead to substantial real change (Rose and Davies 1994). These two forms of change can be combined and used in a discussion about real and formal change and stability.

In *Lesson-Drawing in Public Policy*, Richard Rose (1993: 145ff.) combines two related types of 'governmental' reaction to 'environmental' change.[3] Depending on whether the environmental changes are 'benign' or for the 'worse', policymakers will end up with different combinations of change. The government can either ignore the environmental change or alter programmes and goals. According to Rose, the ensuing four combinatorial effects range from 'policy-deterioration' (the government kept the same goal and the same programme), 'adaptation' (same goal, new programme), 'innovation' (new goal, new programme), 'symbolic gesture, passive acceptance' (new goal, same programme).

The concepts of governmental and environmental change facilitate an elaboration of the concepts of change and stability. In certain instances, the political parties formulate policy goals in advance with the intention to *change* society. At other times, goal *adaptation* to an already profoundly changed society is a more appropriate characterisation of the policy process (Braybrooke and Lindblom 1970; Pierson 1994: 39–50; Rose 1993: 143ff.; Simon 1966; Thelen and Steinmo 1992: 7–10).

Thus, if policy and/or ideological changes were made, they could be described as equivalent to either more or less than would be surmised given the environmental changes. Given a complete fit between policy change and environmental change some would perhaps characterise the relationship as some kind of determinism. Certain changes in the environment political parties face would then 'force' them to take specific action. If, on the other hand, the parties' actions (policy change) were either more limited or more extensive than the environmental changes would suggest, there would be more room for conclusions about the independent role for 'ideas' to influence party choice. In that case party leaders would not merely react passively to environmental stimuli. Nevertheless, as will be shown below, a close fit between environmental change and policy change can indeed hide important elements of political will.

Anyone would understand that operationalising 'necessary environmental changes' would pose a methodologically complicated task. Equally difficult is the operationalisation of 'policy change'. Should we only count the occurrence of 'formal' policy changes? Any reform introducing a new policy element (e.g. a change from flat-rate to earnings-related compensation in the social welfare system) would then be considered a policy change. Lack of any new such elements would equal stability. In many ways, this would be in conformity with common-sense use, with certain advantages such as the minimisation of imprecision.

However, as was indicated above, the definition of change could take on a more refined character, albeit with some obvious problems attached to it. There are apparent analytical rewards by introducing the concepts 'real' and 'formal' and discerning between real and formal change (stability). First, change could be defined as formal change, as was done above. This corresponds to the common-sense understanding of the term. Something concrete and readily observable has occurred and is registered as change.

Second, the relationship between environmental and formal policy changes may be inherently related – i.e. in other words more or less perfectly proportionate to each other – or unrelated to each other. Proportional formal adaptation to environmental change could be seen as equivalent to 'de facto' or real stability in the sense that even though formal changes might have taken place, what has happened is only that the formal change now provides new means to reach the same (stable) ideological goal.

Another version of the relationship would be when formal policy change is larger or smaller than environmental change would have us believe. These varieties would correspond to various kinds of 'de facto real change'. Thus, and as is easily observed, real change will sometimes take place when no formal change whatsoever has been enacted.

Real change comes in two forms. One is disproportionately small, i.e. when formal change has not kept up with environmental changes. Another is disproportionately large, i.e. when substantial formal changes have been carried out without preceding environmental changes. By introducing the two forms of de facto change we emphasise the fact that politics is an important part of the picture. Political behaviour is more than a mere extrapolation of social trends. This is not to say that de facto stability is achieved without political calculation and effort. On the contrary, the point is that stability can also be the outcome of calculated change.

Moreover, with the environment changing, a new policy could be a real break with the past in the sense that now the old goals would no longer be regarded as viable. New goals are set up that just were not contemplated before. But a policy change could also have other objectives than aiming at new goals. To venture a metaphor, change could of course instead be the means to keeping up stability much in the same way as a sailor would adjust the rudder in order to reach the voyage's destination when the wind changes direction. Were the sailor instead stubbornly to tie up the rudder, the ship would drift uncontrollably into unknown waters.[4] In this sense, change is sometimes a necessary ingredient in the craft of creating stability. A voyage into unknown waters will of course also be the end result if there were no targeted destination in the first place. Labour during the final stages of its 1960s cabinet position has been described as that of 'a rudderless ship' (Shaw 1996: 104). It must also be borne in mind, that formal changes can be very different as to the character of the change. Analytically, it is insufficient to limit the study by simply stating that a formal change either took place or failed to occur. The character of change has to be accounted for. Though this is an important point, there seems to be no easy way to dealing with it. Since the interpretation of a formal change takes on different meanings when the environmental context changes, it would hardly be fruitful to formulate a set of formal changes, each with a pre-defined meaning. Instead, the analysis has to provide a more or less exhaustive discussion as to whether a particular formal change is to be interpreted as a way of ensuring that the goal will be reached or not. In other words, whether the sailor's rudder movements will actually help the ship to reach its original destination safely.

Notes

1   Please note that the wording has been reversed from the original's: 'Despite so-called social democratic parties being in power in the United States, the United Kingdom, France, Germany, and Sweden, neo-liberalism continues apace.'
2   This, and all following Swedish-source quotations were translated by the author.
3   This and the following paragraph are adaptations of Hinnfors 1999.
4   I thank my sailing colleague Jon Pierre for providing me with this metaphor.

2

Reinterpreting social democracy

Images of social democracy

Efficiency, full employment and equality. Such would be the brief definition of social democracy (Przeworski 1987: 241). A specific approach towards the market economy takes central stage as the defining ideological characteristic of social democracy. While on the one hand accepting the market economy, the public sector has to correct some of its apparently unavoidable shortcomings. Such a double standard, as it were, squares well with Douglas Hibbs's conclusion that:

> the political success of Labor and Socialist parties . . . effectiveness in socializing the consumption and final distribution (though not necessarily the production) of national income, and hence the locus of distributive conflict, from the market, where capital interests enjoy a comparative advantage, to the electoral arena, where the political resources of the organized working class are more telling. Consequently, in the welfare states (largely the creatures of Labor and Social Democratic political action) the political process decisively shapes the final distribution of income. (Hibbs 1987: 4)

At the core of social democracy rests a belief 'in the primacy of politics and a commitment to using democratically acquired power to direct economic forces in the service of the collective good' (Berman 2003: 142). More or less precise as the definitions may be, some of them run the risk of becoming too vague. 'Reformism' as such offers little help without further clarification (Wickham-Jones 1995: 700). Also, one has to be careful in separating political regimes characteristic of entire countries with those of political parties (Garrett 1998; Huber and Stephens 1998). Sweden may be characterised by a social democratic regime without the non-socialist parties being in favour of or promoting particularly social democratic measures. The non-socialist parties have had precious little time to set their ideological mark on the country by implementing any of their concrete policies.

Typically the following aspects come to the forefront in earlier attempts at defining social democracy: 1) there is a commitment to equality, social justice and social welfare, 2) a large role is envisaged for the public sector, 3) a central feature is a commitment to State intervention as necessary to prompt the market into behaving in a desired manner, so protecting weaker elements in society and promoting economic growth, 4) full employment and sustained economic growth are portrayed as essential targets, 5) the welfare state is seen as crucial to protect and aid those who find it impossible to sustain themselves, 6) as a response to growing problems in the economic sphere, social democratic governments have increasingly employed corporatism – the linking of State, employers and trade unions in a form of social contract (Shaw 1993: 116).

Definitions based on types of organisation, membership levels etc. are excluded from this analysis. However, it might be prudent to remind ourselves that in these respects both parties have changed. The degree of union influence has diminished, mass-membership has decreased and the composition of the electorate changed. Individual rather than collective workers' rights have been augmented, although in comparison, 'British workers' rights . . . remain much slimmer than those of their counterparts in most other EU countries' (Shaw 2002: 6; see also Glyn and Wood 2001: 61f., 291; Howell 2000; King 2002).

When looking for social democratic means available to an overarching public sector we usually find a number of tools but within a rather uniform frame. The catalogue comprises, for example, a capacity to a) equalise the background conditions under which markets operate – restructuring the background conditions that determine what resources people bring to the market, b) enact framework legislation, making the liberal market more perfect through information supply about job vacancies and job-seekers, subsidising the costs of labour mobility, establishing standards of production, subsidising loans, creating incentives to encourage production and reorganisation of industry etc., c) implement functional socialism through the eight-hour day, industrial accident legislation, zoning laws, environmental restrictions, collective bargaining legislation etc. (Tilton 1992: 414ff.). Although less overtly specified Glyn and Wood (2001) list the following criteria: 1) macroeconomic stability, 2) equality, 3) full employment, 4) State activity focussed on active labour market policies and welfare state systems. See also Hay's (1999: 57) related criteria: 1) a commitment to redistribution – distribution within any capitalist society can never be equitable and must be addressed, 2) a commitment to democratic economic governance – the market left to its own will create inefficient and inequitable outcomes, 3) a commitment to social protectionism – it is the primary responsibility of the State to ensure citizens are provided for in terms of health, education and welfare.

With policies like the ones listed above (1–6 etc.), the markets allegedly would approach what is sometimes referred to as a 'planned' character 'where freedom for private initiative is framed or curbed by social control' (Tilton 1992: 417). Particularly tricky, and important, will be to define the character of terms like 'commitment to equality', 'commitment to democratic economic governance'. The meaning of those and similar expressions and terms are by no means uncontested or immediately self-evident. Moreover, social democratic ideology can be defined with reference both to a certain combination of 'themes' (e.g. those mentioned above) and with reference to the character of each theme. So even though the themes of two separate parties (or the same party at separate times) may look the same, the character of the parties might be rather different anyway. Thus a wide but unspecified catalogue of themes, e.g. 'social policy', 'taxation', 'wage policy' and 'family policy', would be very different from a wide but specific set like 'universal social policy', 'progressive taxation', 'solidarity wage policy', and 'sexual equality' (Tilton 1992: 41 ff.). More narrow definitions focus on a single, specified theme, e.g. placing high importance on flat-rate benefits in welfare programmes (Rhodes 1998: 113, which is, however, in contrast to Esping-Andersen's 'Social Democratic Welfare Regime', which puts emphasis on earnings-related benefits; Esping-Andersen 1990: 28), or 'Keynesianism' in order to call a party 'social democrat' (Paterson and Thomas 1986, quoted in Thomson 2000: 8). So when referring to social democracy generally, we should bear in mind that rather different real-life parties correspond to the definitions.

Some parties place more emphasis on some of the themes, while others provide their own definitions of the various themes. Definitions putting an emphasis on the way in which parties in general and social democratic parties in particular organise themselves would form a different approach to the one followed here. Beginning perhaps before and after World War II, social democratic parties have pursued a course with which to attract voters outside their core working-class groups. No doubt this trend has profoundly changed the way the parties relate to their voters. The party leaderships have difficulty referring too much to the industrial worker. As a consequence tightly knit members' clubs are difficult to sustain and the parties take on a less member-focussed character. Membership has indeed fallen in the SAP and Labour but to what extent members were active in the old days and really managed to influence party policies and ideology is an open question (Widfeldt 1999: 144). As regards organisational outlook – class references and probably use of language – both parties have come a long way from their 1940s or 1950s predecessors. However, the present work concerns ideological stability, not organisational character, even though the changing organisational context probably has contributed to a sense of ideological bewilderment among certain segments of party members and voters.

A plethora of other variables and policy areas than those listed above could be considered. What about views on defence policy, international cooperation generally and through EEC/EC/EU in particular, green politics, gender-related questions and so on (see Driver and Martell 1998; Miles 2000; Seldon 2001; Smith and Spear 1992)? Most people would consider these policy areas important and of course the parties have a range of views here as well. In these fields a number of very far-reaching changes have indeed taken place: both Britain and Sweden have joined the EU, although a substantial amount of Europe-scepticism remains in the parties; both parties have changed views on international cooperation generally, holding new views on terrorism, military task forces etc. To analyse these other areas are, no doubt, highly worthy academic tasks.

However, these matters should always be informed by the theoretical problem of the particular study one is carrying out. Standard procedure seems to be that when explicitly trying to define what constitutes social democracy in practice those other areas are usually left out (as shown, for instance, by Shaw's, Tilton's and Glyn and Wood's definitions above). This is an approach which is fully supported by the present author but the point made here is that earlier renderings of social democracy generally fail to accept the logical consequence of such an exclusion: overall empirical images of social democracy ideology should only be based on what is included in the ideology-definition. Thus, if, for example, international politics form no part of the social democratic definition (and usually they don't), such policies should be excluded from conclusions on social democratic ideology. That is not to say that, among the research on social democracy where a wider selection of fields has been selected, all subscribe to the more narrow definition applied here.

Had international politics been part of the social-democracy definition after all, we would have encountered severe difficulties in pinpointing a coherent social democracy anyway. Standpoints on EU and NATO membership, nuclear armament etc. have differed widely between different social democratic parties and over time. That could of course be proof of social democracy either approaching or distancing itself from theoretically defined ideal types, but so far few, if any, authors seem to have come to the conclusion that international politics as such have much to do with the social democratic ideal type. In theory social democracy would define itself as an international movement, which put labour solidarity in front of nationalist concerns. In practice, however, social democracy always seems to have been quick to prioritise nationalism, even during the supposedly more radical early era of social democracy (Douglas 2004). In March 2003, the Labour Government joined the US in launching an extremely disputed military attack on Iraq. Whether that kind of action is reconcilable with social democratic values is not entirely clear. However, in the case of the UK and the Labour Party, a special relationship with the US is nothing new *per se*.

Even though we were to include policy fields like environmental policy and sexual equality we were on safe ground to claim that if anything, the SAP and Labour fare much better today (2004) than their predecessors of forty years ago as far as State involvement in these areas in society is concerned. Indeed '[a] perusal of programmatic statements by the Labour Left in the mid-1980s reveals no readiness to consider the new themes of left-libertarian politics. Ecology rarely surfaces in such debates, and feminism appears only in the garb of equality-oriented socialist feminism, concerned with questions of redistributive justice rather than gender identity' (Kitschelt 1994: 269f.). There simply seems to exist only scant data supporting a view that traditional social democracy came anywhere near radical positions as regards green and feminist issues. Rather the opposite seems to have been the case. The same bewildering differences between different social democratic parties and over time as regards international politics, is found in the case of environmental policy and feminism.

As perhaps anecdotal empirical underpinning to conclusions about clearer adherence to sexual-equality goals forty years after the Golden Age of Social Democracy, one may point to the SAP's inclusion of 'Feminism' in its year 2001 new party programme (SAP 2001), though how far the Party's recent embrace of these views actually reaches is a matter of some controversy. Most would probably agree that the 1960s record of social democracy and feminism was even worse (Ingebritsen 2000).

In the field of green politics we should mention the SAP's new (1997) aim to become a party for the achievement of an 'ecologically sustainable society'

(Lundqvist 2000: 22). Swedish social democracy has always been eager to co-opt new, and challenging, ideologies to mould them into a more easily recognisable social democratic form.

Perhaps even more to the point than vague notions of 'feminism', the SAP's move from supporting the 'one-earner family' with a male breadwinner to supporting the 'two-earner family' with both mother and father gainfully employed is a telling example of how far the Party has changed in the direction of a version of feminism. During the Golden Age, Party ideology on family and gender was focussed on the male breadwinner.

Towards the end of the twentieth century, the Party's explicit view evolved to prevent women from being 'forced' from the labour market to being housewives. This ideological view is mirrored in a constantly upgraded family policy field (Hinnfors 1999), which no doubt carries many shortcomings and might even hold subtle drawbacks from distinctively feminist angles (Ingebritsen 2000) but is still an unmistakable leap forward compared to policies and views during the Golden Age (Hirdman 2002; Sainsbury 1996: 190 ff.).

No one would probably venture into labelling the Labour Party 'feminist' but the Party's drive to include women among its MPs, the recent proposals to increase maternity leave etc. would perhaps indicate that the New Labour Party at least was moving in a less non-feminist direction than its older ancestor during the Golden Age.

As soon as the number of areas is expanded, the notion of a single unified European social democracy becomes increasingly difficult to uphold. And were we to include them, the result could very well be that, in important aspects European social democracy is far more social democratic in the twenty-first century than during the height of the Golden Age. Therefore we should focus on the main areas (Sassoon 1996).

The importance of consistency

With few exceptions (Adler-Karlsson 1967; Heclo and Madsen 1987; Tomasson 1973) – and they seem to have vanished from the discourse – renderings about social democracy do not focus on pragmatism as such. However, contemplating a sample of definitions of social democracy, it is difficult to avoid a feeling about their apparent modest, not to say pragmatic, character. It's eight-hour day rather than nationalisations; it's market perfection rather than market replacement. Above all, references to what could be referred to as economic policy are rare while references to welfare policy abound. Given the modest character indicated above, we have further reason to question whether social democracy has really thrown so much overboard to merit a conclusion about outright neo-liberalism.

So when we utilise earlier research on social democracy, where do we end up? As the rendering above indicates, there is scarcely any shortage of definitions on 'social democracy'. No need for new ones. However, two modest requirements are formulated here. First, we need to take the definitions seriously and actually use them rather than applying double standards for definitions and concrete research.

Second, our aim is to discuss social democracy generally, rather than the Swedish or British variety *per se*. Therefore, country-specific limitations will be of less value here. This generalising aim is upheld with due respect of the shortcomings rendered by limiting the analysis to only two cases, the SAP and Labour.

Given our two requirements, can we still speak of 'social democracy' where there is no Keynesianism or no welfare state? Tentatively the answer to the first question is 'yes', while 'no' answers the second question. These matters will be elaborated on later. If information supply and the eight-hour day, industrial accident legislation and environmental protection were clear and unequivocal signs of social democracy before, why shouldn't they suffice today? Second, with some notable exceptions (Pontusson 1992a and Rhodes 2000), there seems to be a case to hold that rear-mirror images of social democracy during its Golden Age tend to forget the more modest definitions and risk being caught in social democracy's own high-flown rhetoric about a glorious past. Taken to its logical end, such high-flown rhetoric would in practice finally lead to social democracy breaking the frail balance between on the one hand accepting the market economy with corrections and on the other hand replacing the market with State authority. This is not to say that parts of the labour movement, especially within some of the trade unions and at certain party conferences, didn't ever try to shift politics in this more State-oriented direction (Pontusson 1992a). They did, sometimes vehemently. (For a vivid analysis of the rift between party leadership and party grassroots, and between old and new politics, during the 1980s, see Cronin 2004; Heffernan 2000: 66ff.; Wainwright 1987). But the point is that the party leaderships usually were much cooler towards such demands and actually seldom met them with action. Gamble's (1992: 62) point is worth quoting at some length here:

> The second mode [of economic doctrines, i.e. seeking the powers of the nation-state to insulate the national economy from international market constraints in order to build socialism in Britain, as opposed to the first mode which corresponds to realising the party's socialist objectives within the constraints imposed by the international capitalist economy] has been in the ascendancy for shorter periods, but crucially it influenced the programme drawn up by Labour in the 1930s, following the financial crisis of 1931, and the policies of the Attlee Government. It was revived after 1970 and came to dominate policy-making in the party conference and the NEC, although not the leadership (except briefly during Michael Foot's leadership between 1981 and 1983).

Sometimes the conflicts are brought inside the leadership itself to the extent that policy-making takes sudden or unpredictable turns (Radice 2002), but most of the time the leadership has such a broad appeal to various, less vociferous parts of the party that it can sail on untroubled.

Upon closer inspection we realise that definitions of social democracy systematically shy away from any references to what might be termed 'economic policy' (exceptions to this rule would be Kesselman in Paterson and Thomas (1986) quoted in Thomson 2000: 8; see also Moses 1998). Surprising as such lacunae may be in the first place, it is still understandable given that we accept that social democracy has actually been more concerned about correcting the outcomes of the market economy rather than reforming the market economy *per se*. Consequently we are able to formulate a tentative thesis. Change of social democratic economic policy comes about as a result of dwindling economic surplus.

The smaller the economic surplus from which the State can extract resources to allocate to the welfare state, the more difficult will it be to keep up the kind of welfare state which gives social democracy its very *raison d'être*. As a result, only modifications of economic policy – in order to increase the extractable surplus – is possible, given a commitment to a preserved – or even expanding – welfare state. 'Preserved' welfare state should here be understood as permanently within the same 'social democratic' welfare-state category as elaborated by Esping-Andersen (Esping-Andersen 1990: 47ff.). In actual practice Esping-Andersen's broad category allows for many different welfare-state outlooks.

In the present study conclusions on social democracy will be based on the overall ideological views on the relationship between State and market in conjunction with some minor excursions into the fields of economic and social policy.

Reinterpreting social democracy

Somewhere there is a limit to how far market-correcting reforms might go without crossing the line where the market economy is left behind. Social democratic parties face a dilemma. '[T]he dilemma . . . lies in the ability to achieve a more equitable society within capitalism and liberal democracy, without impinging upon consumer choice or entrepreneurial initiative' (Thomson 2000: 1). In their obvious acceptance of the market economy, they have to tread carefully not to abandon their ability to correct the market. In social democracy's obvious subscription to market-correction, it has to tread carefully not to abandon its acceptance of the market economy.

While over the last forty years social democratic parties have indeed made several policy changes in a number of policy fields, the challenge against the view about a new overarching ideology of neo-liberal shape requires an empirical test. In order to refute the neo-liberal label we want to fulfil two requirements. First, pictures of social democracy during the so-called Golden Age of the post-war era as being quite so anti-market compared to present-day stances have to be repainted. Second, we have to prove that the parties are not as pro-market around 2000–4 compared with forty years before.

If the data stand up to the test we will conclude that social democracy is and has always been more or less pragmatic as to the means with which to fulfil its goals. As will become apparent later, 'pragmatic' does not here mean non-ideological. On the contrary, the point is that SAP and Labour ideologies have remained more stable than is often assumed. Our tentative belief is that in practice the overarching goal has seldom strayed far from acceptance of the liberal market economy; it was always fundamental to social democracy.

In such an interpretation, neither globalisation and crises nor new ideas on the merits of free markets posit the challenge to Labour and the SAP. Instead the parties face the strategic task of squaring their old ideas of market-correction with new ones. They have to solve the dilemma of defending the welfare state without leaving the liberal economy, and of defending the market economy without leaving the welfare state. Globalisation, crises and new ideas may change the character of that defence but hardly the core ideological aim of protecting market-weak groups and doing so inside the liberal market economy.

Towards research tools

Political interactions generally are 'predominantly oriented towards the authoritative allocation of values for a society'. The allocation of values – be they concrete or abstract – becomes political when the allocation is regarded as authoritative, i.e. 'when persons oriented to it consider that they are bound by it' (Easton 1979: 50). Stripped to textbook essentials, 'the market' on the other hand entails no 'authority' but is a means of allocating resources based on the demand and supply of these resources. As long as actors in the market reach voluntary agreements to buy and sell at negotiated prices, transactions will take place. These are the terms under which the international capitalist market economy ideally operates (Stiglitz 1997). However, authority 'is a method of control that often works with extraordinary simplicity. Sometimes not even a word is needed; in an authority relation a docile person knows what is wanted of him and does it without being told' (Lindblom 1977: 18). In this sense 'the market' would be equivalent to the sum of the actors operating within the international capitalist economic system.

The market as equivalent to the competitive international capitalist economic system as a vehicle for the pursuit of private profit and yielding the most efficient allocation of resources is the definition used here. Another aspect of the market, i.e. when market mechanisms are used within the State sector in order to increase efficiency, is thus left out of the analysis, but please note that in a few instances the occurrence or non-occurrence of market mechanisms within the State sector will be used as indirect indicators of the parties' views on the market generally.

Since participating in a global market economy involves being part of a more or less interdependent economic system, the SAP and Labour will have to establish whether dependency, i.e. the authority of the market, is high or low. Measuring those views will form our first indicator (out of four) of the parties' views on the market. The indicators will be used as a road map in Chapters 3–8 to test the claim, made in the introductory sections, about social-democratic ideological stability against assertions about a neo-liberal across-the-board triumph.

It is suggested here that the market always constituted a forceful authoritative political actor in the SAP's and Labour's thinking. Even though proponents of the social democratic (or rather social liberal) project believe in improving the market by correcting its outcomes (Shonfield 1965), market mechanisms almost never seem to have been replaced by truly government-planned allocation (Bengtsson 1995). Still, whether the level of dependency is regarded as something positive or negative *per se* is an open matter. Views in this respect will form a sub-category of the first indicator.

Another question, political parties have to pose – and which scholars and text-books pose in abundance – is whether the effects of the allocated resources are efficient or inefficient. Estimations of efficiency obviously depend on normative standpoints but we don't have to take those into account here. Our purpose is simply to find out whether the SAP and Labour themselves regard the market as efficient or inefficient; this is our second indicator.

The third indicator consists of views on the market as a means of distributing surplus resources (Bengtsson 1995). Given that the market is efficient in the sense that considerable surpluses are generated, the SAP and Labour have to ask themselves whether the surplus is distributed fairly or unfairly among the population. Once again we come across a normatively disputed concept, but in this case again we leave it for the parties to decide about the degree of fairness.

The measuring tool sketched above so far constitutes three indirect indicators (plus one sub-indicator) of the parties' views of the market. A more direct (and rough) indicator would be how the parties view the market generally, without any qualifications as regards fairness, efficiency or dependency: positive or negative? (Boréus 1994; Hinnfors and Pierre 1998; McGann Blyth 1999; Pierre 1999). Blunt as this fourth indicator may be, it will be added to the indirect indicators to complete the measuring tool, which will guide the following empirical investigation of the SAP's and Labour's market ideology at the overarching level.

The measuring tool is designed to enable us to render a less black or white picture of the parties' market ideologies. In practice there are a range of different positions between pure market acceptance and utter rejection. The following analysis will rest on the assumption that social democrats (and any party really) are able to express views of different aspects of the market process. The tool is summarised in Box 1.

Box 1 Four indicators and one sub-indicator of ideological views on the international capitalist market economy

> 1   Market dependency? High or low? → Positive or negative?
> 2   Market efficiency? High or low?
> 3   Market distribution? Fair or unfair?
> 4   Market generally? Positive or negative?
>
> Note: The indicators represent four questions (plus one sub-question) social democratic leaderships will have to pose regarding the international capitalist market economy.

Social democracy has always been fairly positive towards the liberal market economy. That is the thesis put forward here. While market-based distribution may be highly unfair as regards social justice etc., the market is still regarded as very efficient. However, unfair outcomes must somehow be adjusted. The following empirical investigation will test whether these views have remained stable within the SAP and Labour or whether major changes have occurred over the last forty years. In the event that the parties find the market to be short of perfect, and we believe this will be the case for the parties we study, a multitude of market-affecting strategies exist. Several basic positions on relations between State and market are possible along a continuum.

The allocation of resources can be left to: a) State-level decisions only: resources are then allocated according to some political authority's notion of needs; b) State-level decisions can be complemented by market-level decisions: while most allocations are needs-based a certain segment of allocations will then be market-based; c) State-level decisions predominate but are corrected by market-level decisions: State authorities then still take authoritative decisions on the allocation of values but with the help of market mechanisms; d) market-level decisions dominate but are complemented by State-level decisions: most allocations then rely on the market mechanism while a certain segment is founded on needs-based allocation; e) market-level decisions dominate but are corrected by State-level decisions: then the market is the major mechanism for allocation but with the State trying to affect how the market works through certain regulations; or f) market-level decisions only (for Bo Bengtsson's presentation and elaboration of these categories, see Bengtsson 1995: 32ff; for a brief introduction in English, see Hinnfors 1995: 175).

Just as with the possibility to hold flexible views on the various aspects of the market economy, indicated by the four market-view indicators there is a range of alternatives from State only to market only allocation in a society. With the State being the sole provider of allocation of resources there will in practice be nothing but public ownership over the means of production – which could be close to some kind of socialist society. Vice versa, market allocation taken to its extreme will include neither any public ownership nor any public sector welfare-state elements whatsoever and this extreme would entail an 'ideal' capitalist society.

There is a number of combinations between market and State available, not all of them being tied to ownership. State financing of privately operated facilities are common solutions to a host of welfare-state services for instance, and so are State regulations of the private sector (Lundqvist 1988). Box 2 gives an overview of the State–market ideological continuum.

Box 2 A State–market ideological continuum

a)   State only
b)   State complemented by market
c)   State corrected by market
d)   market complemented by State
e)   market corrected by State
f)   market only

Note: The categories correspond to a continuum from State-level decisions about allocation only down to only market-level decision. Source: Bengtsson (1995: 32ff.)

Given an empirical outcome where the market-accepting, market-correcting mixture has been stable in the SAP and Labour, we would expect that the bulk of their overarching ideologies has always been a combination of categories d and e. Aware of the problems of generalisation, I would still suggest this applies to social democracy as a whole.

The dilemma social democracy faces is, on the one hand, that as the number of State complements and corrections (categories d and e) grows, the demarcation line to category a, b and c will be blurred. On the other hand, when the number of complements and corrections dwindles, the demarcation line to category f will evaporate. However, replacing old complements and corrections with new ones is possible without affecting the status of the party ideology as regards overarching view on the market.

In all areas and sub-areas the party leaders may consider change. At the same time it is evident that a change in one area might make stability in another area possible. By reducing or increasing the State's market-controlling measures new resources might be made available to preserve or improve welfare state programmes. By reducing or increasing the extraction of resources, the State–market mix might be kept the same.

The whole concept of market-correction, so visible in earlier authors' definitions, presupposes a fundamental view of market efficiency, albeit with unfair distributional consequences (see the four market-view indicators in Box 1). Given an assumption that social democracy should have abandoned a tough stance vis-à-vis the market, and in the light of the State–market categories (see Box 2), it is surprising to realise that earlier authors' definitions of social democracy constantly seem to end up in the State–market categories 'd' (market complemented by State; most allocations rely on the market but a certain segment is based on needs-based allocation) and 'e' (market corrected by State: the State tries to affect how the market operates through a selection of regulations).

Never do the definitions seem to equal any of the more State-oriented categories, i.e. categories a–c. Still, when the same authors draw overarching conclusions, social democracy is mysteriously transformed into a substantially more State-centred political force during the Golden Age and a State-shedding, neo-liberal vehicle today. What we need to sort these oddities out is a new look at the data.

Intriguingly there seems to be rather few connections between developments at different ideological levels. By no means do stable overarching views appear to preclude changing policy standpoints and vice versa. This confusion leaves us with a tentative research strategy: In order to make advances in our knowledge about change (incremental or at sudden formative moments) and stability we need a deeper insight into the relationship between ideas at different levels of abstraction.

Bringing ideology back in

A simple observation about political life is that while certain ideas change, others remain stable. In order to tap the dynamic relationship between change and stability a necessary part of 'ideational' research obviously is to study not only changing ideas but also persistent ones (Berman 2000: 13). Of interest here is the situation when instances of change and stability occur in the same country and in the same actor. Related combinations would be when ideas in one country remain stable while changing in another country (Richardson 1982) or when key actors take up a certain idea rather than another idea (Hall 1992: 96).

One-sided approaches would concentrate either on policy change, emanating from formative moments or more slowly, or path-dependent policy stability (Gourevitch 1986; Hall 1989; Kingdon 1984; Krasner 1984: 241; Rose and Davies 1994; Rothstein 1992; Rothstein 1996). Both suffer from analytical problems. Formative moments always seem to appear out of the blue which reduces the prospective capacity (Hinnfors 1999). Path-dependency approaches border on determinism.

Theories on why party policy or ideology change usually boil down to a version of two broad categories of triggers of ideological change: 1) some kind of external change (economic shocks, party system change etc.), 2) some kind of internal change (new organisation, leaders etc.) (Cortell and Peterson 1999; Demker 1997; Hall 1992; Harmel and Janda 1994; Kitschelt et al. 1999; Müller 1997). However, when taken together these explanatory variables tend to suffer from their inclusiveness, which renders them difficult to falsify. This shortcoming might explain a certain amount of ad-hocness in the literature.

Confusion about what to mean by 'change' and to whom we refer as the changing agent causes uncertainty about how to interpret empirical statements. Obviously one cannot deny that several welfare programmes have been slimmed down or even abandoned, Keynesianism has been thrown overboard and that financial markets have been deregulated. So have the SAP and Labour really stuck so close to their old ideas?

But, the point here is that not all changes merit conclusions that social democracy is a threatened species. At this stage, the best we can say is that the picture is far from clear and the evidence contradictory. What is clear, though, is the need for some clarification concerning the concept of political ideas. Ideas occur at different levels of abstraction, which are not always held apart.

Let us conclude that change can occur at several levels, which are often poorly separated from each other in the literature. For the sake of clarity, it might be fruitful to discern between levels of 'increasing specificity and orientation towards action' (Petersson 1964: 29). One may distinguish between a number of ideological levels. The first, and perhaps most profoundly ideological, contains 'the fundamental view of political reality held by a given school of thought' (Petersson 1964: 29). The second level leaves some of the abstraction behind and approaches more policy and action-oriented ideas (Petersson 1964: 30). Finally a third level is conceivable which approaches day-to-day standpoints 'with recommendations or proposals designed to solve certain sets of persistent problems' (Petersson 1964: 31; see Goldstein and Keohane 1993: 8 ff.; Lewin 1967: 77 suggests four levels; Rose 1993: 145ff. and Seliger 1976 put forward two broader levels).

Policy analysis enables us to relate the three levels to each other. In the following study the SAP's and Labour's overarching views on the status of the market as well as views on a lower ideological level, closer to policy (welfare policy and economic policy) will be analysed. Typically, ideological views will contain three different aspects: 1) images of how the world is put together, 2) ideas about how the world should be put together, 3) ideas about how to improve the world. As would become clear upon inspection of the research tools presented above (see Boxes 1 and 2) the tools cover all three aspects.

It is one thing to define the elements of an ideology ('fundamental views' etc.). Another matter is to decide where the ideology is to be found. How do we as researchers decide on this? Ideology is an analytical concept and there is no concrete object ready to be brought down from the shelf and used in the analysis. This is a delicate matter with no ready-made answers. Approaches have to be avoided, where the ideology is to be found 'everywhere' as well as almost 'nowhere'. In either case ideology is stripped of its function as a variable to be used to explain other phenomena or to be explained by other phenomena.

What, for example, if a certain standpoint was brought forward by the Prime Minister during an informal dinner? Would that be eligible for the researcher to count as empirical underpinning for the party's ideology? What if certain backbenchers fervently back specific policies in opposition to the frontbenchers, would the backbenchers' proposals form part of the researcher's empirical data on the party's ideology? Clearly it is the rule rather than the exception that 'individuals', 'factions' and 'parties' may formulate different views and that these views may develop very differently over time (Laver 1989). An ideological change as such may be allocated to any of these units. However, short of a 'leadership'-sanctioned change we will hardly be able to speak of 'party' change in a more precise sense, at least that is the approach taken here. The present study will concentrate on the top people, i.e. those who hold the formal position to represent the party. In most instances this will be equal to what is the party leadership.

In the UK this will equal the Parliamentary Labour Party (PLP) rather than the Labour Party at large or Conference, with special focus on ministers and shadow ministers. A complicating fact is that the power relations between these forces have varied substantially over the years. Occasionally the PLP leadership is in full command but sometimes it cannot avoid carrying out Conference decisions and policy formulation has been shared with the NEC (National Executive Committee) to varying degrees and with varying organisational arrangements. As always many Conference decisions are open to interpretation and usually the leadership has a way of staying on top of things – a phenomenon equally familiar to the Swedish Social Democratic Party where radically sparkled conferences have taken several far-reaching positions over the years, such as scrapping Swedish jet-fighters – never to be implemented by the leadership (see Pierre 1986: 204ff.). However, during the 1965–2004 period the PLP leadership was probably more in command during the earlier (1965–70) and later (1997–2004) periods. As for the Wilson years Lewis Minkin (1978: 316) claims that '[r]arely in modern times can a parliamentary leadership have appeared as impervious to the policy preferences of its extra-parliamentary supporters as the Wilson Government did in the late 1960s.' Abrupt changes in the Party's policies can sometimes be explained less by true policy reconsiderations but more by new power relationships between the various parts of the Party.

The chosen approach here to focus on party leadership is motivated by the simple observation that no one but the leadership is actually able to carry out any party policy. Even though party conference rulings may often seek to tie the parliamentary leadership no policy will in fact be effectively followed unless the leaders accept it. One example of ambiguous policy-making capacity within the Labour Party is the relationship between the parliamentary leadership and the so-called National Executive Committee (NEC; with substantial formal union representation). The formal right to formulate policies in the Labour Party has been shared by the parliamentary leadership and the NEC. For the better part of the 1970s and 1980s the NEC was dominated by left-leaning activists which managed to influence election manifestos and Conference rulings substantially. Lewis Minkin observes that 'The question "What is Labour Party policy" could often be met by various answers derived from different "authoritative" sources' (Minkin 1978: 318). Even so the parliamentary leadership largely ignored the more radical manifestos and Conference declarations (Shaw 1994: 15). A third source of policy formation has been the TUC-Labour Party Liaison Committee, comprising union members, NEC representatives and parliamentary leaders – so reducing the NEC's influence (Shaw 1994: 8).

Minkin points out that '[t]he existence of these divergent sources meant that the Party and its parliamentary leadership were always subject to the parliamentary and internal as well as the electoral consequences of the resulting conflicts and ambiguities' (Minkin 1978: 318). So in the end we are still left with the parliamentary leadership as the final Party authority. Only the leadership is in a position to weigh the competing views and goals of the party but, overall, election manifestos will be very useful as guidelines to officially endorsed party views (on the usefulness of election manifestos 'to give an image of the continuous alterations in SAP's ideological profile' see Elvander 1980: 227) but, please note, that Swedish election manifestos in their modern form are a touch less elaborate and extensive than the British counterparts. Several manifestos span but a single page.[1]

When the Labour leadership finally let more of the NEC's ideas colour the formal party actions it was largely due to the fact that the 1980–83 leader Michael Foot was actually personally relatively more sympathetic to some of the left's ideas than his predecessor James Callaghan. Moreover, sometimes the character of the union–parliamentary-party leadership relationship was characterised by considerable restrictions for the leadership. Therefore, concentrating on the leadership will not prevent us from nailing down the party line. One reason why the relationship between the parliamentary leadership and the extra-parliamentary party might vary is whether the Party is in governing position or in opposition. When in government the leadership's claim to authority can be regarded as more legitimate.

Generally speaking, there is only one part of the party organisation with the express task of authoritatively defending the party's decisions, namely the leadership. In this respect it is easy to agree with Peter Hall's somewhat laconic observation that: 'Economic policy is . . . made by governments' and governments are made up of party leaderships (Hall 1984: 4). This means that, leaving formalities aside, specific programmes and Conference rulings come to life only when they are officially and in practice backed up by the leadership.

The power of leaderships may be true for most parties most of the time but there are exceptions to the rule – not least in the Labour Party. The long Labour infighting between left and right wing activists came to a head in 1981–83. The NEC's influence peaked and the party leadership was delegitimised but the effect was 'not a transfer of power to the extra-parliamentary party but the paralysis of power'. Labour was 'a rudderless ship that drifted aimlessly in dangerous seas buffeted by storms it was helpless to resist' (Shaw 1994: 22f.). However, by managing to make Michael Foot party leader, the left wing and the party leadership were comparatively at ease with each other. In historical context, Tony Blair's leadership appears to be a particularly strong one (Morgan 2001: 584).

It is also necessary to treat statements by individual party members with a certain amount of caution. The same goes for more or less formal groups, however vociferous and outspoken their statements may be. This means that regardless of how legitimate or illegitimate – in terms of closeness the Party's rank-and-file ideology – we find the leadership's ideological positions and policy decisions, it is still the leadership that acts as the final arbiter of policy decisions. Only in parliament will ideas be able to transform into real decisions and parliament is the leadership's arena.

All political parties occasionally suffer from internal rifts. However, the development in the Labour Party has gone from severe infighting between 1974–83 to a situation after 1997 when 'Party–government relations have been largely free of acrimony' (Shaw 2004: 68; perhaps one should add that Iraq, tuition fees and foundation hospitals have provided fresh material for internal Labour Party disputes lately). Accepting that development for a fact, it seems natural to include a range of party documents, though the election manifesto will form the backbone of the empirical section with continuous data for the whole period. As for 1979–83 especially, Labour Party NEC documents are highlighted in the analysis in order to form a critical test of the market-economy accepting thesis. Over the entire 1965–2003 period the 1979–83 phase is perhaps the clearest case of a clash between different branches of the Party, though probably the 1970–74 period, with its re-emergence of the public ownership issue, could be added as well. With Michael Foot some of the worst rifts could be patched up but the ideological turmoil was of a magnitude to merit special methodological considerations in this case. In case we find clear elements of market-acceptance in the NEC documents as well – which are probably the most radical ones over the entire period in any of the parties – we have a firmer position to discuss the extent of market-economy friendliness within the Labour Party.

A different approach would have been either to regard the party as an entity far wider and far more nebulous than its leadership. That approach would have enabled us to say something about the party as an all-embracing movement rather than as a hierarchical decision-making apparatus. Yet another procedure would have been to make a point about comparing the parliamentary party with activists, party affiliations, unions etc. outside of the party proper (Pontusson 1992a) in order to gauge the strengths of the various power centres within the party (see Cronin 2004 and Shaw 1994). These other interesting angles, however, lie outside the scope of the present study but would be extremely tempting to apply in future follow-up studies. Moreover, at the end of the day the only body with the role of trying to strike compromises and amalgamate different views among party voters, various branches of the party including party activists and what is feasible given the parliamentary strength of the party is the leadership (Sjöblom 1968: 51ff.).

In essence no theoretical or methodological approach is interesting *per se*. The interests of academic quality are poorly served by either theoretical or methodological dictatorship. In a sense therefore anything is possible but then again that is not the case. We have to make a choice among the available alternative approaches. The perhaps unsatisfactory position held by the author is that these matters all have to be guided by the researcher's research problematic (puzzle).

In the following study the research puzzle is focussed on the seeming contradiction between the party leaderships' rather ambitious welfare policies on the one hand and alleged neo-liberal positions by the same leaderships on the other hand. Thus the natural way to go about in this particular study is to concentrate on Labour's and the SAP's fundamental, overarching ideological views as authoritatively formulated by the immediate party leaderships. The ideology on the market economy will also be related to the authoritatively binding policy and action-oriented views on welfare policy and economic policy. In order to operationalise the overarching views we will utilise the categories presented in Boxes 1 and 2.

On top of the ideology-distinction we will have to deal with the problem of parties sometimes paying only lukewarm lip service to their claims (Driver and Martell 1998: 40f.; see also McGann Blyth 1999: 484; Rothstein 1992). Measuring the intensity of an ideological position is easier said than done but still something that has to be carefully handled. One way to go about this problem is to compare the party's ideological notions, e.g. 'planning', 'socialism' or 'freedom' with how the party actually 'operationalises' the notion. This methodological question brings us back to the discussion about three ideological levels referred to above. Comparisons between the second (ideas about how the world should be put together) and the third (ideas about how to improve the world) level will be of particular importance. Thus statements about 'socialism' and 'planning', i.e. an idea about how the world should be put together, of course have a certain ring to them. But the party's direct explanatory references, i.e. ideas about how to improve the world (in the direction of socialism and planning presumably), in the same document or related documents (e.g. a party manifesto or a major parliamentary speech) can be very different. Thus, if the reference were about 'nationalisations' the notion of socialism would be interpreted altogether differently than a statement about 'socialism' accompanied by references to 'voluntary agreements with leading price-setting firms'. The former statement/reference would be pinpointed as far more socialist than the latter.

In the following, party rhetoric will continuously be compared with explanatory references about actions as well as with actual party action. To some extent this reasoning corresponds to Bennett and Åsard's (1997: 16) notions about 'ideology', 'governing ideas' and 'rhetoric'. The thesis about a stable social democratic ideology presupposes stable overarching ideas about how some of the activities between citizens should be decommodified. During different eras this type of basic ideology is rhetorically referred to as, for example, 'socialism' or 'stakeholder society' or 'the people's home' or 'the third way'. My claim is that continuously during the better part of twentieth century all these rhetorical expressions have in fact referred to more or less the same type of society and that the real social democratic governing idea could best be labelled 'the market-correcting society'.

Some would claim that studying ideas *per se* and particularly through textual analysis, is superfluous and that real ideas will show themselves in actual, concrete, action. However, as long as the notion is maintained that ideas (and ideologies) hold any independent power in influencing actual actions one must study ideas and actions separately. Without such separation the arguments will end up in circularity: since the actor acted the way it did it must have held a certain idea (in spite of lack of any independent empirical data to substantiate the claim about the ideological content). There will then emerge a (false) perfect relationship between ideas and actions, something very rare in the social sciences. Moreover, one would deny the self-evident fact that party leaderships sometimes are unable (from various obvious strategic and structural reasons) to carry out all they are in favour of. As long as we believe in restrictions to decision-making the two variables (ideology and actual action) must be analytically separated (Hadenius 1983).

One has to avoid blurring the distinction between what is to explain and what is to be explained (or, in academic-speak, the difference between the independent and the dependent variables risks getting blurred). Therefore I suggest we keep ideas apart from actions. Instead, it will be an empirical matter as to whether the difference between ideas and actions is major or minor. Moreover, differences between the two – and variations over time – will trigger off new fruitful research questions as to when and why such differences (variations) exist.

A related methodological textual-analysis problem is posed by the question of how to deal with changing context. This is a classic dilemma where the same statements might be interpreted differently if issued in differing contexts. Speeches and declarations during Labour's 'winter of discontent' might take on a different meaning than identical (as regards wording and phrases used) speeches during the post-Thatcher era; superficially similar arguments about the welfare state are not necessarily identical if issued when the welfare state is in a state of expansion as compared to when the welfare state has come close to some kind of limit (and that is, as we all know, exactly what has happened with the welfare state).

Though not undisputed, Quentin Skinner (1974, 1978) has elaborated on the need to relate the textual elements to the specific social, political, intellectual context in which they were framed. Even so it is a testing task to present unobjectionable criteria with which to decide the relevance of a certain context. Since 'context' is an analytical concept, how do we actually choose contexts from all imaginable varieties of contexts? Unfortunately there is no immediately available answer but we have to choose in order to avoid getting caught in 'context-means-everything'.

There is one element, though, which one has to be absolutely clear about: What is actually up for measurement? In the present case, I believe I have provided the reader with ample justification for keeping day-to-day concrete actions outside the analysis. Even so, day-to-day activities will inevitably creep into the analysis through the back door in the sense that they form part of the context surrounding the ideology proper. Continuously the ideological development will have to be related to day-to-day development.

It is one thing to acknowledge the need for contextual awareness. A completely different matter is to actually formulate a robust tool for deciding what kind of context is the relevant one. How can these things be known? As always the theoretical problem of the study must take centre stage. Once the relevant contexts have been defined through some form of theoretically based argumentation a still more delicate difficulty emerges. How and with what means do we settle on certain strengths as regards the importance or meaning of the relevant context(s)? Can such things be quantified and how do we go about doing that? If quantification is unrealistic how then do we 'measure' or 'decide' on the 'strength of different contexts?' The best possible way to deal with these matters is to provide the reader with insight into the problem so as to prevent any premature conclusions.

When suitable I will present the reader with contextual data but no doubt there will always be those who feel necessary contextual elements have been left out of the discussion. The reader must thus bear in mind the tentative character of the following empirical investigation and conclusions. This piece of research (or any research for that matter) does not in any way claim to present the only, unequivocal truth. As researchers we are able to provide provisional pictures, well aware of the fact that later research most probably will challenge our views and provide different and better images of our society. My aim in this book is to do exactly that. First, I question the image of social democracy drawn up by earlier research. Second, I provide the readers with a rendering of a part of the truth, which I find has been neglected and underrated.

Let us move over to the real stuff. Labour and SAP standpoints are presented in the following part, where the categories for describing the various ways the parties' approach the market economy introduced earlier come into play. These empirical sections include separate chapters of Labour's and the SAP's market ideologies and conclude with a comparison of how the two parties have handled the central term 'socialism'. Finally, discussions about the ideological state of the two parties and their general strategic dilemma given the encompassing nature of the market crown the account in the concluding chapters of Part III.

Note

1   All Swedish manifestos were generously provided in electronic form by Birger Jerlehag of the *Swedish Social Science Data Service*, a Gothenburg University archives unit; references are made to the electronic versions.

Part II
Market-friendly social democracy

3
Labour's end of the Golden Age

In the past, the Labour Party has been hostile to market forces but more recently the hostility has been replaced by praise. Thus the Party has left its ideological foundations. This view, although obviously with nuances, is permeating several works on Labour. Stuart Thomson's (2000: 7) interpretation that the major social democratic parties, including the Labour Party as well as the Swedish SAP, 'have now become increasingly more neo-liberal than social democratic in character' is distinctly pointing to a rather long ideological distance travelled by social democracy in general and these two parties in particular. Others are equally clear: 'throughout the post-war period [the Labour Party] was social democratic in its stated aspirations and ideology. . . . In opposition in the 1980s it first reclaimed and subsequently repudiated (if gradually) its social democratic aspirations and ideology, as these were again subordinated to economic exigencies' (Hay 1999: 57f.). New Labour's 'dominant logic' is portrayed as neo-liberal, intended to spread 'the gospel of market fundamentalism' and to promote business interests and values (Hall 2003: 19, see also 13f.).

There emerges a view about fundamental change. 'Although cast in the guise of modernisation, the broad economic appeal outlined by "New" Labour has little historical purchase on "Old" Labour. Although it retains some affinity with "Old" Labour, its policy far more closely reflects the preconceptions and prescriptions of the Thatcher and Major governments' (Heffernan 2000: 72). There were indeed several disappointments for the Labour left during the 1960s and 1970s but overall this period, it has been claimed, saw 'the most left-wing statement the party had adopted since 1945' and the *Programme 1973* substantially strengthened ideas about an 'alternative economic strategy aimed to use political power to rebuild economic strength' and 'measures that socialised and collectivised the economy' (Gamble 1994: 172, 175).

Of course several renderings of Labour's market views include shades of grey rather than just black and white. It has been suggested that numerous key elements of New Labour were present already during Wilson and Callaghan, in the sense that reactions against Keynesian economics and a focus on education formed important parts of Labour policies. Meanwhile, '[m]uch of its social and economic

policy . . . shows continuity with the neo-liberalism, privatisation and deregulation of the Thatcher regime' (Morgan 2001: 588). Others would argue that, even
though the Labour Party has veered away from several of its traditional policies
(above all failed to deliver), there is still scope for a future return to more established social democratic positions within a European framework (Wickham-Jones
2000). Several propose that although there is continuity between the present
Labour Government and the preceding Conservative one, there is also, in practice,
continuity with previous Labour governments, though the rhetoric has changed
(Atkinson and Savage 2001: 15; Coates 2001: 300).

The overall impression, however, is the emphasis in earlier research that, while a
number of New Labour policies may remain faithful to a traditional 'government
of the left' (fighting poverty, providing public services), distinct aspects of the policies are state-of-the-art right and pro-market as opposed to earlier anti-market
positions: '[F]iscal and monetary conservatism; the positive value of free markets
and low taxes; the priority accorded to wealth creation over equality of outcome;
and the emphasis on managerial reforms to the public sector' (Driver and Martell
2003: 223). Many scholars propose that although there were disillusionment and
disenchantment about Labour's ability to deliver during the Golden Age of Social
Democracy (Coates, 2001; Gamble 1994: 172; Hay 1999: 57), the Party nonetheless
stood by traditional social democratic values with the aim of gradually, with revisionist measures, limiting the market economy. Today the room for the liberal
market economy within the ideological tenets has expanded.

Given the general view about Labour's ideological development as regards
market views one would expect to find a fair amount of strong market criticism
during the Golden Age of Social Democracy. There would be distinct references to
thoroughly underpinned and elaborated socialist goals, which, albeit through
reformist means, would be the desired outcome of social democracy. If the change
thesis is correct, the criticism should now have been replaced by more uncondi-
tional praise for the market.

A view of stability would instead come in either of two versions. In the first version, one would believe that social democrats were always unerring sceptics about
the market economy. Not only would socialism and a planned economy form the
Golden-Age ideal, but it would also remain as a viable political discourse.

An alternative version of stability would show social democrats as continuous
believers in the merits of the market economy. So, when social democrats freely –
in the sense that they are not caught up in day-to-day political debate – ponder the
merits or shortcomings of the market, what have they said? Has the market been
friend or foe? The point taken in this book is one of much stronger stability than
has been shown by earlier research. Changes in many areas have taken place but
there is a case for claiming that the adherence to the market economy was never
really threatened by either the Labour Party leadership or their Swedish colleagues.
The parties' views of the market were much more nuanced than is often thought
to be the case.

Over and again, Labour's 1966 election manifesto underlined the importance of
balanced public finances. The manifesto stated that: 'the fundamental problems of

the British economy . . . [lie in] . . . the rapid modernisation of our industries and a proper balance between public and private expenditure . . . [without which] . . . the economy was left to the push and pull of the market' (Labour 1966).[1]

This was certainly no politics-shedding party. Nor was it a foe of the market. Rather, the view was that a proper balance had to be struck between the two forces echoing the Party's standpoints two years earlier when the message was to 'encourage industries', 'improving facilities' and 'providing better terms of credit' with the cautious rider that this would apply only when business 'justifies' it (Labour 1964). The basic facts of the market economy were still firmly included in the Party's 1966 manifesto text. Although the market's failures were perceived as necessary to correct, the Party brought forward no pledges to abolish it as such and Labour's 'overriding aim' was the 'pursuit of solvency and the defence of the pound . . . [through the creation of] overseas confidence in sterling' (Labour 1966) and '[t]o maintain full employment and a high level of investment in productive industry' (Labour 1966).

With statements like these, with a clear focus on market 'productivity' and on 'confidence' in the market, a picture emerges, that Labour had a deeply embedded belief in the market economy. Several of the manifesto concepts, like 'confidence' etc., pointed in the direction of a worldview where the market played a significant part. Even though the Labour Party was definitely not a party willing to tear down the public sector, the Party shied away from any real alternative to market competition:

> the Labour Government launched the first serious attack on the rising cost of living. The weapon specially fashioned for this attack is the policy for productivity, prices and incomes, which forms an essential part of the National Plan. Without such a policy it is impossible either to keep exports competitive or to check rising prices at home. The alternative, in fact, is a return to the dreary cycle of inflation followed by deflation and unemployment. (Labour 1966)

Thus, without salubrious pressure from the market, there will be inflation and unemployment. With this central element firmly in place, terms like the 'National Plan' could be used. Competitiveness in the market was Labour's solution to UK's problems at the height of the Golden Age of Social Democracy. In various formulations, this argument was repeated throughout the manifesto and elsewhere (Cronin 2004: Chapter 2). The passage on the role for the publicly owned coal industry is particularly telling: 'The best available estimate of the market for coal in 1970 is 170–180 million tons. We stress that this is an estimate, and in no sense a limitation. Everything depends upon efficiency, costs and the resulting prices. If more can be profitably sold, then no barrier will stand in the way of expansion' (Labour 1966).

In mildly veiled words, what the manifesto actually said was, that even though the mining industry remained in public hands, the market would set its limits and the Party would endorse these limits. According to the text, 'efficiency', 'costs' and 'profits' determined the conditions for the industry. Even the reassuring statement that 'no barrier' would stand in the way of expansion, should the coal be 'profitably sold', was fully lodged in market-thinking. All the Party offered was a calculation, an 'estimate', of the market's needs. Despite the terminology of a 'national fuel policy' this was rather different from a planned, needs-based and politically defined production.

All involved in the mining industry had to meet the market's tough demands. Apparently the Government lacked any kind of 'plan' in the true sense of the word backed by State authority to solve the problems in the mining industry. Little more could be provided than comforting words. Overall, the planning element rested on 'entirely hypothetical figuring' (Goodhart 1965, quoted in Cronin 2004: 69).

The Party's plans for the mining sector involved no threat to the market but were rather a means of finding ways to improving competitiveness. It is extraordinary that the Labour Party's position in these matters (and others) has caused latter-day research to draw the conclusion that the Party wielded strong planning instruments during the Golden Age. And the coal industry was not just any industry. It was one of the most symbolically charged industrial sectors for the British working class.

At the same time as the market was acknowledged as the main vehicle of increased productivity, the Party stressed the need for creating favourable conditions for such a development. In that respect the manifesto presented a mixture of incentives and control mechanisms. While Labour did not want to 'dictate prices, wages and salaries' the party considered 'selective control over the export of capital . . . licensing of inessential buildings' and similar market-limiting actions.

Most readers would probably consider introducing licences to what was described as 'inessential buildings' as rather modest. Once again we encounter a terminology apparently meant to moderate the fact that there were very few means left with which the Party could or wanted to move in a more State-controlling direction. Moreover, according to the manifesto, industry needed help in order to get on the right track towards productivity and competitiveness. To that end, the Government wanted to provide 'purposive financial assistance to key industries', sponsor research councils etc.

Although some of the manifesto's expressions pointed in a State-control direction such as the suggestions about 'selective control over the export of capital', most of the proposals were distinctly market-based with corrective mechanisms. Labour wanted to 'reconstitute the Prices and Incomes Board' but the Party's 'purpose is not to dictate prices, wages and salaries'. Research councils may be 'sponsored' (though there were no proposals about setting up new research councils) and some industries assisted. Helping the market forces along to prudent choices appears to have been the Labour way.

As for public ownership in general, the Party was extremely cautious about any precise promises. The policy was more that of forcing private enterprise to become more competitive by encouraging mergers, takeovers and rationalisation (see Shaw 1996: 78). Big, efficient companies would perform better in the market. To this end the Industrial Reorganisation Corporation (IRC) was set up in 1965 with the express objective of creating large, efficient industrial bodies to increase market performance (Shaw 1996: 78). The overall aim was 'to assist in the rationalisation of British industry and the creation of industrial enterprises that could compete successfully in world markets' (Gamble 1994: 120). So, in spite of the IRC being a body in the State apparatus, it was hardly working in the direction of market replacement. Rather, the opposite was true.

In terms of the research categories utilised in this book, the Party's general opinion about the market in the 1966 Labour election manifesto was slightly mixed. Properly guided, so the argument seems to have gone, the market is a mighty creator of wealth. However, left to its own, the market causes problems, which have to be solved. This is very far from a laissez-faire extreme standpoint but it is still reasonable to classify the Party statements as at least mildly in favour of the market. The whole range of market terminology and the conspicuous absence of clear alternatives to the market's way of operating the economy speak in favour of this conclusion.

As for dependency and efficiency, the clear-cut outcome is that the Labour Party regarded the market as an efficiency agent. The Party acknowledged market dependency and stated no need to change these fundamental conditions. Hence Labour's position will be classified as 'positive' towards market-dependency. On the fairness variable the Party was much more negative, though it remains a bit unclear whether it felt poor people's hardships were caused by the market forces *per se*, or by imprudent Tory Government policies.

The conclusion about the ideology being lodged into an overall worldview about the necessity of keeping policies within the confines set by the international market forces is supported by the contemporary efforts to construct a workable incomes policy. Although superficially of an intervening character, the incomes policy was carried out on the presumption that a spiral of wage and price increases would be devastating. The unions had to be persuaded to hold back their demands. 'Inflation was to be brought under control without sacrificing full employment . . . competitiveness in world markets could be restored only if for some years prices rose more slowly in Britain than in other countries. Without a successful incomes policy, past experience suggested that there was little likelihood of that' (Stewart 1977: 39). The recently appointed Head of the Department of Economic Affairs, George Brown, was given the task. Along with several welfare-state measures (pension increases, rise in income tax, abolition of prescription charges etc.), a Prices and Incomes Board was set up and a 'National Plan' for investments and growth launched. With the words of Michael Stewart in his *The Jekyll and Hyde Years*, 'it was all a dream' (Stewart 1977: 50). The plan was more of a calculating experiment with precious few concrete measures to make the plans come true. Certain measures, such as devaluation were ruled out. Setting annual export growth target at 5.25 per cent 'required a faith big enough to move mountains' (Stewart 1977: 50). Through the sheer size of the figure, the plan acknowledged Britain's reduced world competitiveness. The plan was 'formally interred' in July 1966 (Stewart 1977: 51; see Shaw 1996: 75).

While an underlying, and possibly very earnest, will to 'do' something about market forces can be felt in the efforts to construct a plan, it's equally clear that the Party leadership still implicitly – and explicitly – accepted the overall terms set by the market. The planning intentions, and the concrete measures concerning a national economic policy were 'in ruins' with party activists left disillusioned (Gamble 1994: 172). The new Department of Economic Affairs, set up in 1964 and reflecting an optimism about the technological possibilities to turn industry into higher productivity and efficiency, soon proved to be toothless – a 'cheerleader for planning' (Cronin 2004: 66), lacking any practical means for making planning work rather than a proper planning agency.

Later, devaluation became an option, and the Chancellor of the Exchequer, James Callaghan, presented a Letter of Intent to the IMF recognising the need for improved balance of payments with public-sector borrowing requirements under strict control. Britain was in need of a vote of confidence from the international financial community. In comments of peculiar similarity to later remarks about New Labour, left activists claimed 'that although the Conservatives had been defeated at the polls, Conservative policies were now being imposed on the nation by outside bodies' (Stewart 1977: 85f.).

Four years on, the 1970 election manifesto tried to keep about the same distance to unchecked market forces. 'Without planning, with a return to the Tory free-for-all, people become the victims of economic forces they cannot control' (Labour 1970). At the same time, sentences stressing 'productivity' and 'competitors' indicated that the market's fundamentals were continuously being acknowledged and indeed accepted:

> The biggest challenge facing any industrial nation today, is how to expand the economy without pushing up its costs. The answer lies in increasing our productivity.
>
> Only in this way can we keep our lead over our competitors and ensure an improvement in the real standard of life for our people. . . . If wage increases were now to be linked to increases in production, we should be able to look forward to greater price stability. (Labour 1970)

Playing according to the market's competition rules was Labour's solution. Britain had 'to keep [its] lead over [its] competitors'. While the basic acceptance of the market's characteristics can be inferred by sentences like 'Britain has to pay her way in trade and transactions with the outside world' (Labour 1970), the manifesto also claimed the Labour Party was 'not the creature of private profit' (Labour 1970). Exactly how or in what way the Party was not a creature of private profit was never really spelt out. However, the parallel emphasis on welfare-state measures, i.e. corrections to the market's outcome, show that the party felt that profits alone did not guarantee prosperity for all. A 'disastrous cycle of Stop-Go ... and scandalous neglect of such essential community services as houses, schools and hospitals' told a story of mounting needs of corrections of the market's 'push and pull' effects.

The goals about proper public guidelines for the market were still intact in the manifesto, including a number of corrective measures, such as training programmes, investment grants, and industrial reorganisation incentives. At the same time the Labour Party was particularly clear about the need for balanced balance of payments. National accounts in the red formed no part of Labour's policy.

Keynesianism had indeed been 'largely unchallenged', but without ever having to cope with insufficient demand, the model's solutions of public borrowing and tax reductions had never been put to the test (Cronin 2004: 62).

Overall, the Party's market ideology remained fairly stable between 1966 and 1970. If anything, this early period offered few examples of what has here been referred to as 'state-enforcing' research categories. The mixture between plain market-acceptance and vague allusions to plans and steering indicate that the Party had to contemplate how old tenets should confront new realities. It also illustrates the fact that decisive moves away from the old tenets were probably taken long before.

Shifts from the rather positive attitude towards basic facts of the market economy, expressed during the 1960s, emerged in the 1974 (February) manifesto (reflecting the left wing's gaining of dominance on the NEC; see Hatfield 1978). These moves are indicated in Table 1, which presents a summary of Labour's 1965–2002 market-ideological development. For 1974, the Party's 'General opinion' about the market was 'Negative', while the views on 'Dependency' were emphasising the negative effects of high market dependency. Whether the market economy was really efficient or not became much more of an open matter, which visibly differed from earlier periods when the Party had been decidedly more positive. While still recognising the importance of productivity, the Party proposed to take:

> Land required for development ... into public ownership, so that land is freely and cheaply available for new houses, schools, hospitals and other purposes. Public ownership of land will stop land profiteering. [The party will] substantially extend public enterprise by taking mineral rights ... take shipbuilding, shiprepairing and marine engineering, ports, the manufacture of airframes and aeroengines into public ownership and control. (Labour 1974a)

As the Government's 'first priority', a 'determined attack on inflation and the appalling overseas deficit' was promised. At the same time, the former Tory Government was accused of allowing huge deficits to accumulate and of borrowing hundreds of millions of pounds (Labour 1974b). Labour's alternative was the new deal, which included a 'social contract' with a number of market correctives and a few market complements to sustain full employment and redistribute wealth (through taxation) to the poorer sections of society.

The energy crisis had hit the world. Among other things, the Party suggested 'strict price control on key services and commodities'. All in all, these measures indicate a distinctly cooler attitude towards the market than during the Golden Age of the 1960s. The Party unequivocally stated that public ownership had to be extended, even if the range of industries targeted appears to have been slightly incoherent. In the 1973 Party Programme, some major industrial sectors were indeed listed for nationalisation (or at least 'public control and participation') such as the North Sea oil industry, as well as the docks, aircraft industry and shipbuilding (Labour 1973: 32ff.).

As for the strategically important financial institutions, the manifesto became more evasive. The text was veiled and vague. Studies were 'under way' about 'what kind of publicly owned institutions will best suit the role we wish them to play'. The readers were not given information about the status of the studies referred to. Whether the future role for industry would be in a more State-controlled direction or not was never settled. Finally, pharmaceuticals were to be the focus of 'some element of public ownership in the future' (Labour 1973: 35).

Although the suggested increase in public ownership was rather limited and could be interpreted as a short-term reaction to the oil crisis, the documents showed a willingness to discuss complements to the market. Most allocations would still rely on the market but certain segments (though still very few) of the market would be based on some kind of needs-based allocation. However, the market was still the backdrop against which the Party leadership envisaged its policies. Public ownership was a way of trying to make better use of market processes and competitive mechanisms. As the terms set for a new National Enterprise Board (NEB) showed, the Government relied heavily on market outcomes. The NEB was to operate on commercial criteria and remained distinctly toothless during its lifetime (Stewart 1977: 217).

Overall, the manifesto was still a market-correcting document. Such a conclusion is underpinned by the apparently market-economy friendly introductory paragraph to the October 1974 manifesto with its emphasis on productivity, competitiveness and high investment. According to the manifesto, those things were all needed to get Britain back on the right track and – readers were led to believe – it was the Government's responsibility to make those things happen in a 'new deal' (Labour 1974b) – a concept, which is a popular slogan recycled by the later New Labour Party. But the manifesto was also a fervent statement about the need for social justice for everyone, not just for property speculators who 'grow wealthy looking at empty office blocks' but for coal miners, 'the weak, the poor, the disabled' (Labour 1974b).

The 1973 Party Programme had oscillated between market-hostility and market-acceptance. On the one hand, Labour wanted to use 'price controls . . . new public ownership . . . economic planning, and . . . new industrial powers' (Labour 1973: 13). On the other hand the Programme admitted that '[w]e cannot escape from the reality that for a major world trading nation, such as Britain, events in the outside world can sometimes work to the detriment of our own standards of living. . . . [O]ur exports must not be allowed to become uncompetitive against those of our leading competitors among the industrial countries of the world' (Labour 1973: 16).

Moreover, even though nationalised industries were to 'plan the national economy in the national interest', the firms were still to act on the same international capitalist market as the Programme had shown Britain would have to stay competitive against. The more radical proponents of NEB takeover of private companies wanted public ownership to 'change the public-private balance' and to alter the old planning techniques [italics in original]' (Judith Hart, quoted in Hatfield 1978: 158). At the same time, they were still willing to use 'competitive stimuli by giving a lead on investment' and would 'reduce private monopoly by inserting public enterprise competition' (Eric Heffer, quoted in Coates 1980: 90). Thus, public ownership would be a means to make better use of market processes and competitive mechanisms, rather than replacing the liberal market economy as such. Even leading Labour left intellectuals seemed to share this view. Though close to the Cabinet, Stuart Holland expressed many of the British left's standpoints in his *The Socialist Challenge* (1975). In spite of scathing criticism of the increasing strength of large near-monopoly multinational companies (the 'mesoeconomic sector' with almost government-size planning-like capacity), Holland still acknowledged the liberal market's role as such – or at least found no real means for replacing it. The problem with large companies was rather their enormous profits, made possible through lack of proper exposure to competition. Real public influence would also change the way companies outside the public sector operated:

> If a socialist government were able to ensure direct control of the strategic decision-making in a range of leading companies, and were able to exploit its state power to coordinate the planned expansion of such firms to fulfil new economic and social objectives, it would thereby have transformed the conditions and constraints under which the remaining firms in the mesoeconomic sector could operate. This would result from the information on the real structure of costs and profits in the meso-sector which it could secure from its own companies, plus the harnessing of the leadership of dominant market power in the public rather than the private interest. (Holland 1975: 159f., see also Chapters 2–4)

In other words, Holland foresaw that new public owners would bring new intentions with them and they would also create more transparent information structures to those who operated on the market. But it would still be a market and the companies would still have to be competitive. In some instances, the left's project went further by proposing to protect the economy from the international market. While '[t]he British economy would remain a major trading economy . . . [it would be] no longer burdened by an international currency, a deteriorating balance of payments on visible trade, and an internationally oriented financial and business sector' (Gamble 1994: 178f.). This view seems to have been outside the core of the Party.

The point here is not that Holland or any of his fellow renewers of the ideological left of the Party wanted anything like 'New Labour' as such. The rhetoric, the views on internal decision-making structure, on the stance on public ownership, the volume of public sector involovement etc. were all different from what was to come later. However, the absence of any true suggestions to the basic operations of the market bears testimony to the lack of alternatives. Holland emphasised the need for 'information on the real costs and profits'. Let loose, the market's actors will pervert the way they relate to each other by hiding information. With more altruistic public-sector owners, the real facts would emerge and the market's outcome would, consequently, be different.

Other, more moderate forces, such as the 'main exponent of social democratic theory in Britain in the 1950s, Anthony Crosland', were convinced Government could influence industry without wholesale public takeover (Crosland 1956;

Holland 1975: 24; Shaw 1996: 115), something, which was, in fact, not proposed by Holland either. More resigned moods were also present, as shown by the Department of Economic Affairs' (staffed by several influential persons, among them Crosland) 1969 planning paper *The Task Ahead*, which rather bluntly stated that 'what happens in industry is not under the control of the government' (Department of Economic Affairs 1969).

Without playing down the strength with which the groups to the left were critical of the market, a paradoxical picture emerges of the market eating itself into the very centre of their criticism. Of course these groups were aware of the internally divided Labour Party and had to tread carefully in order not to cause too much alarm among more conventional social democrats. Even so the results have to be interpreted as a sign of the tremendous difficulties of ridding the Labour Party of its adherence to the market.

Overall, important groups in the Party did change their views about public ownership. From having been a dead issue in the late 1960s, the ownership option suddenly appeared in central party documents in the early 1970s. It appears, and this is perhaps a surprising result, that the views on the market and on ownership were not mutually excluding. It was absolutely possible simultaneously to be in favour of both the market and of public ownership. Indeed, increased public ownership would lead to improvements in the way the market functioned and 'towards state-initiated restructuring of British capitalism on a large scale' (Coates 1980: 96). Obviously, everyone wasn't happy with this de facto capitalism, which involved the same 'shedding of labour' (Coates 1980: 96) as any other capitalist rationalising process.

The general impression, then, is that the Programme conveyed a message that basic facts of the market economy were there to stay, but that the Labour Party wanted to alleviate the effects of the market. This strategy was far less than the radical parts of the Party wanted (Coates 1980: 86ff.; Hatfield 1978: 151ff.; Stewart 1977: 216ff.) but again the market-conforming policy prevailed among those who finally set their marks on the Party's ideology.

If the Labour Party texts turned away somewhat from the market in the aftermath of the oil price shock in 1974, the formulations were back on more familiar ground a couple of years later. However, the return to more outspoken market acceptance did not prevent Labour from accusing the Tories for letting 'crude market forces' free (Labour 1979). According to Labour, laissez faire would lead to 'soaring inflation, rising prices and growing unemployment'. The perceived uncaring attitude behind those effects would cause 'misery for millions of the most vulnerable in our community' (Labour 1979).

Moreover, distinct elements of the public ownership theme from five years before were still present. The 1979 manifesto claimed that, 'wherever we give direct aid to a company out of public funds, we shall reserve the right to take a proportionate share of the ownership of the company' (Labour 1979). This said – and it was still some distance away from a firmly expressed aim in the direction of leaving the market economy – the Party went a long way in using market rhetoric: 'Nothing so undermines a nation as inflation. Not only does it make the family's task of budgeting more difficult, it is a threat to jobs and a standing invitation to our overseas competitors to invade our markets' (Labour 1979).

According to the manifesto, the Conservatives had 'failed to control the supply of money', while the Labour Party wanted to set the 'task of bringing inflation down to 5 per cent' and to 'ensure that consumers are not exploited by monopoly producers or unfair practices'. Monopolies render a market economy less efficient, and by sentences like these, the Party could show a conviction to ensure real – and fair – competition became the hallmark of the British economic system. These paragraphs were very close to the 1974 formulations. The Party claimed to be 'deeply concerned to enlarge people's freedom' and to give 'high priority to working for a return to full employment', although full employment 'must go hand-in-hand with keeping down inflation'. There is little to indicate other than that the notion of the market was firmly entrenched in Labour's language.

The Party had set an optimistic target of 3 per cent economic growth per annum. In order to be able to deliver, the economy had to function well and Labour explicitly stressed the positive effects of the market economy – with due respect paid to avoiding the 'crude market forces' advocated by the Tories: 'In order to take full advantage of these opportunities, we must improve our industrial competitiveness at home and abroad – and that means making sure our industries adapt to new markets and technological change' (Labour 1979).

As a safeguard against private industry malpractices, the public sector was given a role by the manifesto to outline 'positive strategies' for industry, aid in investment, and provide training and retraining programmes. Finally, the Party pledged to use a limited amount of public ownership, but only where 'possible' and only as a means to give direct aid to a specific company.

But for the most part, the Party actually issued statements about the authoritative character of the market economy. Industries had to 'adapt to new markets and technological change' (Labour 1979). In essence, this can only be interpreted as Labour's acknowledgement that government planning had to be distinctly weaker in comparison to the broad outcome of the market. What the Party could do, and pledged to do, with a number of more or less binding promises, was to ensure ordinary people were not hurt in the maelstrom of market forces. By trying to work to upgrade the public sector, some of the hardships endured by the many could be alleviated.

In the research-analytical terminology used in this book, the overall picture of the measures, taken together, neatly corresponds to the State–market category where the State is supposed to wield several tools to try and affect and correct how the market operates. Instead of public ownership (with some exceptions), a selection of regulations will lead to the desired outcome. By no means is the State thought to be powerless, but the power is more or less restricted to work within the confines of the market economy. That was exactly the strategy the Labour Government had practised during the latter part of the 1970s. Stricter limits to public expenditure had been introduced in 1975, unemployment had been allowed to rise without utilising any Keynesian measures and the sterling crisis of 1976 had led the Government to accept monetary targets (Gamble 1994: 194).

1980–86: Socialism on the agenda

Labour's sudden well-known, but temporary, radicalisation after Margaret Thatcher's 1979 electoral triumph is easily detected in the 1983 election manifesto. Under the heading 'Emergency programme of action', a host of actions were presented. Labour would 'launch a massive programme for expansion' to end mass unemployment, which was presented as the number one goal. In order to pay for this, Labour wanted to reintroduce a key State-planning measure: exchange controls. The intention was expressed as preventing 'currency speculation and to make available – to industry and government in Britain – the large capital resources that are now flowing overseas' (Labour 1983). Capital was the enemy and through the documents, there is still to be felt the desire to actually do something radical about the state of affairs at the time. The willingness to produce an alternative to the openly market-praising Conservative Government – and perhaps to the earlier Labour administrations – is almost palpable.

The Labour Party's interest in 'real' socialism during the early days of the 1980s took central stage in the party's National Executive Committee's 1981 *The Socialist Alternative*, Statements to the 1981 Party conference. Probably the most radical centrally located branch in any of the two parties (Labour and the SAP) during any period since World War II.

As expected, socialism was no longer a mere rhetorical figure in *The Socialist Alternative*. At the heart of the text was a commitment to 'common ownership'. The long-term goal was said to 'substitute private ownership by these diverse forms [public enterprises, workers' cooperatives, municipal ventures and ownership by workers' capital funds] of common ownership' (Labour, NEC 1981: 11). The basic argument behind common ownership was the capitalist economy's inner drive to 'move in search of the highest private profit and [to treat workers] as disposable, to be discarded at will'. 'Social control of production' should replace 'the anarchy of the market' (Labour, NEC 1981: 11).

Apparently private ownership was to have no role in this framework for a socialist Britain. A reasonable conclusion about the meaning of 'social control' would be that it presupposed a distinct role for the working class, or at least strong State powers. To make people unemployed or even to force people to move to new jobs without their consent would violate the social element. Instead, emerging in the documents was a picture of a benevolent State intent upon organising society in such a way as to ensure steady employment and catering for the needs of consumers and workers. Profit-seeking market speculators would then have to accept a secondary, or even negligent, role in the economy.

But even so, there was an intriguing – and astonishing – ambivalence to be felt in the text. Planning, it was claimed, 'will be able to steer jobs directly into *the regions*, and to create new jobs to replace those which die' (Labour, NEC 1981: 21, italics in original). The text conveyed a message of determination to create and protect jobs. Surprisingly, the same text acknowledged the fact that even in a new economic system, jobs would actually 'die'. But, how could the jobs 'die' given that ownership was common and social production had been introduced? One would have thought that with social control of production in place and with private ownership more or less abolished, the Party would be certain new jobs would emerge and multiply according to social needs rather than simply risk dying away. The contradiction leaves one to question the conviction with which the Party actually wanted to reform the economic system and abolish the market economy. Rather, a more plausible conclusion is that the Party was still ready to accept the basic elements of the market economy but contemplated stronger means than before, with which to correct the market's outcomes.

Moreover, 'small businesses' were apparently excluded from the need for common ownership. They should even be 'encouraged' by Labour's policies (Labour, NEC 1981: 21). The same ambivalence was shown when the NEC condemned the 'failures of the free market' on one page only to urge, on the next page, the need to raise 'the level of productivity right across industry and make it much more responsive to technical change and to changes in demand – particularly in world markets' (Labour, NEC 1981: 19f.). Although the message clearly was to emphasise that the market system was about to be brought down, it is equally obvious that the NEC's version of how this was to be done presupposed the market economy was somehow to remain. The two stories do not square.

That the NEC should underline the core socialist issue – public ownership over the means of production – is perhaps less surprising, given that the drift towards revisionism during the 1960s was more of a Party leadership phenomenon than something that permeated the Party in a broader sense. There was still support for traditional socialist measures within the Party's rank and file as well as the unions. As soon as they managed to win strategic influence over Conference, their policies became visible once more (Minkin 1978: 326).

However, the tough, pro-active NEC, so full of initiative and socialist drive, was actually allowing itself to indirectly accept a system where British industries merely reacted passively to changes in the international market. This conclusion was unexpected. One cannot but conclude that although the document was written by highly committed authors, even given internal NEC conflicts, free to elaborate with only minor limitations about future responsibility, the sheer force of traditional market-thinking still had a firm grip over the proposals.

Important parts of the 1981 NEC statements were not included in the 1983 election manifesto. This transformation of policies on the way from activist centre to the parliamentary party leadership is an important reminder about how cautious we should be about equalling activist proposals with authoritatively binding party documents. In the 1982 Party Programme the Party's ownership aims were somewhat reduced. Now, private companies were manifestly accepted alongside public ownership and the Programme explicitly stated that '[w]e do not say that common ownership will need to reach down into every aspect of economic activity' (Labour 1982: 9). The goal was to give 'the community decisive power over the commanding heights of the economy' (Labour 1982: 9). Also 'joint ventures between public and private companies' had been added to the list of public ownership forms (Labour Party: 9). Overall, the role for new common-ownership enterprise was downplayed. The range of industries to be affected by nationalisation was reduced to electronics, pharmaceuticals, health equipment and building materials (plus other sectors 'as required in the national interest' (Labour 1983: 11)). Besides, the increased attraction of the market was shown by the proposal to give 'far more freedom [to public enterprises] to raise funds on capital markets' (Labour 1983: 11). A more determined way to deal with the market economy would perhaps have been to reduce the influence of capital markets, in many ways the very epitome of the international capitalist market economy. Instead, the Party proposed broadening the market's sphere.

The NEC's 1981 Statements included a section criticising the fact that the market was dominated by only a hundred companies and therefore didn't function properly as a market (Labour, NEC 1981: 20). Consequently, public ownership must be used to make sure research, innovation and guidance generally was assured. Ironically the size of the largest companies was partly the effect of Labour's own policies during the 1960s when it was felt that too many companies were of sub-optimal size and had to be pushed to merge in order to be competitive on the market. A special so-called Industrial Reorganisation Corporation (IRC) was set up for this purpose, although in absolute numbers the IRC's influence was rather limited (Woodward 1993: 88; see Beckerman 1972a: 191ff.). The IRC operated under a pragmatic philosophy promoting productive efficiency rather than market efficiency and utilising persuasion rather than coercion (Beckerman 1972a: 193). In both instances, Labour's express policies tried to intervene in the way the market system operated rather than replacing it altogether.

Earlier manifestos were rather matter-of-fact in their comments about the fundamental requirements upon the economy, exerted by the market forces. This manifesto was no exception but expressed willingness to give governments an important role: '[W]e will also work with other governments – especially socialist governments – to bring about a co-ordinated expansion of our economies' (Labour 1983).

But in the midst of indisputable market scepticism, not to say hostility, there was a clear element of perhaps surprising ambivalence in the manifesto. On the one hand, and echoing the February 1974 manifesto, Labour wanted to 'introduce back-up import controls, using tariffs and quotas ... to achieve our objectives of trade balance ... [and] establish a significant public stake in electronics, pharmaceuticals, health equipment and building materials; and also in other important sectors, as required in the national interest'. These passages all correspond to a vision where 'the market is complemented by the State' or even in some instances bordering to 'the State being complemented by the market'. In analytical terms, this was therefore a radical shift away from the Party's position five years before.

But on the other hand, 'we must ensure that our trade and balance of payments contribute to our expansion. This means maintaining the pound at a realistic and competitive rate' without which interest rates would surge and the balance of trade be damaged. 'A competitive exchange rate will assist British exports abroad and make British goods more competitive at home' (Labour 1983: 9). Also, the Programme drove home the point that 'public borrowing is financed, through the financial institutions and national savings, without disruptive or damaging changes in interest rates' (Labour 1983: 9).

Obviously, terms like 'realistic' and 'competitive' have to be defined. One can hardly see any other interpretation than where 'realistic' and 'competitive' exchange rates are those set by the international capitalist economic system. The programme offered no alternative definition of 'realistic'. As for 'competitive', the text is definitely within the boundaries of market terminology. A society permeated with the will to allocate resources according to 'needs' would hardly pay much attention to 'competition' as such. The two terms contradict each other. In fact the phrases were strangely reminiscent of how, twenty years earlier, the Conservative Chancellor Selwyn Lloyd commented on the role of the so called National Development Economic Council (NEDC or 'Neddy'): 'What the Council must do is to set an ambitious but realistic target figure. Both sides of industry, the Government and indeed all sections of the community must be prepared to face up to the practical consequences involved in its achievement' (quoted in Stewart 1977: 48 f.).

In Labour's own words, no matter how vital a certain welfare reform might be, it would apparently have to wait until the public funds were there to handle borrowing properly. The capital market was the final enforcer of interest rates. The manifesto stated that 'disruptive or damaging changes in interest rates' had to be avoided. Once again, core Labour formulations point in the direction of a tacit acceptance of market forces. While these sentences hardly praise the market, they certainly provide support for the conclusion that the Labour Party has had severe difficulties avoiding the logic of the market even when some of the rhetoric points in another direction. These latter views are thus clearly indicative of market terminology and correspond to a distinctly market-correcting worldview. Moreover, the same randomness as was encountered in the 1974 manifesto about the range of industries targeted for public ownership can be found in the 1983 document. This would indicate that the Party's readiness to offer a clear-cut planning-oriented belief system was limited.

Given our earlier hesitation about using data from both opposition and government years, it is interesting to compare the 1974 (October) and 1981–83 statements. In both cases the Party took noticeably left positions. In both cases the lid was lifted to let out the power question in the form of suggestions that major industries should be considered for public ownership. However, in 1974 Labour was a governing party (albeit only since February) whereas the Party formed the Opposition between 1979 and 1983 (and beyond). Despite the different structural power position, (Government/Opposition) policy positions were similar. Another example of similar policy positions in spite of different Government/Opposition positions would be to compare Harold Wilson's Golden Age Labour Party with Neil Kinnock's mid-1980s Party. Although differences exist, both parties stand out as full-blown examples of market-accepting parties. Beginning in Opposition with Gaitskell (1955–63 Party Leader), 'the Party revised its policy in connection with public ownership. . . . And by the later years of the decade [under Harold Wilson and in Government], so complete was the apparent transformation that a new gloss was given to the analysis of the events of the crisis years. . . . [T]he revisionist Gaitskellites thereby "won the post-war battle for the soul of the Labour Party"' (Minkin 1978: 325; last section quotation in Haseler 1969: 253).

So, although the Party was distancing itself considerably from the market economy, there was still noticeable adherence to the fundamentals of competitiveness as well as to the market as a wealth-creating vehicle. The same equivocal posture was shown in the sections about controlling inflation. For all the statements about 'controls', 'price commissions', 'monitoring' etc. – no doubt designed to convey a message of a government in control – the Party was unexpectedly lukewarm in its approach to inflation. All that was said was that the 'controls will be closely linked to our industrial planning, through agreed development plans with the leading price-setting firms' (Labour 1983).

Once again, behind the term 'plan', with its obvious overtones of political power and socialist determination, was to be found an alternative interpretation. What would be 'agreed' upon in the plan was, obviously, to be set by the international capitalist market system. The Party's rhetoric squared rather badly with what was actually said on concrete measures.

Phrases like the market's 'leading price-setters' denote that the competitive, market-successful firms should take the lead. No information was provided about what would happen if the 'leading' price-setting market winners were to refuse to participate in any 'agreed development plans'. There was nothing to indicate that the firms would then have been forced by the Government to comply. Again, the Party's elaboration on concrete measures was decidedly at odds with what was said in the more sweeping rhetorical sections. As soon as the Party introduced clarifications as to what lay behind terms like 'planning' and 'control', the planning element paradoxically seemed to disappear. This ambiguousness is not the case all the time of course. Several concrete measures were indeed provided to strengthen the State. But overall, Labour seems to have accepted the market in much the same way as the Rehn–Meidner Model for Sweden worked twenty years before; to enable the market to function better than if it was left on its own (more about the Rehn–Meidner Model later in the section about the SAP).

Sometimes social goals were explicitly put in the first place. The proposed setting up of an NEB would receive powers to buy shares in British industries. But, even then there was a distinct reliance on the market's terms: 'As it is intended to invest in potentially the most profitable areas of industry, NEB should, in the long-term at least, make profits it can reinvest' (Opposition Green Paper 1980: 12). A Green Paper was extremely cautious by saying that '[w]e must here enter a caveat. The above is an impressive and extensive list of aims. We must emphasise that NEB could not carry out all of these at once, or indeed even over a fairly long period' (Opposition Green Paper 1980: 20). Thus, even for the so radicalised 1983 Labour Party, the unexpected conclusion is that the Government basically should rely on the market economy and in some instances aid the economy into becoming more competitive in the market. Briefly, this is a conclusion also drawn by Shaw: 'Hence, in this respect [attention to public ownership] – a point invariably overlooked – Labour's programme in 1983 amounted to a move towards accepting a predominantly privately owned economy, albeit one which subjected market forces to a complex system of state regulation' (Shaw 1994: 13).

Voluntary agreements were outlined but in the end price-setting companies should prevail. Companies, which were not up to market standards, were left to adapt (to market forces obviously). Behind the rather high-flown rhetoric it appears that, in practice, the State would lack decisive clout to replace or even affect the market in any considerable way.

The same unexpected acceptance of grim market forces appeared in a paragraph on food prices where Labour wanted to 'buy our food where it is cheaper, on world markets, following Britain's withdrawal from the EEC' (Labour 1983). One would have thought that buying at the lowest price on international markets was exactly the way the international capitalist market were supposed to function. How this could act as a socialist vision is not entirely clear – unless one subscribes to the view by Lord Morrison of Lambeth (1940–51 Labour Minister and 1951–55 Deputy Leader of the Opposition), that 'Socialism is what a Labour government does' (quoted in Walker 1987: 188).

Of course, the reader might feel that mention of cheap world markets in this paragraph could be considered to be irrelevant to the State–market debate and significant only as an anti-EEC argument. This may very well be the case, especially considering Labour opted in favour of EEC withdrawal at that time. However, one is still struck by the manifesto using market terminology as such. An equally plausible, alternative, angle would have been something more appealing to solidarity-conscious voters inside an anti-EEC framework, e.g. about supporting poor countries by buying outside the rich man's EEC, or something similar. Criticising the planning-oriented EEC with market-biased phrases seems to sit badly with a socialist strategy in mind. One way of creating cheap food is to let the world market work without politically induced levies and taxes – this is in effect what the manifesto stated. Thus, the Labour Party tacitly adhered to the controversial standpoint that the world's poor could be helped through the market forces.

Characteristically, the 1983 manifesto blamed Mrs Thatcher and her Government rather than the market economy as such for Britain's troubles. She 'worships the profit motive' and the Government has 'forced up interest rates and kept the pound too high – a combination that has crippled British industry, and helped lose us markets at home and abroad' (Labour 1983: 5, 8). With the pound back on realistic levels, so the argument appears to have gone, British goods would once again be successful in world markets.

In summary, then, the 1979–83 position pointed in several directions. No doubt the rhetoric towards the market economy was negative generally. Unemployment and unfair distribution of wealth were pictured to come in the wake of Tory free-for-all market economy. On the other hand, Labour went to surprising lengths in accepting the advantages of well-working markets. The Party conveyed an image of the market as efficient – it produces goods at low cost – Britain depends on the market economy and the economy relies on British firms being competitive. With Labour's policies, so the Party claimed, the market dependency may in the future be somewhat reduced but not replaced.

Note

1   For the overwhelming part of the following data, electronic versions have been used. In such cases page references cannot be given. Data based on Swedish Parliamentary Minutes, 1965, 1975, 1985 and 1995 were all gathered by Robin Skoglund (2000). All other data was gathered by the present author.

4

Labour's new era?

Already four years later, much of the radical words had evaporated. It has been suggested elsewhere (Driver and Martell 1998: 14) that 'The 1987 manifesto was essentially a watered-down version of the 1983 document.' According to this view, 'the modernization of the Labour Party began in earnest' only after the 1987 election defeat. One has to be cautious about ideological data, and the magnitude of change is by no means self-evident. However, even though the 1987 manifesto still retained considerable determination to combat unemployment and poverty, the proposed means had changed completely. Roughly, the Party was back to where it stood in the 1960s and at the end of the 1970s. Traces of socialism may have remained symbolically but hardly substantively (Ross 2000: 26).

The shift is indicated in several ways in the 1987 election manifesto. By enumerating a few policy fields and raising a warning finger that 'all other programmes that require substantial public finance must take lower priority in terms of timescale and public resources' (Labour 1987), the Party showed two things. First, there was a rather narrow limit to public spending and thus to the public sector as a whole. Second, the public sector was manifestly described as a means to achieve certain ends but not an end in itself. The prioritised sectors were 'the health, housing, social services and crime-fighting services', i.e. the 'classic' areas of market-correction in a social liberal market economy.

Labour did not shy away from 'prudent' borrowing but, taken as a whole, the Party accepted the forces of international competition, which impose technical change on the economy. As an example of this standpoint, the following manifesto sections are illustrative. Labour urged the 'country to . . . make the best use of computers and information technology to develop the modern means of making a living' (Labour 1987). Rather than controlling exports, imports and exchange rates, like in 1983, Labour wanted to 'attract and retain British savings and investment in Britain' through the tax system.

Under an expressed concern for 'British savings', echoing the 1983 nationalist phrases, Labour did in fact say the market couldn't be forced, but only attracted. A more unequivocal statement about market acceptance is hard to find, short of overt praise of the market. A needs-based and State-controlled system of allocating resources seems to have formed a very slim part of what the Party actually was ready to stand behind in the documents. Though concern for 'British' needs was present, the manifesto acknowledged the view that the game had to be played according to the overall rules of the market. Given the terminological radicalism surrounding Labour in the aftermath of Thatcher's 1979 victory, and under the leadership of Michael Foot, these results are paradoxical. In essence, the content is close to the 1966, 1970 and 1979 manifestos.

The long road travelled from the 1983 policies is reflected in the TUC's and NEC's joint 1987 programme *Work to Win* where any references to nationalisations or common ownership have disappeared. The programme gave a clear example of policies aimed at enabling the market to function, rather than replacing the market:

> Modern industry competes by innovation in product and process and sustained innovation requires investment in machines, in ideas and in people, together with the creation of a framework of economic policy within which that investment can bear fruit. This investment cannot be left to the vagaries of the market. It requires consistent government support in education and training, and in research. And it requires that investment projects can go forward on the basis of a commitment to providing a long-term stable framework of financial and industrial policy. (Labour, TUC-NEC 1987: 6)

Already, two years earlier, Labour had left the old emphasis on common ownership. Under the new slogan 'A New Partnership – A New Britain', a familiar old standpoint of helping industry overcome the market's requirements was formulated. Apart from a brief paragraph on public and co-operative enterprise, with BT as the only concrete example, the *Investing in Britain* Programme was a catalogue of proposals on how to help industry modernise and increase competitiveness. The list included such things as 'joint discussions with firms and unions' in order to 'identify priorities for investment . . . provide financial assistance' to firms (Labour 1985a: 7) and setting up a National Investment Bank with the objective of providing 'industry in Britain with the long-term finance it needs on the right terms and conditions' (Labour 1985a: 11).

In a familiar vein, rather reminiscent of earlier proposals about 'voluntary agreements' between business and government, the programme now stated that firms and unions should carry out 'joint discussions'. The same contradiction between rhetoric about stated goals and rhetoric about how to achieve the goals dominated the NEC's 1984 Statement to Annual Conference. In this statement on the one hand, Labour was said to 'extend the frontiers of public enterprise in sectors that were vital for the future' (Labour, NEC 1984: 15). On the other hand, no sectors were actually named for nationalisation. Only railway electrification and better telecommunications were explicitly targeted for increased public investment (Labour, NEC 1984: 6). The market's key function was made clear by stating that 'there is no reason why total employment in manufacturing should continue to fall – *provided* British industry can capture a larger share of a growing market' (Labour Party, NEC 1984: 11, italics in original; see Labour, NEC 1985). Market acceptance can hardly be stated more clearly or unequivocally short of actual praise.

In a similar programme, *Working Together for Britain*, Labour extolled public investment under the headline 'Rebuilding Britain', but now the investment plans concerned infrastructure and schools and hospitals rather than publicly owned industries. Instead, industry was to be boosted by setting up 'Enterprise Boards', which were to assist industry to modernise (Labour 1985b: 10, 14). So, even though concrete proposals were modest a few years earlier, the new programme clearly meant a further reduction in ambitions and plans. The emphasis was gradually being transferred towards creating a favourable business atmosphere and a generous welfare state, instead of owning the means of production. In fact the element of more hard-line public enterprise proposals, which existed just before 1983, more or less vanished. The left's influence collapsed with remarkable swiftness. In terms of policy formulations, the modernisation of the Party began almost immediately after the 1983 defeat.

The more forthright attitude of market-acceptance found its way into the 'Policy Review', set in motion in 1987. Labour had 'laid out a series of far-reaching proposals designed to correct market failures' (Wickham-Jones 2000: 16). The 1989 *Meet the Challenge, Make the Change* report stated that 'the market and competition are essential in meeting the demands of the consumer, promoting efficiency and stimulating innovation, and often the best means of securing all the myriad, incremental changes which are needed to take the economy forward' (Labour 1989: 10). This clear market-correcting view was the next step in the party's move towards harmonising its rhetoric with a surprisingly robust view about the market economy. Apparently, the time had come for a more straightforward, overt, acceptance of the market and to claim that it was 'essential' for the nation's well-being.

If outspoken praise of the market was less evident in the 1987 manifesto, it was definitely to be found in 1992. The central elements of market-acceptance were still the same though, only more visibly elaborated in the 1992 text. Already on page 1, the Party stated that '[a]t the core of our convictions is belief in individual liberty.' Then followed what in essence conformed to the fundamentals of a market-accepting, but market-correcting, credo.

> [F]or liberty to have real meaning the standards of community provision must be high and access to that provision must be wide. . . . [T]he rights . . . must . . . belong to all men and women. . . . [G]overnment . . . must work to build prosperity by properly supporting research, innovation, the improvement of skills, the infrastructure and long-term development.

Contrary to earlier manifestos (with minor exceptions), the 1992 manifesto turned explicitly analytical on the role of government:

> Modern government has a strategic role not to replace the market but to ensure that the market works properly. Other competitors in Europe and elsewhere recognise that industrial policy must be at the heart of economic policy. It is the government's responsibility to create the conditions for enterprise to thrive. Business needs sustained and balanced growth, with stable exchange rates, steady and competitive interest rates and low inflation. We will deliver them.

As the earlier documents have shown for the early 1980s, Labour expressed negative views towards the market generally and towards the economy's dependency on
market forces. To some extent the Party standpoints were mildly sceptical in the
earlier part of the 1970s as well. Those two periods seem to be rather exceptional.
Towards the end of the 1980s, Labour was on its way back to the position it held at
the height of the Golden Age (1965), i.e. that the state of the economy depends on
market forces, which was regarded by the Party as positive. In *Looking to the Future*
(Labour 1990), the Party laid out its views on the relationship between public
sector and private enterprise with the slogan '[b]usiness where appropriate: government where necessary' (Labour 1990: 6). However, never before had this been
more clearly phrased than in the 1992 manifesto.

Few developments took place between 1992 and 1997. Perhaps the Party leadership felt the 1992 manifesto had been a touch too market-economy friendly and
now believed there was a need to distance itself from totally embracing market
ideals. The Party now claimed:

> The old left would have sought state control of the economy. The Conservative right
> is content to leave all to the market. We reject both approaches. Government and
> industry must work together to achieve key objectives aimed at enhancing the
> dynamism of the market, not undermining it. (Labour 1997)

Though very little was explicitly said about controlling or planning the economy,
much the same prioritised policy fields emerged in the 1997 manifesto as in most
of the earlier manifestos: education, unemployment, the NHS and family policy.
Especially in the paragraphs on the NHS, the manifesto's rhetoric resounded of
distinctly anti-market phrases. A typical example of anti-market elements would
be the following section: '[I]f you are ill . . . there will be a national health service
there to help; and access to it will be based on need and need alone – not on your
ability to pay' (Labour 1997). A more clear-cut example of market-correction is
hard to imagine. The idea is that the market cannot be left alone; its outcomes have
to be corrected. Unequal distributions of income were, then, something the Government should seek to affect (Thomas 2001: 70). In a way, the Party had now
completely found its way back to its Golden Age outlook bar the planning rhetoric. The market economy was portrayed as good for the economy but its outcomes
had to be corrected and the correction-side to it was not to be taken lightly.

Labour's firm belief in the market – with a wide range of market-correcting
mechanisms – was further borne out by Tony Blair in his 2000 Labour Party conference speech. The speech was something of a praise of active government. It
seems that Blair wanted to show his and his Party's determination to correct the
outcomes of the market, and that the Party had become 'bolder' (Annesley and
Gamble 2004: 148). Blair gave a view about a rather traditional social democracy
(Annesley and Gamble 2004: 157), a society where weak groups like the low-paid,
pensioners, schoolchildren, sick and unemployed needed – and were entitled to –
far-ranging public services at high standards:

> The NHS was the greatest achievement of the post-war Labour government. It was
> based on a single, clear, enduring value: that healthcare should be based on need not

ability to pay. Some objected to that principle then. Some urge us to abandon it now. But this party, the Labour Party will never abandon what was one of the greatest civilising acts of emancipation this country has ever known. (Blair 2000)

By also accusing the Tories of regarding youth unemployment as 'a price worth paying', Blair communicated that there were definite limits within which the market should stay inside: 'Unemployment is never worth paying' (Blair 2000). Already in 1997 Blair had pledged that his 'greatest challenge' was to 'refashion our institutions to bring the new work-less class back into society and into useful work' (Blair 1997). How far did Blair then in reality stretch his ambitions? Several elements in the text indicate that the aim went further than mere rhetoric. Instead of general phrases about the negative effects of unemployment or sympathy with the unemployed, Blair actually took the risk of pledging that unemployment was 'never' worth paying. He also pledged 'never' to abandon the NHS, rather than just being in favour of the NHS in more general terms. Data like these indicate that the Labour Government still held the view that far-reaching political measures were vital in order to correct the market's outcomes. Unlike the earlier period when formulations about 'planning' and 'socialism' were frequent, there was more conformity in the Labour documents between concrete proposals and style during the latter half of the 1990s. Almost all references to 'planning' and 'control' were gone, while the list of market-correcting measures remained more or less intact.

When Labour returned to office in 1997, several – though not all – of the union rights, which had been scrapped by the Tories were reintroduced and in some cases enhanced, including the fundamental right to be represented by a union (Coates 2000: 130f.). The Party's post-1997 relationship with the unions has had a mixed record. Several policies have received the express blessing from the unions (e.g. parental leave extensions, increased funds to the unions, government support to troubled industries) while others have been fiercely contested (e.g. relations with the CBI, EU questions, PFI policies). The union–party link became an important issue during Blair's second term in office, when some unions threatened to hold back their financial support to the Party, while Blair on his part, initiated a debate on State funding, which would reduce union influence over the Party (Ludlam 2004). On this, Blair had become outspokenly hostile towards free-for-all markets: 'And we have introduced the democratic right, delivered after 100 years of trying, to be represented by a trade union should you want it. That was our choice. Not to leave you at the mercy of markets. Not to walk by. Not to say: tough, sink or swim' (Blair 2000). Obviously, the speech has to be set in context. Much in the same way as the more militant left part of the Party around 1980 wanted to convey a message about an energetic party with socialism on the agenda, Blair wanted to portray himself as the protector of the welfare state. The 1983 Labour Party had few concrete alternatives to the market economy and of course no-one knows exactly to what extent Tony Blair's New Labour was prepared to alleviate poor union conditions. There is always a risk that commitments are 'largely rhetorical', where 'the goals are not aligned with means to secure them' (Wickham-Jones 2000: 16). Nevertheless, in this case Blair followed up, by strongly committing himself to public-service improvements, by addressing the choice between 'a Government with the strength to invest for the long term, or a Government that cuts our public services' (Blair 2000); and with a tax-system in place to provide the services necessary: 'So when the Tories say: we'll cut Labour's investment and give you tax cuts, it's a fool's game. We will cut tax for people as we can, but will do it in a way that lasts not at the expense of the very stability and investment on which the wealth and security of millions of families depend. So that is my explanation. That's why I won't take the easy way. Because that way we cannot reach our journey's end' (Blair 2000). Make no mistake. In the sense that 'old' social democracy was eager to show its commitment to the welfare state by proposing budget-enforcing tax increases, Blair is all 'new'. But in its new version the Party will cut taxes only 'as we can'. The message is very cautiously phrased to please all camps but the only real promise is that investments will not be cut. Blair's statements show that he was prepared to go to great lengths in order to commit himself in concrete terms to stand behind a welfare state far more ambitious than the neo-liberal version.

Blair also added a commitment to substantial NHS and school investments. Almost every sentence of Blair's speech reflected arguments, which correspond to views about market corrected by the state. This was indeed a Party friendly to the market economy, but one firmly dedicated to correcting the market's effects. While some of the means were distinctly new, the element of 'alleviating social risk' was traditional. 'Men and women of working age are being moved from State dependency to the labour market, while the state is adopting the role of making the labour market fairer and developing policies to support families' (Annesley and Gamble 2004: 157). This kind of policy was a continuation of what had been introduced already before Labour came back to power (Thompson 1996: 284). At the same time, and as further evidence on Labour's market views, Blair's Chancellor, Gordon Brown (2000), rejected 'absentee Government', which he claimed was the legacy of the earlier Tory Governments. Brown pictured 'least Government', with 'their exclusive reliance on markets' as the main reason behind worklessness and deprivation. Those illnesses had to be tackled with 'established responsibilities of Government'. In the 2002 budget, taxes were raised but already in the lifetime of the 1997 Parliament windfall taxes and various alterations in the tax system increased public incomes considerably (Stephens 2001: 196). At the same time, Brown has had no difficulty in praising the market as in his 2002 statement: 'Labour is more pro-business, pro-wealth creation, pro-competition than ever before' (*Financial Times*, 28 March 2002). The Prime Minister's pledge to improve public services was reflected in the Party's 2001 election manifesto, which in its entirety was a commitment to the importance of the public sector: 'The whole country depends on high-quality public services. We have a ten-year vision for Britain's public services: record improvement to match record investment, so they deliver high standards to the people, all the time, wherever they live' (Labour 2001: 17).

'Investment and reform' was the double-sided phrase echoing throughout the manifesto, indicating that the Party was firmly devoted to protecting the public sector as a necessary correction to the market. Later on, Gordon Brown went one step further and pledged the Government and the public sector would offer not just minimum standards, but the 'maximum possible range of services' (Brown 2004). He went on and defined Labour's goals in contrast to Conservative philosophy. Labour, he said, is 'planning for the long term, building from strong foundations – and reject[ing] Tory free market short termism and opportunism' (Brown 2004).

Behind Brown's attack on free markets lay his conviction that 'public services are good [not just] because we owe obligations to each other as neighbours that go beyond calculation and contract. Not simply out of altruism: because we do feel, however distantly, the pain of others. Because we do believe in something bigger than ourselves' (Brown 2004). Brown's statement echoed old social democratic ideals about the merits of collectivism and social inclusion (Miller 1989) and shows a distinct determination that the liberal market economy has to function in combination with public-sector market-corrections.

Although rather modest, there was also to be felt an element of State planning in the Party's 'new regional economic policy', corresponding to aspects of the category concerning market complemented by the State. Correction was, evidently, not always enough in this view. In some instances, tougher action than utilising 'Job Transition Service[s]' and 'anticipat[ing] change, handl[ing] restructuring and enabl[ing] businesses to move into high-skill, high value-added product markets' (Labour 2001: 13) had to be taken by public authorities to prevent undesired outcomes, e.g. regional economic differences: 'Sitting back and leaving regional problems to the market is not acceptable. The causes of disparities within and between regions must be addressed. The new regional economic policy must be based on boosting regional capacity for innovation, enterprise and skill development' (Labour 2001: 13).

Amid criticism that the Party had abandoned its welfare-state goals, the Labour leadership did actually take the opportunity to really speak out about the role for the public sector. The reason for the clarifications can, of course, only be guessed at. However, a plausible conclusion would be that perhaps the Party leaders felt they had been overly cautious about not upsetting the City in the aftermath of the 1997 election victory. In a speech shortly after the 2001 elections Tony Blair went even further than the election manifesto:

> Our public services symbolise that spirit of community [where investment is put before tax cuts]. Universal public services are right today just as they were right more than 50 years ago. Collective provision, not the market, is the best way of ensuring that the majority get the opportunity and security that the few at the top take for granted. (Blair 2001)

These statements show remarkable similarity to Labour's earlier market-correcting standpoints. In terms of the market-view indicators applied in this book, the Party leadership's observations corresponded to the view that the market may be a formidably efficient generator of wealth, but is still an unfair generator when it comes to distributional results. 'The few at the top' are too few. The majority face unfair terms and will have to be helped along with 'universal public services' based on a tax system. A year on, the manifesto's pledges were turned into real policy when the 2002 budget revealed record real increases in NHS funding of 43 per cent over a five-year period, with various tax increases to back up the reform (*Financial Times*, 18 April 2002), though technically, compulsory contributions to the so-called national insurance were raised rather than income taxes. Even though the Party's general opinion of the international capitalist market was undoubtedly positive, there were also clear elements of hesitancy and negative objections.

However, despite the curious fact that the international capitalist market was hardly mentioned at all in the manifesto, except for the criticism quoted above, this was still a Party with a rock-solid belief in the merits of the market economy. An indicator of this belief was the Party's wish to reform parts of the public sector, triggering criticism from Party members and trade unions (see *Financial Times*, 16 July, 24 September 2001). The Party wanted to give a greater role for the private sector to provide public services. However, the Party made it very clear that the Government should set the targets and that private provision should not affect the cost at the point of consumption. The Government would still decide on fees etc. (Blair 2001; Driver and Martell 2003: 44f., 79ff., 166ff.; see Lundqvist 1988; Prabhakar 2004).

Labour 1965–2002: from market acceptance in practice to market acceptance in theory and practice

The Labour Party has worked with the market in several ways and has been able to use a range of different positions between outright market-acceptance on the one hand and using more guarded terms on the other. The liberal market economy has never been totally rejected. In the midst of criticism there has been a constant allusion to basic market principles about efficiency, competitiveness and flexibility. During brief periods frustration over the market economy has been tangible and documents rife with criticism. However, it is a clear sign of the extent to which the liberal market economy has been entrenched in the Labour Party's thinking, that alternative visions of economic systems have been more or less absent. When alternatives were offered they have had the character of improvements rather than replacements. Make no mistake. The Labour Party has included plenty of groups, activists and leading individuals who were deeply distressed about the functioning of the liberal capitalist market economy. Several would have preferred entirely different policies than those favoured by the New Labour Party. But at the same time as the uneasiness with the nature of things has been almost tangible at times, it remains equally clear that the leadership, and indeed most of the principal critics of the market economy, have been so permeated by allusions to how the market functions (and should function), that we may conclude the Labour Party's ideology rests firmly on the market. Indeed this attitude is evident both when the market economy is praised and when it is criticised. The positive attitude taken by Labour of market processes is fundamental to its reformist project.

In sum, the Labour Party's views about the market have undergone some fundamental changes. It is also fair to claim that overall, market acceptance was always an important part of the Party's ideology. Table 1 presents a summary view. Please note that although the Table 1 characterisations for each research category (introduced in Chapter 2) may appear deceivingly exact and clear-cut, there is need for some analytical precaution. The entries ('high' etc.) are all based on a qualitative understanding of the empirical data rather than on strictly quantitative measurement. No general word count or similar methodology has been utilised. Instead, the underpinning of these qualitative measurements is to be found in the continuous discussion and argumentation as they have unfolded in the empirical section.

The immediate impression from Table 1 is the overwhelming stability over the entire forty-year period. Labour's overall view on the market has been fairly positive throughout. Whereas the economy is pictured to be dependent upon the market and though the distributional outcomes are unfair, the market's efficiency has been regarded as high. As we have seen above, a leading theme in the documents has been to claim that the market's unfair effects render market-correcting measures necessary. Despite the fact that the list of corrective means in election manifestos etc. has been fairly long and elaborate over the entire time period, the opposite has been true of 'market-complementing' measures. Very few proposals of that, more radical, kind have been suggested. When such propositions have been brought forward, most noticeably around 1981, they have always been connected with indications of a basic acceptance of the international capitalist market economy. Occasionally these indications have been indirect and we have had to resort to a somewhat close reading of the party documents to find them.

Table 1 Labour Party ideological views on the market 1965–2002 as measured by four indicators and one sub-indicator

	1965	1970	1974	1979	1983	1987	1992	1997	2002
Dependency*	High/	High/	High/	High/	High/	High/	High/	High/	High/
	Pos	Pos	Neg	Pos	Neg	–	Pos	Pos	Pos
Efficiency	High	High	–	High	High	High	High	High	High
Distribution	Unfair	Unfair	Unfair	Unfair	Unfair	Unfair	Unfair	Unfair	Unfair
General									
opinion	Pos	Pos	Neg	Pos	Neg	Pos	Pos	Pos	Pos

*Including evaluation of dependency

At the same time the exceptions to the stability-conclusion cannot be denied. Scepticism towards the market has indeed been obvious in the Labour Party but hardly so during the Golden Age of Social Democracy, which was firmly planted in market-accepting soil. The 'underlying closeness of [Labour's] relationship with private corporate capital is not new in Labour Party terms' (Coates 2001: 300). However, at the level of very vague and high-flown rhetoric, socialism as a concept was still vivid during the Golden Age. But, let it be clear that, already then, the notion of socialism had lost most of its content. In the sense that socialism was another word for the good society, the concept was full of substance but only so long as the good society took the shape of an ambitious welfare state rather than an alternative economic system.

These overall conclusions are sufficiently underpinned even though we acknowledge the fact that common ownership of the means of production was still included in the Party's Constitution as late as 1994.

It is somewhat of a paradox that Labour's well-documented confidence in its planning capacity, based on war experience and the 1945–51 Governmental position and given extra focus in the 1960s, should end so unglamorously (Cronin 2004: Chapter 2). Self-confident and with a record of achievement, the Party, one would have assumed, would go about the task with determination when resuming office in 1964. The result was the opposite. Some of the failures can probably be explained by unfavourable international economic circumstances but the very hollowness of the planning activities suggests that a more plausible explanation is that hardcore planning sat very uneasily with the Party's market ideology. As long as planning stood for efficiency and creativity, the ideas were easy to reconcile with the liberal market economy (which did not prevent the weak planning authorities from failing anyway). More far-reaching ambitions were almost negligible and fell outside the Party's overarching goals.

The 1974 position was somewhat of a deviation from the quite firm belief in a guided market (not least in the key 1966, 1970, 1979, 1987 and 1992 manifestos). Even more so, the 1981–83 period swayed in a distinctly radical direction. This is no news. What is less well known is that even in the midst of radicalism in the period's manifesto, programme and the NEC, the Party showed clear, though perhaps grudging, acceptance of the international capitalist market's mechanisms.

Overall, competitive, market-successful firms were supposed to constitute the driving force of the economy as much in 1965 as forty years later. In order to make them competitive and successful in the market, the State was portrayed as a necessary guiding force. Left on its own, the market would instead revert to imperfections, monopolies etc. In this sense the State was regarded as the essential final supervisor. But the ultimate goal then, was to force the market to behave in an ideal way more than replacing the market's allocation mechanisms with State-controlled allocation. Finally, the allocation had to be corrected according to some criteria of need. The proper institution for such corrections was the welfare state.

The Party's planning offensive during the 1960s will hardly change our overall conclusion. The planning agencies were left without any proper means to carry out real planning. Their work appears to have been resting on guesswork more than on carefully conceived plans for production etc. What is more important though than the wrong-footed outcome as such is the fact that the Party's whole idea behind the planning offensive was crafted in market-conforming terms. The planners may have lacked mechanisms for making the plans into reality but their intention was to make industry more efficient. The whole industrial sector was believed to be backward and class biased with no real understanding of modern management and scientific skills (Cronin 2004: 66). Getting inside industry itself would have provided a way of 'removing the fetters of social conservatism' (Cronin 2004: 66).

What is felt post-1979 is instead a determination, sometimes verging on desperation, to find the proper means to correct the market's outcomes. So much had been tried during the 1960s and still the results were little more than bleak. More interference, more voluntary agreements between business and government, improved and expanded publicly financed infrastructure and more common ownership solutions were the typical new answers. But rather than replacing the market, the 1983 Labour Party favoured some additional State complements to the market on top of the wide array of already existing market-correcting means. In a few instances, such as particular NEC documents, the determination to correct the market crossed the line where 'market replacement' would perhaps be a more pertinent phrase.

Towards the end of the research period Labour once again became somewhat more firmly outspoken about the merits of the public sector. This is shown in a significantly more elaborate analysis on the unfair distributional effects of the market economy. Several determined ideology statements about protecting the welfare state and about the darker sides of the market economy were issued after 1997.

At the same time, of course, the defence of the public sector was carried out against a backdrop of explicit and indisputable support for the market economy. An explicit aim of the incoming Labour Party Government in 1997 was to earn the confidence from Business and to prove that Labour could run the economy smoothly and capably (Annesley and Gamble 2004: 149ff.; Keegan 2003: 242; Panitch and Leys 1997: 261; Stephens 2001: 185ff.; Wickham-Jones 2002: 468). Even limited versions of socialist rhetoric were dropped. However, should anyone have doubted Labour's willingness to correct the market's outcomes, the Party leadership appears to have felt an urge to emphasise its longstanding commitment to market-correction.

The feeling that New Labour was more about talk than delivery has become a widely discussed problem, as the 2003 media frenzy after the resignation of Alastair Campbell, the Downing Street Director of Communication showed. Much of the criticism focussed on the Labour Party's obsession with how proposals were packaged rather than their content. Spin-doctors in place of real politicians with obvious problems of empty rhetoric has been the image of modern politics generally and the Labour Party in particular (*Guardian*, 30 August 2003; *Financial Times*, 30 August 2003; Franklin 2004). At the same time, criticism of the Party's failure to stand up to its stated goals is by no means new but something of a recurring theme for the past decades.

5

SAP's end of the Golden Age

Just as with Labour, comments on the SAP's ideological development has included statements that the SAP has fallen 'victim to the ascendancy of neo-liberal economic thought' (Lindvall and Rothstein 2004: 2; Blyth 2002; Thomson 2000: 7). Even though substantial welfare-state improvements have been implemented, e.g. in the family policy field, these authors claim that the programmes are largely an effect of 1970s efforts than testimony to contemporary ideas about the strong State and that the results are unsatisfactory (Eduards 2002; Lindvall and Rothstein 2004: 12f.).

Although the Swedish society in the 1960s and 1970s may not have been altered from a capitalist to a socialist State, the distribution of income, earnings and wealth in Sweden still being primarily determined by the private sector, a view has prevailed that in the long run these basic terms would be altered 'because of the way in which the labour movement's ideological commitment to egalitarianism has affected worker's attitudes' (Scase 1977: 164f.). Until the end of the 1980s, 'Sweden seemed immune to worldwide political trends in a conservative or neoliberal direction. [But s]uddenly, this success story unravelled in 1989–91' (Pontusson 1992a: 305). Thus, it has been suggested that in the early 1990s the 'spell was broken' about 'how a decent society should be organized' (Lindvall 2004: 156). According to such a view, the Golden Age politics behind full employment – strong faith in the Government's capacity for social problem solving, and in corporatist decision-making, all based on the idea of the State intervening in the market economy – was finally abandoned not only in practice but also at the level of ideas and norms (Lindvall 146ff.). The State 'is no longer an instrument for the political parties that dominate the *Riksdag* [The Swedish Parliament] to steer and change society' (Lindvall and Rothstein 2004: 19; please note that in several respects Lindvall as well as Lindvall and Rothstein include most of the *Riksdag* parties, which they claim all subscribed to a more or less social democratic planning ideology; see also Garme 2001: 135). The SAP has even 'cognitively locked [itself] into these new ideas [neo-liberal laissez-faire ideas]' (Blyth 2002: 237f.). That would have been an exceptionally long stride from the view that the SAP crowned the Golden Age period by re-emphasising its adherence to replacing the capitalist system's concentration of power to a few private actors by a socialist system where each citizen equally influenced the terms of production (Elvander 1980: 225f.).

Whether market-driven 'economism' purportedly dominating SAP ideology today will dominate in the future is an open matter. 'Looking back in history, it seems as though economic liberalism and State interventionism have followed each other in a kind of pendulous movement. When the currently dominating economism and the doctrine of low interest and low inflation will give way is of course impossible to predict' (Pierre 1999: 50f.).

In spite of the flow of literature on the SAP's ideological change, the question mark from Chapter 1 remains: Has the the SAP really become a neo-liberal party? Has tough market hostility been replaced by downright market friendliness?

With World War II well behind them, Labour as well as SAP ideologues could think more freely about their real objectives. Tage Erlander, the then Swedish Prime Minister, emphasised the importance of international economic conditions in Parliament's 1965 general debate on the economy. He went on: 'Of course we have benefited from the dynamic developments of the world economy' (*Riksdag* Minutes FK 1965/3: 28, Erlander).

That the Swedish economy was directly dependent on the world economy was underlined by Erlander's Finance Minister, Gunnar Sträng, who claimed that 'the 1964 Consumer Price Index is mirroring increased import prices'. He went on to say that in spite of tough international competition, Swedish industry had increased its market shares (*Riksdag* Minutes AK 1965/3, 30: 32, 67, Sträng). Sträng's obvious position was that market exposure leads to efficient companies. The view about the market's distributional effects was clear according to Sträng: 'We accept an order where sectors and professions without the same opportunities to rationalise their activities as others have, adapt to the wage-levels ... of the [sectors] which are able to absorb wage increases' (*Riksdag* Minutes AK 1965/30: 34, Sträng).

If the market forces are let loose, unacceptable injustices will follow against which the Government has to act. Income differences, particularly those caused by 'social and economic privileges', were targeted as unacceptable, while differences emanating from 'differing work efforts, skills, responsibilities and degree of initiative' would be accepted (SAP 1960 *Party Programme*). Later on, the last clause was cut off in an attempt at radicalising the Party.

In general, the Party strengthened its views on how the market economy's outcomes would be corrected. Very clearly the standpoint emerged that true freedom for citizens was a matter of acting *through* the public sector as against a view where freedom was reached by distancing oneself *from* the public sector (SAP programme *Resultat och reformer* [Results and Reforms] 1964: 10; Elvander 1980: 228).

The 1966 local elections were a clear disappointment to the SAP who made severe losses (until 1970, local elections were of national significance as they affected the indirectly elected upper *Riksdag* chamber. Constitutional reforms led to the unicameral *Riksdag* as from 1970). The Party leadership felt great concern about creeping signs of economic slowdown, structurally related unemployment and the negative social effects caused by rapid farm closures. A vitalised ideological debate ensued, crowned by the 1967 extraordinary Party Congress (SAP and LO 1968; SAP and LO 1969; SAP and LO 1972).

As during the end of the 1950s, focus was on industrial and economic policy. However, in spite of concerns about the damaging social effects caused by structural change, the Party leadership's main target was to support even faster changes. Only by creating top-of-the-league industries able to meet the toughest international market competition could Sweden remain ahead of other leading industrial nations. Industrial policy was aiming to secure such competitive edge for industry. The centrality of the early market-economy friendly approach is borne out by Birgit Karlsson (2001) in her study on Swedish approaches towards West-European economic integration 1948–72. According to Karlsson's data, Sweden's (i.e. the Social Democratic Cabinet's) principal view was to keep trades policy separated from foreign policy. In dealing with the then EEC Swedish official negotiators wanted '[o]nly economic considerations ... to decide on purchases and sales of goods. The ideal was a free market, without customs or other regulations, and this market was to be global' (Karlsson 2001: 67).

At the same time the 1968 *Program för aktiv näringspolitik* [Programme for an Active Industrial and Enterprise Policy] emphasised the need for 'security in change'. In order to achieve such security the programme advocated massive public sector support like job-seeking centres, removals allowances, setting up a State-run investment bank, support to the regions, more active State companies and environmental policies. 'Equality' was the catchword at the 1968 Party Congress. (SAP 1968a , Myrdal 1968: 188ff; SAP and LO 1968: 6ff; 26–39, 40–51, 68, 75, 82, 85; see Pierre 1986: 112–20). The Prime Minister, Mr Erlander developed his, and the Party's, views in a book sometime before the 1968 general elections:

> Demands on the public sector will increase. . . . Our demands for freedom, equality and solidarity will be realised through expanded public resources. . . . The government sector must control developments in a planned manner. (Alsterdal 1967: 6f.)

Undoubtedly the Party leader wanted to communicate a feeling that with social democracy, society would indeed be in firm hands. There would be a plan and politics was to take the upper hand over the market. However, it is equally clear that the planning element referred almost exclusively to market-correcting measures. The renewed ideological debate post-1966 may have contained a gush of socialist and State-force rhetoric, but proposals for concrete measures – and concrete measures too – told a different story. These measures made up for an ambitious programme for market-correction rather than market-replacement. Granted, there was an element of planning, at least on paper, in the State-run investment bank and regional support but hardly to the extent as to merit an alternative conclusion.

The SAP was perfectly aware of the dependency of the Swedish economy on competitive international market forces, but since these market forces created highly efficient companies, the dependency was deemed to be positive even though the ensuing distribution of values in society was unfair and had to be dealt with through welfare state measures and, in the SAP's case, 'solidarity wages'. In a 1969 analytical comment, Sträng held that 'the most important objectives of our economic policy: full employment, rapid growth and a more equal distribution of income, require a considerable effort on behalf of the government' (Government Proposition 1969:1, app. 1, p. 9). At the same time there is no doubting the Party's commitment to giving the public sector a substantial role in the effort to create efficient economic development:

> [T]he Party wants an increased involvement on the part of the public sector and wage earners in a policy for full employment, workplace security, diminishing income gaps and towards fast economic development. We reject bourgeois policies, which increase the concentration of power in private hands and which is contrary to the interests of the wage earners. (SAP 1968b)

Whether these 1968 manifesto sentences presupposed State-controlled allocation of resources or tacitly accepted the market economy topped-up with generous welfare-state programmes is not entirely clear. The market economy as such was left outside the document, which concentrated on sending a message to the voters that Sweden would be a more equal society by means of the public sector.

One would have thought that the SAP should have entered the 1970 election campaign from a unique vantage point given the extremely successful outcome of the 1968 election. The Party had secured more than 50 per cent of the overall votes cast, something which is exceptionally rare in the history of democratic elections. This favourable position should have opened the parliamentary door for radical ideological reforms if the party leadership had really intended such a development.

In fact the manifesto was radical in the sense that it would be hard to imagine a more fully developed credo in favour of the welfare state and on the need to correct the outcomes of the market economy. However, it was not a radical document in the sense that any alternatives to the capitalist market economy were suggested. It is perfectly clear that such alternatives were off limits. On the contrary, the non-socialist parties were accused of pork-barrel politics, which the SAP considered detrimental to the economy, would lead to weakened government financial policy, increased inflation and harm foreign trade.

The Party professed a willingness to provide the voters with an alternative economic policy, but the offer was hardly a true alternative. The catalogue of corrective improvements was impressive with a number of proposals about health care, regional development, education, support for the elderly and for families with children, public transport etc., etc. (SAP 1970). But it was not an alternative to market capitalism. On the contrary, the text was bursting of hints about prudent economic policies with budget balance in the focus.

The 1970 election returned the party to office, though this time round at a more normal 45 per cent minority level (with Sweden's proportional electoral system, translated into 45 per cent of the seats). In spite of the slightly weakened position (in the sense that the 1968 result was even better, but quite normal seen over an extended time period) there was once again in the 1973 manifesto the familiar combination of welfare reforms and implicit (sometimes rather explicit) support for the market economy:

The most important task [for the Party] is to safeguard everyone's right to work and to secure greater influence for workers and professional employees as regards their working life. Social democracy will not accept the free play of economic forces to decide over peoples' work, health and security.

Sweden's economy is strong. We compete successfully on the export markets. The foreign currency reserves are at record levels. Sweden enjoys Europe's lowest inflation. … The progress will be used to increase the living standard of broad sectors of the wage earners, improve conditions for pensioners with the lowest pensions and pursue a reform policy for solidarity. This is in the interest of the whole nation. (SAP 1973)

No doubt the expression that social democracy will 'not accept the free play of economic forces' suggested a less than positive attitude towards the market economy. Equally clear is the fact that the Party did not envisage an alternative type of economic system. On the contrary, the Party praised itself for managing the market economy effeciently. The text informed readers that Swedish export was competing successfully and that the currency reserve was full and inflation low. These latter examples rather point in the direction of market-economy acceptance. Therefore the only plausible interpretation of how the Party wanted to tackle the free play of economic forces is that corrective measures rather than alternative economic forces would be used. The long list of conceivable reform proposals supports such an interpretation.

Ten years after the peak of the Golden Age there was still scant proof of direct criticism of the market economy. Instead the Government was outspokenly positive about its merits. Gunnar Sträng equalled a 'closed economy' with that of a 'totalitarian economy' (*Riksdag* Minutes 1975/16: 131 f., Sträng). Sträng claimed that the Government supported 'a commitment for enterprise expansion which will improve competitiveness in order to increase export incomes and [support] domestic industries, thus limiting import needs' (*Riksdag* Minutes 1975/16: 132, Sträng).

Sträng expressed the Government's general understanding, and acceptance, of the Swedish economy's market dependency. Concepts like 'competitiveness' presuppose a market economy and Sträng chose to talk about this rather than indicating any attempts at replacing the need for competitiveness through radical reforms of the economic system. Along the same lines, Prime Minister Olof Palme propounded a view that market efficiency was a precondition for the economic surpluses necessary to finance the public sector: 'A powerful commitment to industrial investments is a precondition for employment increases … [in] the public sector' (*Riksdag* Minutes 1975/97: 137, Palme).

While Palme did not here confine industrial investments to the private sector only, he did in fact juxtapose those investments with the public sector. Indirectly readers were thus led to believe that the bulk of investment, which would keep up employment in the public sector, had to emanate from the private sector. In the same debate Gunnar Sträng once again underlined the importance and desirability of competitive companies:

The whole technical and general development is such that companies inevitably have to expand and grow in order to be efficient. If they want to sell across the globe, which

> major Swedish companies do, they can't come small. There is no wrong in acting big
> as long as they respect social and labour market legislation enacted in this House and
> guarantee steady jobs and fair wages. (*Riksdag* Minutes 1975/97: 82, Sträng)

The actors on the international capitalist market have to follow certain rules and the Government sets those rules. But as long as that requirement was fulfilled Sträng acknowledged that companies have to accept the conditions set by the international capitalist market. If that market has forced companies to merge into big companies it's something the Government cannot or will not change. Competition on world markets is tough but Sträng apparently wanted Swedish companies to join the Party in order to reach sufficient levels of efficiency. When it came to the market's distributive effects, Sträng was clear-eyed: '[Companies] may be big or small, the essential is that our political power is such that Capitalism's unpleasant sides cannot overgrow but are kept on the straight and narrow' (*Riksdag* Minutes 1975/97: 82f., Sträng).

In sum, then, the 1975 position on how to view the market was that of accepting the nation's dependency on the market economy, which was deemed to be efficient and positive generally. Although the distributive outcomes may be unfair the Government obviously regarded them as correctable.

The prominence of the social sector as the key to a truly market-correcting ideology was emphasised in the new Party Programme. Once again the social sector was targeted as the focus for planned governmental control (SAP 1974: 9, 34ff.; SAP 1975: 16ff.; 33ff., 41ff.).

> [W]e have to make sure the principles of the market economy will not become the
> leading canon for production and distribution of welfare-related social services. In
> our view this will be the only possibility to fulfil, for the whole people, the major
> unfulfilled needs for social services. . . . Naturally, the aim of expanding government-
> run services is to increase people's welfare and to improve their living conditions. (SAP
> and LO 1974: 7, 13)

Please note the rhetorical move to describe the market in rather critical terms but to confine the scope of the description to the welfare-state sector. The Party wanted the welfare state to remain a corrective of the market, not emulating the market. A decade later the Party gradually began to accept the idea that certain parts of the welfare state operated according to market rules.

Perhaps the apex of the SAP's considerations about how to tackle the capitalist market economy is found in the 1976 election manifesto, the election in which the SAP lost its government position for the first time since 1936. The public sector, including public companies, was praised in the manifesto. But rather than providing true alternatives to the market's way of allocating resources, the public-sector companies were described as successful. Sentences like 'The National Wood Industries Company was built on the ruins of private sawmills gone bankrupt in the 1930s. 2,600 employees in *Norrbotten* [a heavily forested region in the extreme north; huge, almost half the size of the UK, but very sparsely inhabited with only about 250,000 people] are now provided for' conveyed a message that public sector companies can actually make it better in the market than some private companies.

If the 1950s and 1960s saw a social democracy convinced that market-corrections were necessary in a market economy, the 1970s ideological revival proved to the Party leadership that even more corrections would be necessary. In *Tillsammans kan vi göra ett bra land bättre* [Together We Will Make a Good Country Better; 1976] the social sector was pinpointed as the essential tool in creating a good society and without which even the core of democracy would be reduced to 'formalities only' (Palme 1976: 19, 80–7). While the market economy carries with it substantial advantages as regards overall productivity etc. the harsh competition will allow the risk that entire regions will suffer. Therefore powerful corrections would be necessary and the social democrats believed they knew how to come to grips with this problem:

> The regional allocation policy has contributed to expansion in more than 1,000 companies in 266 places. . . . This has provided employment for 26,000 people.
> The Government's measures for education, healthcare, care for the elderly, expanded nursery system, support for the disabled and other urgent services have increased peoples' security. Another consequence has been new job vacancies. A tax policy showing solidarity with the low-paid workers has provided the necessary basis for these measures. A bourgeois [non-socialist] tax policy will jeopardise the welfare of the citizens.
> Special tax equalisation subsidies, recently drastically expanded, mean citizens in tax-weak councils have been provided with a basis for ample services.
> Our policies have contributed to the increase in employment in the manufacturing industry and to increased public services in the [sparsely populated 'Forest'] regions. The downward population trend has turned. We know we are on the right track. . . . [S]ocial democracy and the unions will continue the struggle against the concentration of private enterprise. Citizens of *Norrland* [northern Sweden] and other [sparsely populated 'Forest'] regions are entitled to the same employment opportunities as the rest of the country. A bourgeois [non-socialist] free-for-all policy would be disastrous to this work. (SAP 1976)

Towards the end of the 1970s economic recession had hit Sweden with rising unemployment and surging budget deficits. After having lost government power in 1976, the SAP fought the 1979 elections on a fiercely pro-public-sector election manifesto but with few concrete pledges. As regards market ideology, free-reign capitalism was criticised but without offering alternative planning-based policies:

> All over Europe strong right-wing forces are now attacking welfare state policies. In places they have gained political power. Their aim is to let loose the market forces, limit the social welfare and public sector tasks, increase economic inequalities and strike back on demands for work life co-determination. It is all being justified by capitalism's demands for economic progress. So far the results have led to increased unemployment and increasing social antagonism. (SAP 1979)

With all due respect to the SAP's effort to steer the economy in a more planning-oriented direction by means of so-called wage-earners' funds the funds were rather toothless. There were tight caps on the amount of private shares they were allowed to control. An ironic fact is that they were actually designed to operate on the stock exchange market on the terms set by the market. Even so, the 1982 election mani-

Gothenburg 11 February 2008

Dear James,

We briefly met at Leeds university during the 2005 PSA conference when I commented on your excellent *New Labour's Pasts* volume. I really appreciated your book and your work and since then my own title *Reinterpreting social democracy. A history of stability in the British Labour Party and the Swedish Social Democratic Party* has been published by MUP. Partially they cover similar areas.

Enclosed you will find a copy of my book. Hopefully you will not find this too pushy.

All the best wishes

Jonas Hinnfors
Professor
Department of Political Science
University of Gothenburg
PO Box 711
405 30 Gothenburg

festo contained a substantial amount of criticism of the market economy and even disbelief in the market's ability to create surpluses sufficient enough to support the whole population. There was even a Marxist hint at capitalism's inherent tendency to revert into recessions:

> Social democracy always represented the third force, an alternative to capitalism as well as communism. The need for this alternative becomes all the more obvious when neither capitalism nor communism can manage basic societal problems.
>
> Our country is now hit by the same malady as the capitalist Western world. The Moderate Party [the Conservatives] is inspired by the forces in the US and UK who want to use the economic crisis to roll back the development to a harder society in which egoism has become a virtue and the poor its victims.
>
> What employers label 'Operation Roll-Back' has commenced, and its target is full employment and social welfare, care for the children and the elderly – solidarity. This entails the most severe threat since the thirties against the edifice of welfare around which social democracy has united generations of Swedes.
>
> The bourgeois [non-socialist] parties have confidence in the 'self-healing powers of the market.' But the economy will not heal itself. We are facing social cut backs and growing unemployment. At the same time we are having huge public and foreign trade deficits, record levels of inflation with investments and construction for the future plunging. . . . In order to secure future investments, incomes and pensions increased capital formation and savings is necessary. This will only materialise with the participation of the wage earners and provided the wage earners gain means to influence that the money is spent on investments rather than on speculation, and that wage earners receive a share in the values created. This is why the social democracy has proposed the establishment of wage-earners' funds. . . . Wage-earners' funds form an essential part of the efforts to solve the economic crisis. Our welfare and social security can only be founded on a strong economy. (SAP 1982)

These are strong words. The SAP was close to lifting the lid off the box where the question of ownership had been stored for the better part of the twentieth century. The genie of socialism was almost out. Free-for-all markets were described as detrimental to the economy and thus to the welfare state. According to this view, unemployment would inevitably follow in he wake of capitalism. The Government must intervene. Workers need a share in the benefits of the economy. The answer was an ever-expanding welfare state and the wage-earners' funds.

The welfare state was fiercely promoted as the bulwark against the negative effects of the market. This is evidence that the Party still wanted to keep the market economy, however detrimental its effects. There was a curious ambivalence in the Party's views here. This was reflected in the fact that no real alternatives to the market economy were provided. It was also reflected in the fact that the wage-earners' funds, which were portrayed as the step away from the market economy, were actually extremely weak devices and ineffective as vehicles for taking over the private sector. Still this is the strongest expression of considerations about the role of ownership within the SAP's authoritatively binding documents during the entire research period.

Other documents were more modest, which further proves the point that these were times where strong beliefs inside the party leadership stood against each other. At the very same time as the wage-earners' funds purportedly took the Party nearer to real socialism the party chairman, Prime Minister Olof Palme elaborated on where social democracy was heading: 'The social democrats want to continue on the welfare construction, but it has to be at a pace the economy can handle. We promise no new cost-demanding reforms' (Palme 1982: 24).

In the wake of Palme's cautious standpoint about protecting the welfare state without any new reform sprees, the programme *Framtid för Sverige* [Future for Sweden] emphasised the unwavering view that privatisations and cut downs in the public sector had to be prevented in order to guarantee social welfare. However, a distinctly new element was that the programme now referred to the social sector's relative share of the national economy rather than the absolute share. Indirectly this position would imply that in times of economic slow-down the Government might have to cut down some welfare programmes – but still keep their relative share of the national economy.

Juxtaposed to the 1982 manifesto with all its emphasis on the public sector and eloquent rhetoric about the defects of the market economy, the *Framtid för Sverige* programme validated the conclusion about the role for the public sector. Rather than offering the Government with a powerful tool for changing the very foundations of the economic system – as certain formulations in the election manifesto indicated – the public sector was described as a corrective instrument. There was a definitive cap on its use. Over and above a defined level it may even become counter productive. Had the Party believed in the merits of a new economic system any reference to weaknesses of such a new system, would have been anathema. Our overall conclusion about this time period will therefore be that no real thoughts about moving away from the market economy were given by the Social Democratic Party leadership. The planning-oriented formulations were meant to show the party's fervent motivation to protect the welfare state as a powerful corrective mechanism to the market economy. Such emphasis was strategically motivated as the non-socialist parties, which had held government position between 1976 and 1982, had proved to be far less welfare-state retrenching than might perhaps have been expected. The SAP had to educate the voters that social democracy really was the indisputable guardian of the welfare state.

At the same time as the programme claimed social democracy to be a safeguard against social sector retrenchment, the role for the public sector was pictured to be that of providing the (private) industrial sector with a guiding framework. With a well-functioning framework, industry would operate smoothly enough to create sufficient surpluses for the public sector to use for social support. No longer were further tax increases perceived to be possible as instruments for national budget balancing (SAP 1981: 31ff., 46ff., 51ff.; Feldt 1982: 9ff., 17f., 24f., 36ff.). Though high taxes actually were no major part of the traditional Swedish model, they had definitely taken centre stage during the Golden Age upgrading of the Swedish model (taxes as per cent of GDP 1950, Sweden: 21.0 per cent, UK: 33.1 per cent; 1965, Sweden: 35.6 per cent, UK 30.8 per cent; Steinmo 2003: 33). To state that there was a limit to taxes was essentially the same as saying that there was a limit to the Swedish model, or at least that the model could not be developed much further along the old lines.

While for a few years towards the end of the 1970s, the public social sector was described as the basic guarantor for welfare, the 1984 programme *Framtiden i folkets händer* [The Future in the Hands of the People] gave this role instead to an efficient (private) industrial sector. Suddenly there was a limit – vague but still a limit – across which the public sector was not to expand (Feldt 1989).

It took only a few years for the Party to get back on track. Most of the veil of planning was lifted off already in the 1985 election manifesto. Not only were voters offered arguments about the need to support (free) enterprise by creating favourable conditions for investment and research, but a new element was introduced by pinpointing the welfare state as a sector where reforms to increase efficiency and the quality of the service provided were necessary. 'Renewal' was the catchword:

> Social democracy's most important goal is employment to all. That is why the economic policy continuously has to aim for renewal and development of our country's economy and enterprise. The successful politics to lead Sweden out of the economic crisis – the politics of the third way – shall continue.
>
> A social democratic policy after the elections should be aimed at taking down the inflation and to stimulate the development of trade and industry through investments and research. This way we will create employment, balance in our foreign trade and increased resources for private and public consumption. Sweden needs profitable small-sized companies as well as successful large-scale enterprises. . . . The Swedish welfare society will continue to rely on the public sector as an important foundation. The reform of the public sector will continue to make it more efficient, more service minded and providing citizens with more choice and influence. (SAP 1985)

This was a time (the 1980s) when the overall rhetoric definitely changed character. Gone was most of the socialist prose. The Finance Minister was one of the more outspoken proponents of the new idiom:

> The big units, the hierarchical organisation, poorly operating markets . . . should all be elements in a critical analysis. . . . Which then are the conclusions we should draw? The first one is that we should stop backbiting the market economy. . . . As is well known the market economy . . . has won a total victory over its only known alternative, planned economy.
>
> According to our party programme the market economy can only be accepted in certain circumstances. This should be the other way round – only in certain circumstances and on certain markets is a planned economy superior to market solutions. (Feldt 1989; SAP 1990: 18)

> There are only two methods we can use [to cut down structurally based red figures in the national budget]. Either we reduce public expenses or we raise taxes. . . . [I]n reality there is but one alternative: cutting down the level of public costs in relation to national incomes. . . . [The public sector] must not take resources from other sectors to the extent that these sectors run into serious imbalances. (Ahlqvist and Engqvist 1984: 72, 100; see SAP 1990: 153, 180ff.)

At the same time, the Party clearly positioned itself in favour of the universal welfare state. This is not to say more selective ideas had formed any major part of the ideology since the 1950s but somehow the leadership must have felt a need to make things clear in this respect (Hedborg and Meidner 1984; SAP 1990: 175ff.).

All considered, one should not overestimate the change in ideological direction. There was indeed a distinct new open readiness to accept the market economy but this was first and foremost a question of new language. In the former Golden-Age era, the market economy was accepted and found to be the only possible means for reaching decent levels of living standard. In the 1980s almost all praise for planning etc. faded away and was replaced by more outspoken acceptance of the market economy, sometimes praise.

As regards concrete measures there was hardly any change. In many respects the Party was even moving in the direction of a more consolidated public sector. And the range of public sector policies was by no means diminished. All the well-known ingredients were there: day-care, job-seeking centres, allowances of various kinds etc., etc.

A slight change of focus occurred around 1979. The change consisted of four clarifying elements. First, instead of emphasising the need for new reforms the leadership concentrated on the defence of what was already achieved. Secondly, instead of exclusively defending unified government solutions, the new view allowed for freedom of choice within the realm of the public sector. Thirdly, the support for universal welfare state solutions became more outspoken and distinct within the Party's rhetoric. Fourthly, market mechanisms emerged more clearly as elements in the Party's rhetoric.

For the second time since the 1950s influential groups within the Party seriously discussed possible roads to take when taxes and public finances fall short of keeping the public sector at desired levels. Earlier, when public finances were under less strain there was less need for these clarifications.

6
SAP's new era?

Any claims about SAP moves in either market-criticising or market-praising direction are still unsubstantiated in 1985. The Party leadership was still aware of the market's highly efficient, though unevenly distributed outcomes. Kjell-Olof Feldt, the new Finance Minister since 1982 underlined market success as the key to keeping unemployment at bay and that unfair effects had to be corrected through State policies:

> [It is necessary] Sweden enjoys another three years of growth and that this growth . . .
> is allocated to the sector exposed to competitive forces. . . . Also required is that the
> Government backs an active redistributing policy. (*Riksdag* Minutes 1984–85/167: 50
> ff., Feldt)

Finally, towards the end of the period, one would expect at least some traces of a more market-economy friendly attitude than in the preceding decades (or at least that would have been the expectation from those who claim the SAP has moved in a truly neo-liberal direction). But such signs are scarce. In the SAP's book, the market continued to be an agent of efficiency upon which the Swedish economy was highly dependent, thus forcing Swedish companies to make necessary restructurings. In this sense Göran Persson has walked in the footsteps of the legendary Golden Age Finance Minister Gunnar Sträng. Mr Persson, who was later to become Prime Minister but who still headed the Department of Finances in 1994 stressed the role of free enterprise: 'To a very grand extent, new jobs must emanate from free enterprise. We want to contribute to swift reformation and development of companies' (*Riksdag* Minutes 1994–95/57: 33, Persson).

Apparently, Persson felt it to be the job of the Government; in the 1990s as much as in the 1960s to make sure the market economy does not get stuck in inefficiencies, monopolies and biased competition. But government should not replace the market. However, in spite of the general consensus on the merits of free markets the Government was at least as critical of free-for-all markets as ever. Persson was very explicit on this point:

> Alas, Olof Johansson [the then leader of the Centre Party], there were neo-liberals
> in the Government you were in [the 1991–94 non-socialist Government]. That

Government utilised the basic strategy of the neo-liberals: Cut taxes for society's better off, let the market take care of the rest and all will be well. That did not work in the USA, not in the UK and it will not work in Sweden either. Olof Johansson will not escape responsibility. It cost Sweden enormous sums. It led to a different Sweden, not least at the municipal and regional levels where various privatisation measures further strengthened the neo-liberal effects. (*Riksdag* Minutes 1994–95/57: 40, Persson)[1]

This is hardly a neo-liberal in action. Göran Persson may be sternly in favour of the liberal market economy but insofar as the outcomes are concerned he did not regard State corrections as superfluous. The same view was expressed in the 2000 Party programme draft, which though avoiding the term 'socialism', labelled SAP 'anti-capitalist': 'Social democracy is an anti-capitalist party. However, the market economy is regarded by social democracy to be an efficient method of distributing goods and services. Still, political counterforce is needed to prevent improper imbalances' (SAP 2000).

Some caution is still merited. Anti-capitalist the Party may be but a clear indicator of its basic acknowledgement of the market's merits is the trend towards using market mechanisms as a tool in several sectors of the economy including the welfare state. Privatisations, utilising private entrepreneurs and introducing purchasing-selling arrangements within the State sector became more common since the middle of the 1980s (Blomqvist and Rothstein 2000; Hinnfors 1992: Chapter 3). Though at a general level the party was still forcefully protecting the welfare state as a means to safeguarding the population.

Social democracy will never contribute to undermining Sweden's economy. That is why new reforms have to be fully financed. Primarily new resources will have to be used to increase security and fairness. That will have to take precedence over tax cuts.

Our country is too small for major conflicts. There is instead call for a new sense of concert to modernise Sweden and make her more secure. We want broad agreements right across traditional boundaries and barriers.

We want a fully employed Sweden where income gaps narrow and greed is pushed back. We want to create a society where economic, social and ecological forces rest in balance with each other.

Sweden has to be held together – between people and regions. Good quality welfare in the whole country is a precondition for regional fairness. We will increase, not decrease the utilisation of regional tax equalisation. We want to evolve a regional development policy taking into account local and regional commitment. We want to carry out targeted efforts for IT use and out-of-campus education. We want to carry out the biggest commitment on infrastructure in modern time – in major cities as well as in rural areas. (SAP 2002)

The message was mixed. On the one side, the party leadership obviously acknowledged the fact that the market economy creates inequalities and greed and that these inequalities had to be dealt with via regional support, welfare state measures etc. The economic sphere had to be balanced by the social and ecological spheres and major tax cuts were not on the agenda any more. On the other hand the market economy was solidly in place in this document and 'conflicts' should apparently be avoided at any price. The mirage of revolution has cleared and its proponents have left the stage.

However, the extent of this trend is still somewhat limited (Svensson 2001) and with the market-state ideological continuum utilised here many of the reforms fall inside the category 'State corrected by market' where State authorities decide but with the help of market mechanisms.

SAP 1965–2002: the market as an efficiency agent

Much as for the Labour Party, the SAP leadership has been extremely cautious about veering too far from the fundamentals of the market economy. Almost without exception the SAP's alternative visions for the economic system have been well inside the existing system. We are now in a position to say something empirically educated about the 1965–2002 period as a whole as regards the SAP's overarching views about the merits and shortcomings of the market economy. To what extent has the party's market ideology set off in a more market-economy friendly direction or are things pretty much as they used to be? Table 2 gives an overview.

Table 2 SAP ideological views on the market 1965–2002 as measured by four indicators and one sub-indicator

	1965/66	1970	1974/75	1979	1983/85	1987	1992	1995/97	2000/02
Dependency*	High/ Pos	High/ Pos	High/ Pos	High/ Pos	High/ Pos	High/ Pos	High/ Pos	High/ Pos	High/ Pos
Efficiency	High	High	High	High	High	High	High	High	High
Distribution	Unfair	Unfair	Unfair	Unfair	Unfair	Unfair	Unfair	Unfair	Unfair
General opinion	Pos	–	Pos	Pos	–	Pos	Pos	Pos/ Neg	Pos

* Including evaluation of dependency

It might come as a surprise to those who claim social democracy has abandoned a 'political power' view in favour of a 'market power' view, but over the years there is substantial stability in these matters.

Refraining from ownership as a means of correcting the market is far from a 'new' social democracy measure. In the words of former Swedish Prime Minister Tage Erlander, the demand for nationalisation had been pushed into the background. Instead the role of the public sector is that of an overarching body rather than an all-powerful commander (Shaw 1993) providing equality through a 'cradle-to-grave' welfare state (Gray 1996) and economic policies. In conjunction to this phrase, it is strange how strong the notion of 'cradle-to-grave' has been in spite of the fact that the 'cradle' part actually is a very new phenomenon. Substantial numbers of day-care places and sufficient lengths of parental leave periods (paid) is a very recent (post Golden Age) trend. Apart from child allowances the public sector took on few cradle arrangements.

Sweden, like most countries, is depending on international capitalism and there is not much the party leadership can do about it. However, dependency can be a good thing as long as the outcomes are positive. With only minor exceptions, the SAP have found the dependency rewarding and in general have been positive towards the market.

Note

1   Please note that although the lack of titles ('the Right Honourable' etc.) in *Riksdag* debates might surprise English-speaking readers the habit is in full conformity with modern Swedish usage.

7

Parties with a socialist record?

Labour: socialism in the closet

With two social democratic parties, both strongly rooted in socialist tradition, it would be interesting to assess the status of this concept in party documents. Assuming that socialism stands for a vision of a different society than that formed under liberal market economy, the distance between the parties and socialism is a contributory indicator of the status of the market in their ideologies.

It is easy to claim, that socialism is less popular in the New Labour Party than in the old Labour Party. In fact the very term has become something of a taboo, expelled completely from policy documents. This was not always the case. The 1966 election manifesto did not shy away from this word. On the other hand, it was only used once and in the somewhat peripheral sense (although extremely important to those affected) that '[f]or years socialists have crusaded to redress the grievance of the leaseholder who loses his home without compensation when a long lease comes to an end' (Labour 1966). Leaseholders had obvious similarities with workers as regards living conditions. However, focussing on the working class proper would have been even more to the point, especially given the rather limited space permitted by the manifesto. So even at the height of the Golden Age of Social Democracy, the manifesto was focused on topics other than socialism. This applies equally well to the 1964 manifesto. Seemingly the manifesto presented a programme for socialism by announcing that things like full employment; industrial expansion (including 'a sensible distribution of industry throughout the country'), improved traffic and transport conditions, reduced inflation and 'a solution to our balance of payments problems . . . will only be achieved by socialist planning' (Labour 1964). However, by clarifying what lay behind the energetic formulation 'A National Plan', by enumerating policies like encouraging industries and firms to export more through tax inducements, providing good terms credit for business plus a number of 'encouragements' to modernise British industry the 'planning' part of the plan disintegrated. These measures were far from replacing the market with State-allocation according to needs

Alternative visions about a future socialist State towards which social democracy was powerfully striding, albeit with reformist steps, formed no part of the image communicated by the mid-1960s Labour Party. By all means, socialism as a term was present, but watered down to the extent that its meaning was lost. Looking back, one cannot avoid the conclusion that socialism as such was something those responsible for the manifesto were wary of.

SAP: the forbidden word

If Labour has put socialism in the closet, they have, in fact, used the term to some extent. The SAP record is even more clear-cut. Not a single SAP election manifesto refers to 'socialism' during the entire 1965–2002 period (elections to the *Riksdag* were held 1964, 1968, 1970, 1973, 1976, 1979, 1982, 1985, 1988, 1991, 1994, 1998 and 2002). Swedish election manifestos are rather short affairs. Even so, the total lack of references to socialism is a clear indicator of the party leadership's cautious attitude towards more general goal transformations in the future. If anything, this echoing silence tells us something about the standing of socialism within the Swedish Social Democratic Party. In a sense socialism appears to be a concept defunct of meaning, indeed without any meaningful use whatsoever in the Party's ideology. It is remarkable how the party leadership must have lost all conviction that socialism was worth fighting for. It is true that political parties face a pressing task to present some kind of concrete reform proposals during election campaigns. Vote-getting promises have to fill the manifestos. Even so, one would at least have thought that a few inspired formulations about a future better life called socialism would have been used as a way of mobilising the working class. This has not been the case.

The leadership must have felt that references to socialism, in however mild or diluted form, were no particularly useful vote-getting strategy. These observations would, perhaps, not have been entirely surprising in the overall ideological climate of the early twenty-first century. But that socialism was put in the closet already during the height of the Golden Age is more unexpected. Surely some elements of the Party must have thought socialism worth fighting for openly in the efforts to attract voters. Most probably some parts of the SAP and the workers' movement did this but apparently not when voters were addressed in this formal way.

The total absence of socialist references is yet another strong indicator that SAP never seriously contemplated any radical moves away from the international capitalist market economy. Had the concept of socialism been included in the manifestos the Party would have had to face either of two alternatives. Either socialism had been equalled with something like a strong welfare state, correcting the market, i.e. the model for society SAP relies on in practice. Such references may not have been embarrassing as such but the voters might have interpreted the evident lack of anything more than what was already realised in the existing society as empty and hollow. Better then to use 'social democracy' rather than 'socialism'.

The other option would have been to refer to socialism without defining it. That would have been yet another tactic of hollowness. The fact that neither of these roads was taken points in the direction that the leadership actually wanted to use the socialist word as little as possible since they did not want it to materialise.

'Dedication' to socialism?

The 1970 Labour manifesto was equally low-key on the mentioning of socialism. Apart from a statement on the final line of the manifesto, that the Party was 'dedicated' to socialism and the information that Willy Brandt, German Prime Minister, was talking to East German and Polish leaders, only a single reference was offered. On the other hand this reference actually tried to elaborate on the definition of socialism: 'It is true – and it is a truly Socialist shift in priorities – that we now spend more on education than on defence, and that in the near future the health and welfare service expenditure will also exceed defence spending'.

As an attempt to define socialism the section was rather limited. As is shown by the document, the same list of priorities emerged here as in almost every single year, including the 2002 elections (and 2002 was not an election full of socialist rhetoric). Education, health and welfare services take top priority. What is just as clear is the lack of any developed elaboration on socialism. There were no references to any kind of alternative economic system. Instead, the readers were provided with the list of public sector corrections, which has become an important part of all Labour documents. Therefore, the conclusion is, that the Party's ideology rested firmly on a belief that the market economy works well as a surplus-generating agent. In many ways, this view about the market's role – a trigger of 'privately-generated economic growth' (Coates 2001: 300) – was at the core of the Golden Age Party. The surplus needs a fair distribution, hence the emphasis on the welfare state.

The February 1974 manifesto was a touch more elaborate. The statement that 'power in industry [should be made] genuinely accountable to the workers and the community at large' hinted at the proof of the pudding: Power. According to this view, pious attempts to strike voluntary agreements with employers would never count as real steps towards socialism. Contrary to most other documents, this manifesto did actually dwell on the need for true shifts in power. On the other hand the reference was only indirect and the other items on the list included familiar phrases like:

> Bring about a fundamental and irreversible shift in the balance of power and wealth in favour of working people and their families. . . . Eliminate poverty wherever it exists in Britain, and commit ourselves to a substantial increase in our contribution to fight poverty abroad. . . . Achieve far greater economic equality – in income, wealth and living standards. . . . Increase social equality by giving far greater importance to full employment, housing, education and social benefits. . . . Improve the environment in which our people live and work and spend their leisure. (Labour 1974a)

At the same time as the phrases rang familiar bells about improvements in the welfare state, they undoubtedly offered more radical versions of market-correction than before. '[F]undamental' and 'irreversible' power and wealth shifts in favour of working people were held up as goals rather than just 'shifts'. Poverty should be 'eliminated' and 'far' greater equality should be achieved. There is no mistaking the aim to correct the grim outcomes of capitalism. However, the radicalism quickly vanished. Most of the references, especially the power angle, disappeared six months later. In the October 1974 manifesto, focus was once again on equalling socialism with milder corrective measures destined to create a kinder and gentler society:

> What we as democratic socialists maintain is that when the going is toughest it is more than ever necessary to base our policies on social justice, to protect the weak, the poor, the disabled, to help those least able to help themselves, and to maintain and improve their living standards.
>
> We are a democratic socialist party and our objective is to bring about a fundamental and irreversible shift in the balance of wealth and power in favour of working people and their families. (Labour 1974b)

A new kind of rhetoric cropped up in 1979, when the manifesto held that '[w]e reject the concept that there is a choice to be made between a prosperous and efficient Britain and a caring and compassionate society. As democratic socialists, we believe they complement each other' (Labour 1979). Tony Blair could very well have formulated these sentences twenty-five years later; only he would perhaps have dropped the word 'socialist'. The power question appeared to have been relegated to second-rate status no less then than within New Labour.

Early SAP manifestos did speak of 'a strong society able to counter the forces of the free market' (SAP 1970), and 'a strengthened position for employees ... [through] democratisation of labour relations' (SAP 1970). Overall SAP was at least as low key as the Labour Party with very modest, and more or less unspecified suggestions, about 'the reformation of labour conditions including its democratisation' (SAP 1973). The Social Democrats would 'not accept the free play of economic forces to decide over people's work, health and security' (SAP 1973) but proposals were weak. Apart from these rather mild attempts to formulate anything resembling an alternative economic system with at least some focus on the question of power over production, the manifestos contained – across-the-board – an abundance of familiar welfare-state reform proposals. And, as so many times before, the proposals hovered around education, health and regional policies.

Short-lived revival

Radicalisation swept over both Parties 1979–83. As could be expected, the 1983 Labour manifesto tried hard to send a tougher message both qualitatively and quantitatively speaking. Still, references to the power question were gone (although it has to be remembered that the manifesto actually promised to give a larger role to common-ownership enterprises, which indirectly related to the issue of power). Apart from claiming that socialist governments have the 'right' policies the manifesto became concrete mainly in the defence of the National Health Service. The NHS was described as 'a commonsense example of democratic socialism in action'. There were also references to full employment, exchange controls and regulating direct overseas investment and other typical examples of market-correcting measures (Labour 1983). As a socialist belief system, with its supposed concrete information about what was really behind the term, the text is surprisingly brief. On the other hand, were we to consider commitments to support the NHS as true examples of 'commonsense . . . democratic socialism' the Party was decidedly more outspoken. But then, we must also acknowledge the fact that the present Labour Government's effort to undo the effect of decades of neglect and under spending of the NHS is as socialist as what Labour promised in 1983.

Equally surprising, is the relative abundance of mentioning of socialism four years on, in the 1987 manifesto which, incidentally, was the last Labour manifesto with any direct use of the term 'socialism.' Once again the text included phrases – quoted here at some length – which pointed in the direction of Tony Blair and New Labour:

> Labour's objective is to broaden and deepen the liberty of all individuals in our community: to free people from poverty, exploitation and fear; to free them to realise their full potential; to see that everyone has the liberty to enjoy real chances, to make real choices. . . . Commonsense and the common interest require that the Tory philosophy of selfishness and short-term gain is replaced by the democratic socialist philosophy of community and caring, of investment in people and in production. . . . They are essential too if we are to generate the wealth needed for the security, care and opportunity fundamental to the individual freedom of women and men of all ages and origins. When our country faces the common pressures on the environment, the common dangers of crime, the common costs of unemployment, under-investment and under-performance together, our country has every commonsense reason to meet those challenges together. . . . It means collective provision for private use. The British people know that this is the most effective way for them to secure their freedom as individuals whilst meeting the moral obligations which they feel towards others and seeing that fairness is a way of national life, not just a fine word. (Labour 1987)

As a piece of eloquence this is an excellent text. In comparison with other manifestos, the formulations were very close to the Party's more recent rhetoric (on policy continuity underlying a 'surface of rhetoric', see Coates 2001). The content was laden with implicit references to the liberal version of equality in opportunities rather than equality in results. Terms like 'community', 'caring', 'full potential' and 'real chances' dominated. Equally clear, is the fact that the Labour leadership staid well away from any reference to the power-over-capital question. Collective provision for private use, i.e. an efficient public sector, rather than nationalisations was brought forward as the solution to the country's problems. Chief among the troubles were 'pressures on the environment, the common dangers of crime, the common costs of unemployment, under-investment and under-performance'. The Party claimed 'our country has every commonsense reason to meet those challenges together.' There were no references as such to the power over the market (in that sense, the interpretation made here about 1987 being a 'terminological' break with Labour socialism, corresponds to that made by Panitch and Leys 1997: 237, who emphasise the effects of the so called 'Policy Review', which was set in motion by Neil Kinnock in 1987, as the real step away from 'making the party into a vehicle for socialism'). Colin Hay takes their argument one step further and claims 'that by the completion of the Policy Review – and, perhaps some time before that

– Labour had ceased effectively to be a social democratic party, committed as it had by then become to a pervasive neo-liberal orthodoxy'. Still, in the sense that a welfare state is tantamount to some sort of power over the distribution of the market's surplus, the power-issue was present. And, though 'socialism' was off, the range of public-sector measures was certainly not 'neo-liberal.'

In order to be able to give analytical underpinning to how far or how close to socialist ideals the Labour Party has been, some kind of criterion is necessary. To claim that there was no doubt at all about Labour being clearly in favour of an alternative political and economic model ('socialism'), an element of express references to the exact meaning of this alternative would have to be revealed in the documents. This has not been the case. Over the years, the list of welfare-state programmes reappears continuously. In a few instances, the list was complemented by elaborations on nationalisation of certain industries. Even when nationalisation was given such status, the documents included passages, which distinctly rested on the assumption that the market economy would be left untouched. Alternative economic systems practically never formed any part of the Labour Party's market ideology.

As for the term socialism, the references have been few, obscure and ambiguous. The difference is striking, compared to the high degree of elaboration and the extensive space given to the familiar range of corrective measures, which all fit into the traditional market-economy framework. The documents include long and detailed discussions about welfare-state reform, both as regards improvements of existing welfare programmes and extensions into new fields. One cannot but conclude that socialism is a term, which, even during the Golden Age of Social Democracy, has been used more as a tribute to the historical tradition from which the Party emerged, than as an indicator of what kind of society the Party wanted for the future. In effect then, the Party made the fundamental changes concerning the State–market question long ago, but let some traces of its State-oriented past linger.

Some references to power over industrial production temporarily occurred in the 1979 and 1982 SAP manifestos, where, in interesting similarity to the Labour Party, a similar period of radicalisation took place. 'We have to continue democratising the economic sphere and renewing work life' (SAP 1979) was a phrase hinting at the need to come to grips with unequal relationships between employers and employees. The so-called wage-earners' funds, which finally were brought to the voters in 1982, after endless muddling and shuffling in the party, were briefly mentioned in the 1982 manifesto. Somewhat remarkably the funds were not overtly connected to the question of collectivist ownership and power over the means of production which were the intentions in Rudolf Meidner's (LO economist) original proposal (Meidner 1975). Instead the manifesto listed several other economic reasons for introducing the funds:

> It is crucial to bring down the huge deficits in the Government budget and in our foreign trade. To secure future employment levels, incomes and pensions will need improved capital formation and increased savings. That will only be possible through wage-earners' cooperation and given that wage earners gain influence so that the

money is used on investments – not on speculation – and that the wage earners will get their share of the created resources. (SAP 1982)

Most probably the leadership was eager to downplay the risks of the funds. The employers and non-socialist parties were furious about the whole idea. Emphasis on capital formation and the need to keep the public budget in balance were efforts to pour oil on troubled waters but could hardly please left-of-centre social democrats who wanted decisive steps towards real workers' power. Any party may be excused of playing its cards as strategically wise as possible but the emphasis on deficit fighting is a clear indicator the party leadership never really embraced the wage-earners' fund ideas wholeheartedly. From the beginning it was more of an LO (the powerful Swedish confederation of blue-collar workers) project than an SAP plan.

Whatever the interpretation of these lines, they were the last SAP manifesto references to the hotly disputed funds. Already in 1985 the manifesto placed great emphasis on the need for 'profitable small enterprises and successful big companies' (SAP 1985). The funds have vanished from the text through a back door (though they were still operative until the 1991–94 non-socialist Government abolished them; they were never reintroduced when the SAP regained power in 1994, since then funds are a non-issue).

On the other hand, the party programmes reveal a somewhat different picture than what emerge in election manifestos and speeches. Neither capitalism nor communism has been actively endorsed as the SAP's way forward. In bewildering contrast to what was said in manifestos and elsewhere, the 1975 party programme was relatively eloquent on 'democratic socialism.' According to the programme:

the concentration of economic power in the hands of the few will have to be replaced by an order in which every human being as citizen, wage earner and consumer will hold the right to influence the direction of economic production and distribution. . . . A democratisation of the economic sphere will presuppose that citizen influence will be effective at all levels of the economy. The entire economic sphere will have to be co-ordinated in a planned administration under citizen control' (SAP 1975).

In rhetoric at least, planning and direction over the means of production and over the economy were brought to the agenda. The core question of socialism versus capitalism was indeed tackled here. However, the meaning of 'planned administration under citizen control' turns out to be a little obscure. Behind the comparatively tough phrases lay familiar proposals about public sector health care and social security plus references to the need for scientific and technical progress, which would be important tasks for the public sector. Rather than reducing the dependence on the international market the Party wanted through the programme to 'strengthen the position of individuals in order to make them stronger and better prepared to endure the changes caused by changing forms of production which emerge as a consequence of new technical and economic conditions and with immediate impact [on society] brought about by the internationally dependent economy' (SAP 1975). By continuing the efforts to decrease income differentials the programme wanted to 'equalize consumers' ability to affect the economy through their actions in the market. As far as income distribution, tax levels, welfare state measures the programme was indeed tough.

When it comes to the market economy as such the aim was less clear. While the programme did not shy away from dwelling on the subject of who shall hold the right to influence conditions of production, the ownership question *per se* was more or less off limits, though not completely. The passage about the importance to 'transfer into public ownership or under public control, natural resources, financial institutions and companies to the extent regarded as necessary in order to safeguard common interests' (SAP 1975) indicated a preparedness to move ahead in the direction of nationalisations.

On the other hand there was no information whatsoever as regards the scope of nationalisations. How much is 'necessary'? When are common interests 'safeguarded' and what exactly is a 'common interest'? Since no proposals to nationalise anything (apart from minor symbolic measures) where brought forward in manifestos, speeches, government bills etc. during the period covered by the programme the conclusion here is, that the party leadership was rather happy with the status quo.

In stark similarity with Labour's rhetoric around 1983, words such as 'planning', 'control' and 'influence' seem to lose their meaning. Why all the tough words when little else than more of the same type of market-correcting means was intended? Behind all this rhetoric most probably rest two circumstances. First, there were true compromises between those who wanted to speed up a process towards a more clear-cut socialist society and those who felt a need to pull the emergency brake in alarm. Second, the grand words had perhaps other, mobilising, aims than providing direct guidelines for what the party was actually going to do. Words fill symbolic meanings and to allude to the core sentences about the means of production being transferred to the hands of ordinary people, the authors could hope to encourage hesitant voters that social democracy stood for something completely different than the non-socialist parties.

Back to normal

Up until 1994, the Labour Party's constitution included phrases which had distinct socialist connotations: 'the common ownership of the means of production, distribution and exchange, and the best obtainable system of popular administration and control of each industry and service.' Given the party's extremely few efforts to provide any day-to-day policy measures of any kind to realise the 'common ownership' and 'popular administration and control of each industry and service', it is surprising that these passages should have remained as long as 1994. The fact that they did is an example of the extent to which symbols and reverences actually mean something to us. Parties need more than day-to-day policies to convince their followers. They need visions, even though the visions are considered impossible to realise.

The new version of Labour's constitution talks instead of 'common endeavour', 'a dynamic economy', 'a just society', 'an open democracy', and 'a healthy environment'. No doubt the symbolic change this revision entailed was substantial even though the new views had taken root within the Labour leadership long ago (Peele 1997: 91). Whether words and phrases like 'open democracy' carry the same visionary force as 'common ownership' is an empirical question.

Almost in tandem with the Labour Party's march from 'old' to 'New', the SAP had formulated a new, revised programme in 1990. In many ways the changes brought the programme more in tune with the party's actual policies and ideological standpoints. Capitalism and Communism were still equally criticised for inhumanity and lack of understanding of the real needs for necessary security and fairness in society. 'Democratic socialism' on the other hand was described as a 'fight for freedom'. The real character of the democratic socialism was said to set free 'human power' needed to contribute to society's build-up. In its pure form 'democratic socialism is founded upon a trust in people's willingness and ability to create a society characterised by togetherness and human dignity in harmony with what nature is able to carry in the long run' (SAP 1990).

The 1990 programme made direct reference to the ownership question. 'Ownership', the programme stated, was not the social democratic way. 'Rather . . . a more suitable method to ensuring public influence over the mode of production is through various ways of influence over production and the distribution of the production's outcome' (SAP 1990).

The programme did indeed mention the need to nationalise banks, credit companies and insurance companies. The difficult point for the Party was to define the 'various ways of influence over production and the distribution of the production's outcome.' A paragraph later in the programme the Party's definition stated that 'environmental protection, regional distribution, nationwide employment opportunities and social services available to everyone.' These were the actual measures by which the Party leadership regarded democratic socialism to be fulfilled. It is unclear whether the leadership by these references regarded the state of democratic socialism as something worth striving for in the future or something, which had already materialised in the real world.

The market mechanism as such was briefly elaborated upon. 'Market mechanisms provide a quick and convenient system of signalling between producers and consumers. Apparently the market mechanism constitutes the basis for economic activity. However, the market has several shortcomings.' Therefore the market had to be guided through 'framework legislation' in order to make it function in a desired manner. Aware of the market's limitations the programme also listed a number of areas, which lack any real market price. Consequently there would have to be politically based corrections in certain spheres of life. At this stage, and given earlier years' SAP development of attitudes towards the market, it comes as no surprise that the subjects mentioned in the programme were those of social care and education (SAP 1990).

One cannot escape from the feeling that democratic socialism in this version has little to do with socialism in its more classical version. Democratic socialism is much closer to the familiar market economy with a number of generous welfare state elements and with a top-up of public ownership in a few selected areas. There might also be a number of public policies designed to force the market to behave in an acceptable way.

The present SAP Party programme was carried in 2001. Although references to 'democratic socialism' are by no means gone most traces of traditional elements of socialism still visible in the 1975 and 1990 versions have now been swept away. 'Democracy does always hold the right to formulate the terms for the economy and to set the limits for the market' (SAP 2001) is perhaps the closest we get to the older programmes' paragraphs about the role for the public sector. To 'hold the right' is not entirely the same thing as wielding that right and few passages in the programme give us much hope that any far-reaching actions will be taken in any very market-limiting way.

The programme explicitly denounces public ownership as such as a way to abolish insecurity, injustices and lack of freedom. Economies based on public ownership have not been able to rid themselves of those problems. Instead the way forward is founded on 'participation, co-operation [and] a multitude of [influencing the economy, which are all supported by] government rules for private enterprise, economic policy, labour-market wage-bargaining agreements, labour rights legislation and consumer legislation, growing consumer cooperative movement and a strong public sector.'

The programme goes to great lengths to elaborate on the role of the market. The market economy is regarded as a natural part of the economic sphere as long as the democratic sphere sets the limits for the market's activities. The price mechanism is described as an efficient way of communication between consumers and producers but the public sphere is always needed not only to correct the market's outcomes, which in many ways cannot fulfil perfectly legitimate needs of social care etc. but also in order to make sure the market really behaves according to the rules of free competition. Left on its own the market's inner tendency is to pervert into monopolies. As a safeguard against capital concentration the public sector is indispensable by setting fair rules of the game without which the market will destroy itself (SAP 2001). A more clear-cut example of the combination of market-acceptance and the need to correct the market's outcomes and behaviour is hard to get.

As so many times before, this document is an eloquent example of the emphasis social democracy places on the need to correct the market's outcomes. In a mixed economy, so the programme states, social care and education are areas, which will always need the public sector. Social rights like education and social care 'belong to everyone regardless of income' and have to be excluded from the market's principles of distribution.

Socialism in the distance

There is no denying that followers to the two Parties once wanted 'socialism'. At the same time it is clear socialism has left the Parties' documents and, thus, the conclusion is that it has left the Parties' ideologies. However, the key matter would rather be whether socialism was ever, since 1965, included in the ideology behind the phrases. To some extent a future, better, society – sometimes by the name of socialism – was indeed held up as motivational cue during the Golden Age. In that respect social democracies have changed compared to the 1974–87 period and certainly with the Labour Party. This is real change and it has occurred twice. Before and after the 1974–87 period, socialism was in the distance, more like a mirage than a concrete image of how a future society should be organised. After 1987 even the mirage has evaporated. Between mid-1970s and mid-1980s the mirage gained somewhat in clarity as a concept but the proposals about the organisation of a future society were still extremely vague and few. Neither did the Party place quantitative emphasis in the documents on waving the socialist flag nor did it make much effort to elaborate qualitatively on what exactly socialism stood for. The market economy has taken centre stage in the Labour Party's ideology. The effort dedicated to socialism in the manifestos is telling in the sense that so extremely little has been said. The character of the texts has been perfunctory rather than an indication of radicalism. It is also evident that, with very few exceptions, in Labour's thinking, socialism has come to mean something very close to what Labour had already tried to achieve in practice: An extensive welfare state, active labour market policies, more or less organised cooperation between employers and employees and an element of companies owned by the public sector. In truth, socialism appears to have been a mirage.

All in all, and seen over the entire 1965–2002 period, socialism has lost most of its meaning in the SAP manifestos and Party programmes as well. In the beginning there were at least some elements of an alternative economic system to be found in the references about the future. The references were few and were always balanced by elaborations in the text, which took the bite off the earlier sentences. Public ownership of the means of production was still something, which could be referred to, as a possible alternative in a future democratic socialist State but the extent of public ownership was never explicitly put on paper. Vague notions of 'to the extent necessary' were hardly enough to give an overall picture of a party striving to leave the market economy. Nor were the tasks of the public sector specified other than that they should bring new efficiency.

Over the concluding four decades of the twentieth century the SAP have accepted, and even praised the positive effects of, the market economy (Table 2). While the distributional effects have always been regarded as negative, no less so in 2004 than during the Golden Age of Social Democracy, the market as an efficiency agent is nothing new to social democracy. On the contrary, that has been a leading theme of the Party leadership for at least the last third of the twentieth century. The fact that we are unable to pinpoint a single reference to socialism in the Party's election manifestos over the entire 1965–2002 period corroborates this conclusion.

Set in a context where no election manifesto or indeed hardly any major spokesperson explicitly elaborated on how to interpret the democratic socialism we are left to conclude that welfare state, market economy and an element of public ownership comprised the social democratic vision of society. Until the late 1980s the Party sometimes wanted to call this mixture 'socialism.' Later the mixture remains roughly untouched but the label has been removed. As a revolutionary vision – though of course with reformist measures – it always fell short of qualifying as a true alternative to the existing economic and political system. As the repeated criticism from left-of-middle party members and from left-wing groups outside the Party probably proves, such a conclusion is not too far-fetched.

The whole debate about wage-earners' funds, which peaked during the 1970s showed that important elements inside the social democratic movement wanted to take the ideology at least one full step to the left. They realised that the power question had to be addressed. The point I have made is that even though those forces were strong, eloquent and manifold the party leadership never really contemplated letting them have their way. The struggle between the forces might have been close at some stage, but the cautious formulations in the Party programmes plus the total silence on socialism in the election manifestos bear witness of the strength of the status-quo proponents within the Party. As time went by the status quo group also managed to rid the leading Party documents from the disharmony between different parts of the rhetoric they endorsed.

That both Parties have treated socialism with caution is an understatement. The term has been a source of encouragement but has formed a very limited part of the parties' messages to the voters. Overall the term has been conspicuous more through its absence than its presence. The ideological repercussions for the Parties' market ideologies of lavishly using the concept of socialism would perhaps have been too unpredictable given socialism's implicit, and explicit, notion of alternative ways of organising society than through the market.

Part III
The nature of social democracy

8
Full circle back

The positive attitude taken by the Labour Party and the SAP of market processes is fundamental to the reformism project to the extent that it forms the very *raison d'être* of social democracy, yet it is one that has been neglected in earlier research. Although confined to two parties the study shows they have been remarkably similar. This fact and the fact that we have spanned several decades with ebbs and flows of ideological debate contribute to extend the conclusions to social democracy more generally.

Over the last thirty years the SAP and the Labour Party have come full circle back to the entirely market-economy friendly, but still market-correcting, position the Parties occupied in the 1960s. In spite of different policy histories, different parliamentary contexts and different organisational structure, there are surprisingly small differences between the Parties' ideologies. They emerged during the Golden Age of Social Democracy as Parties with high regard for market efficiency and a view that the respective economies were highly dependent on world market behaviour. The same overall views remained at the turn of the millennium.

Likewise, both Parties still stand behind essentially the same views as to the need for market-corrections. The collection of such corrections is fairly stable. In 2002 (and indeed in 2005) as well as in 1965, information supply and job-seeking support for the work force, health services and education continuously form the backbone of the Parties' suggested corrective measures. Only the rhetoric about future public ownership takeovers has vanished from the Party leaderships' language. The veil has come off and we are able to see the parties' true ideologies in clearer light.

At times the market economy has been harshly criticised but never to the extent that any real alternative has been offered, not even in the radical early 1980s. Basically the criticism has usually ended up in a somewhat wider collection of market-correcting measures and – less common – a relatively limited increase in public ownership. However, precious little indicates that the Parties' leaderships should have left the market-correcting (or market-complementing) attitude in any single year.

Let us take a look at the overall picture (Table 3) where both Labour and SAP market views are presented for the entire 1965–2002 period.

Table 3 Labour and SAP ideological views on the market 1965–2002 as measured by four indicators and one sub-indicator

	1965/ 66	1970	1974/ 75	1979	1983/ 85	1987	1992	1995/ 97	2002
Dependency*									
SAP	High/ Pos	High/ Pos	High/ Pos	High/ Pos	High/ Pos	High/ Pos	High/ Pos	High/ Pos	High/ Pos
Labour	High/ Pos	High/ Pos	High/ Neg	High/ Pos	High/ Neg	High/ –	High/ Pos	High/ Pos	High/ Pos
Efficiency									
SAP	High	High	High	High	High	High	High	High	High
Labour	High	High	–	High	High	High	High	High	High
Distribution									
SAP	Unfair	Unfair	Unfair	Unfair	Unfair	Unfair	Unfair	Unfair	Unfair
Labour	Unfair	Unfair	Unfair	Unfair	Unfair	Unfair	Unfair	Unfair	Unfair
General Opinion									
SAP	Pos	–	Pos	Pos	–	Pos	Pos	Pos/Neg	Pos
Labour	Pos	Pos	Neg	Pos	Neg	Pos	Pos	Pos	Pos

*Including evaluation of dependency

With obvious exceptions, stability is characteristic of the Parties' ideologies about the market economy. In 1974 and 1983 Labour played with the idea of keeping the market forces on tighter reins, but even so the differences with other periods are astonishingly small. Even accounting for the 1974/1983 deviances we still have no reason to accept the notion that social democracy should have moved from a distinctly State-authority Golden Age ideology to a clear-cut present-day market-favouring and neo-liberal ideology. There have indeed been ups and downs in the market-acceptance but no specific trend in any direction.

With an array of market-correcting measures the two parties firmly present themselves as full-blown social liberals in the Golden Age as well as forty years on. At no point socialism seems to be a real possibility, at least as far as moving in a decidedly State-centred direction – if for a moment we recall the State–market categories 'a–f' in Box 2 in Chapter 2 – is concerned. Typically education, health care and family support are targeted as the major market-correcting sectors. In this respect the parties' goals are extremely stable over time and between the countries in spite of all the differences as regards country size, economic position on the world markets, Party history etc.

The step is very long between 'market complemented by the State' and 'State complemented by the market'. Even during Labour's most outspokenly radical period in the early 1980s the role for government was portrayed as aiding the economy into becoming more competitive in the market. Companies successful in the market should be allowed to set the standards to which less successful companies have to adapt. The list of sectors, destined to be taken over by State ownership, was much too short to merit any definite conclusion of a major change in Party policy in these respects. And please note that this conclusion does not deny Labour's strong criticism of how the market actually worked. To be sure, the Party wanted extraordinary means to force it into acceptable behaviour.

The Swedish Party is somewhat more stable in its attitudes towards the market. State ownership is never really suggested as a viable alternative to market-correction of the traditional type. Wage-earners' funds were discussed, and implemented in a modest form, in the beginning of the 1980s, but the implemented funds were actually to rely on market forces in the first place, were set a fairly low ownership ceiling and were never meant to reach anything resembling what we here label 'State complemented by the market.' So in actual effect, the funds contributed to boosting the Stockholm stock exchange during the 1980s. They were never (in their final form) meant to be able to take over Swedish industry and the Party leadership never endorsed any of the more radical versions. The funds were a pet project for the Swedish blue-collar union LO rather than for the Party's leadership (see Pontusson 1992). The unions pressed on for the funds after 1979 and the leadership simply had to come up with something to respond to these pressures, which in some versions were rather radical. The diluted final proposal was much criticised for being toothless but proves the point made here about the Party leadership's cool attitude towards socialising Swedish industry (see Feldt 1991).

Never was Labour any closer to a State-commanding position than in 1983. And even then the Party was firmly planted in market-economy-accepting soil. As was shown earlier, the 1983 Labour position was close to the market-based Swedish Rehn–Meidner Model in operation during the 1960s. In both cases the models rested on the view that the government should guide the economy into becoming more competitive in the market. The labour force should be encouraged to move to the productive jobs in the market-exposed sector of the economy. There should be an ambitious public sector to help workers and employers finding each other. In that way pockets of poverty and economic backwardness would be forced out of the economic system, but it would also mean rather drastic removals of the working force to where the internationally profitable industrial sectors were situated (for an overview of the basic characteristics of the Rehn–Meidner Model see Pontusson 1992).

In their turn the 1983 beliefs about labour-market policies were not very far from Labour's later policies. The 1997 manifesto listed a long range of government-led activities to attract the workforce to the competitive sectors of the economy. Of course we all know that the 1983 version of Labour tried to be far more radical in its use of words, references etc. than the present-day version of New Labour. This difference in context can be interpreted in two different ways. On the one hand the more radical context then might lead us to believe that the Party at that time actually meant more with its promises than its 'New' version. The whole atmosphere surrounding the early 1980s documents created a feeling that Labour was a Party willing to go ahead and actually do something.

On the other hand, behind the radical phrases the lack of any real alternatives to the traditional economic and political order of liberal democracy provokes a feeling that the 1983 Party leadership was hesitant about what it wanted to do. To the critical mind the conclusion would then be that Labour was promising more than it could deliver (a disturbing similarity to later political debate about the status of the Labour Party, see Coates 2001; Wickham-Jones 2000). And although the promises were wrapped in what seems to be shining paper the content was more or less old.

The somewhat more radical position of the Labour Party in the early 1980s was shared with the SAP, which launched its wage-earners' funds at the same time. Even here the likeness is striking between the two parties. Both were radicalised at about the same time, and to some extent this radicalisation was based upon the shock of not being able to hold on to power during the economically tumultuous 1970s. Both parties sent out mixed messages about the radicalisation. A few years later SAP took the same road back to a more clear-cut market-correcting attitude as Labour did. Perhaps SAP was a touch more sceptical to the market towards the end of the period but especially post-2000 the difference is minor.

Compare Gunnar Sträng's (the then Swedish finance minister) 1969 statement on the role of government with the 1997 Labour manifesto. Mr Sträng's 'the most important objectives of our economic policy: Full employment, rapid growth and a more equal distribution of income, require a considerable effort on behalf of the Government' (Government Proposition 1969:1, app. 1, p. 9) was closely echoed by Labour thirty years later:

Government and industry must work together to achieve key objectives aimed at enhancing the dynamism of the market, not undermining it. (Labour 1997)

Never forget: in 18 Tory years, unemployment trebled. Families of three generations with nobody bringing in a wage. Record youth unemployment. And what did they say: it was a price worth paying. Unemployment is never a price worth paying. The New Deal has helped nearly a million people with work or training, the largest ever jobs programme Britain has seen. . . . That was our choice. Not to leave you at the mercy of markets. (Blair 2000)

The difference between the supposedly Golden Age, left-leaning 1969 Swedish minister (on any account the former agricultural farm-hand Sträng was decidedly old school) and his latter-age allegedly neo-liberal British counterpart is one of degree rather than character. Perhaps Mr Sträng hinted more at Government having to force or guide the business community while Tony Blair perhaps put more emphasis on business and government working as a team. Whether the parties are to be classified as tough or lean on the market forces is a question of theoretical indicators and we need to use the same indicators over time. With the indicators utilised here neither the SAP or Labour has ever been particularly tough. Nor have they been particularly soft since market-correction is a distinct, not to say essential, social democratic characteristic as defined in this book.

The parties are new in their apparent determination to scrap most of their alternative 'visions' about socialism and overtly stand behind the liberal market economy. But, at the same time they have been able to carry out the string of new market-conforming policies, such as deregulated currency markets etc., and still remain faithful to their old ideologies of market-correction. The new economic policies were possible to implement because they did not break with the parties' core ideologies, which have focused far more on how to correct the market's unfair results than to replace the market as such. The parties have utilised a range of measures to establish such corrections but the outlook of social democrats towards economic issues, and in particular, their relationship with the market has had an important element of stability between these two parties across polities as well as over time.

The recurring theme of enabling capitalism

As one of the very symbols of the Swedish Social Democracy during the Golden Age stood the so called Rehn–Meidner Model for wages and productivity The Model's founding fathers were LO economists Bertil Rehn and Rudolf Meidner. The Model yields a suitable preliminary indication of the position that market forces enjoyed during that time. For all the Model's rhetorical overtones of planning, its specific aim was actually to fine-tune the economy according to international market forces in order to 'obviate' the 'inflationary fires' (McGann Blyth 1999: Chapter 9; Tilton 1990: 195ff.; see Rehn 1957) or – in Linda Weiss's (1998: 95) rather grim words – 'a central aim of the Rehn–Meidner programme was to squeeze low-productivity firms and industries, forcing them to upgrade or exit from the market.'

In fact the Model can be described as an 'articulate expression of the labor movement's commitment to the free market economy' (Pontusson 1992a: 62). According to Meidner himself the model represented the 'culmination of market-conforming thinking and unwillingness to plan or steer within the labour movement' (Hedborg and Meidner 1984: 202). Rather peculiarly, Patrick Dunleavy in a way catches the essence of the Rehn–Meidner Model in his description of what he considers form the constitutive elements of 'New' Labour. Dunleavy claims that the purported centrism:

> reflects an outward-looking response to globalization, to the reduced powers and competencies of the nation State in the modern age. It re-focuses on the 'core competencies' of national governments in the 'post-modern' period, conceived as facilitating the UK's economic competitiveness via re-skilling and education, encouraging long-term investment, creating flexible and adaptive labour markets and industrial structures, and retuning the welfare state to reduce dependency and encourage self-reliance. (Dunleavy 1997: 13)

Inflation was seen as a cause of unemployment, thus it had to be battled. Whether, in practice, one of these two goals was superior than the other is down to hair-splitting. Rehn and Meidner saw the necessity in fighting inflation in order to be able to create real redistributable surpluses and to stabilise the economy. Increasing prices would 'hamper productivity, and thus the increase in the standard of living' and would also harm foreign trade so 'that full employment could no longer be maintained' (LO 1953: 82).

Nor were latter-day opinions about a strict relationship between wages and productivity foreign to the Rehn–Meidner Model (LO 1953: 94). On the contrary, Rehn and Meidner explicitly warned that wage increases would affect Sweden's international market position. Moreover, rather than the expansionary fiscal policies in times of recession expected of Keynesianism, a somewhat restrictive approach, more reminiscent of what neo-liberalism argues, was applied (McGann Blyth 1999: Chapter 8).

The entire Rehn–Meidner Model was geared around relentless market forces, which it never really tried to diminish. Rather the model's focus was to handle the international market economy and make the best of it. By pushing the more protected domestic industrial sectors to apply the same wages as the highly productive trade-dependent sector, which was exposed to international market competition, the pressures of international markets were reproduced throughout the economy. The ensuing increase in overall productivity would create a taxable surplus to transfer to the welfare state.

The Rehn–Meidner Model was a clear-cut example of social democracy in practice. The aim was to free resources for the welfare state, which was seen as the central vehicle in correcting the market economy's unfair results. At the same time the policy, which usually went under the name 'solidaristic wage policy', literally forced every little remote part of the country and all economic sectors to endure the cutting edge of the international capitalist market forces and to drive those who lagged behind out of business. An essential part of the solidaristic wage policy was to keep wages down in the profitable sector, so that workers in this sector would not unduly outperform their less fortunate comrades in less productive parts of the country. At the same time wages in the more low-performing sectors were to be kept as high as those in the top-performing sectors. One consequence of these policies was the increasing profits in the market-exposed sector because business could benefit from the relatively modest wage demands. The relatively high wages in the not so productive sectors also contributed to the rapid closure of industrial sectors, contributing to a general exodus from remoter parts of the country to the major southern cities. The transformation was given an extra boost by generous government removals subsidies, jobs training etc. That was the face of the Golden Age of Social Democracy in Sweden. The welfare state expanded but it rested firmly on a true understanding, and acceptance, of the market economy's demands (Swenson 1989).

Even with deregulated capital markets, including freed National Banks with inflation-curbing on their agendas, the Social Democrats do not seem to have travelled very far. With most of the economy exposed to international market forces, the public sector could help companies become efficient. The resulting surplus is transferable to the welfare state. It is fair to say that the Golden Age had more of grand words and maybe a true belief in the prospects of planning but hardly any real intention of letting those words and prospects materialise.

Exchange controls and politicised National Banks were in place during the Golden Age and maybe the abolishing of these are indications of a more unrestrained acceptance of the market's conditions. On the other hand, the post-war economies were extremely dependent on USA and the Bretton-Woods system with questionable economic manoeuvrability for Swedish and UK Governments.

Utilising our continuum of State–market closeness, one can hardly characterise the Rehn–Meidner Model as anything other than market-correcting. Granted, the means of correcting were many and ingenious but corrections they were. In no way was market replaced by State mechanisms. On the contrary, when push comes to shove, the difference between acceptance of market forces in the post-1990s version and the Golden Age's idea of removing 'hindrances for a market economy of the type that the classical economic theorists dreamed of' (Hedborg and Meidner 1984: 275) is limited. The change is one of degree rather than character. In terms of our market-view indicators (categories 1–4, see Box 1 in chapter 2), the Model corresponds to high marks for market efficiency and dependency. Nor does the Rehn–Meidner Model warrant any conclusions about market hostility. The whole point of the model was to accept the market while compensating for its unfair results.

The post-war welfare-state expansions, which in both countries have been labelled security 'from the cradle to the grave', indicate a deeply felt willingness to correct market outcomes, rather than offering alternatives to the market. Parties of all political colours have utilised an extensive number of measures of what is known as 'social liberalism'. Politicians support consumers or producers who risk being losers on an unregulated market. This kind of political presence in the market is often regarded as a means of lubricating aid for better market efficiency and is present in most Western democracies. Rather than replacing the market the overarching aim is to improve it (Bengtsson 1995; Lewin 1967; Pilkington 1998: 13, 16, 24; Shonfield 1965). Should capital flight occur as a consequence of these correctives, politicians may reach a point where policy reconsiderations grow imminent.

With Stephen Driver and Luke Martell, we may claim that only the means have changed and that the well-being of the least well-off has not been given up on, 'their well-being is now seen as better delivered by the success of capitalism than its dilution' (Driver and Martell 1998: 47). According to this view the Labour Party's change is one from stressing the importance of enabling the capitalist economy to function rather than stressing State ownership as part of the economy. Be that as it may. State ownership definitely was part of both SAP and Labour rhetoric in the 1970s when 'wage-earners' funds' were on the Swedish agenda and (re)nationalisations on the British.

However, refraining from State ownership is by no means new to social democracy. It might be held that social democracy has come full circle back to its 1940s/1950s position when redistribution rather than State ownership was deemed central. Interestingly, none of the definitions of social democracy referred to above by Tilton, Shaw and others (Chapter 2) includes State ownership as a defining variable of social democracy. On the contrary, all seem to emphasise the exact opposite: That one of the essential elements of social democracy is the precedence 'functional' socialism takes over ownership socialism.

Moreover, 'enabling' capitalism to function in order to sap the surplus of means for the welfare state appears to have been at the centre of social democratic thinking long before Tony Blair and Göran Persson. The Rehn–Meidner Model can be described in no other way than an 'enabling' model. Its fundament rested on the market economy no less than later types of market-enabling methods. Fundamental changes in the character of the international market economy probably have reduced the scope for pro-active rhetoric about market steering, State-ownership and planning. This said the point here is that the old rhetoric was by no means free from – in fact it was full of – elements based on enabling the capitalist economy to create a redistributable surplus.

Eight-hour day, industrial accident legislation...

Let us then once more remind ourselves about the modest character everyone seems to accord to the notion of 'functional socialism' even during the heydays of the Golden Age: Eight-hour day, industrial accident legislation, zoning laws, environmental restrictions, collective bargaining legislation etc. (Tilton 1992: 414 ff.) or equality, social justice and social welfare, a large and active public sector, full employment (Shaw 1993: 116). Social democracy has always been about 'the success of capitalism [rather] than its dilution.' The means have changed but social democracy was hardly about the dilution of capitalism during the Golden Age. Nor is it so forty years later.

The overall conclusion is that, contrary to earlier research, SAP and Labour have remained surprisingly stable in their views on the market. State-control rhetoric is easy to detect but under a thin veil of 'planning', 'control' etc. (sometimes even 'socialism' is used) the more market-economy friendly, market-correcting ideology lurks.

Today much of the veil has been lifted off so that the Parties' rhetoric is freed of most of the State-planning language. The market-economy-friendly attitudes that were always there, lie exposed more nakedly today. This is indeed a substantial change in how the parties communicate to the voters and members. Words of encouragement are not unimportant. As such the change may of course have led to disillusionment among certain segments of voters as well as members and elite groups. Other segments of the followers might feel more attracted by the change. An element of insecurity about where the Parties stand ideologically has gone.

Indirectly the change is an indicator that the very particular 'social democratic way of life' has gone. The reverence shown to certain phenomena perhaps functioned as a means to tie followers closer together. Familiarity with a common language could make people feel secure and thus help the Party leadership to 'hold the flock together' (Lipset and Rokkan 1967). That rhetoric has approached actual ideology will then have had the consequence that the flock may not recognise its fold.

Even though the change has hardly meant any substantial deeper ideological transformation in the sense that they have become less eloquent or less specific when it comes to market-correcting proposals the change is evident. The old language is gone. What in those days was perhaps only indirectly clear (reliance on the market) is now brought out into the light. By doing this the SAP and the Labour Party no more stand out as particularly separate from most of the other parties in the party system (we only have to think briefly about the basic policy similarities between the Liberals and Labour and between the Swedish Liberals and the SAP to realise this).

Maybe the Party leaders have sensed the danger of becoming too close to their competitors. At least the new or reborn fervour surrounding policies, which somehow could be connected to the 'old' welfare state, bear witness of this. NHS commitments in the UK, family policy improvements etc. in Sweden are easy to connect rhetorically to the old traditions within the Parties. Whether these efforts are serious and will be sufficient to make the voters and members feel at home in the parties will perhaps become clear in the future. Too many references to PPP Hospitals and similar departures from old ways of handling the public sector might prove extremely dangerous in this respect. Too many 'free schools' in Sweden (however publicly financed they may be) might prove equally risky for the the SAP.

Indeed, with our findings, it is quite intriguing how the thinking behind 'a third way' (Giddens 1998) could ever have been understood as a new phenomenon. By no means is such a notion novel to social democracy. Instead, the choice between outright market capitalism and unrelenting State socialism has always (in modern times) been an easy one to social democracy in the UK and Sweden. The third way – enabling capitalism to function, combined with market-correction with a whiff of market complemented by the State – has always been preferred by the parties. We have reason to believe that the third way always constituted the very *raison d'être* for social democratic parties. As for Sweden, a perhaps anecdotal testimony to the pragmatism of the Golden Age is the quote by Marcus Wallenberg, the then leader of the gigantic Wallenberg industrial empire, from a letter to the leader of the Swedish blue-collar union (LO) that he would like to 'praise your efforts to keeping the balance between desirable social progress and an efficient, productive Swedish business world' (quoted in Olsson 2000: 339; on the 'formation of an inclusivist coalition between big business, labor and the state' see Blyth 2002: 113).

But the opposite of this conclusion is also possible. In one sense the third way is and has been the social democratic way of dealing with the relationship between market and politics. But perhaps it is just as fruitful to think about the third way as an empty concept. To the extent that very few parties in any party system actually propose completely freed markets everything turns into shades of social liberalism. Far from being a case of either/or most parties place themselves somewhere along the social-liberal continuum. Perhaps the SAP and Labour have been a touch more 'social' liberal than others but their modern history is difficult to tell apart from most major political alternatives, which rely on the market economy with a greater or shorter list of corrections.

Let us remind us about the core characteristics of social democracy. Efficiency, full employment and equality (Przeworski 1987: 241) based on a belief 'in the primacy of politics and a commitment to using democratically acquired power to direct economic forces in the service of the collective good' (Berman 2003: 142).

Central to such an analysis are the words 'power' and 'direct economic forces.' What do we actually mean when we claim that something is 'directed?' How much do we have to direct and what exactly is it that we direct? The same vagueness mars the 'efficiency, full employment and equality' words. When exactly is something efficient? What do we mean by 'full employment' and when is something 'equal?' Welfare state programmes, taxes etc. are all excellent examples of democratically based power used to direct economic forces in the service of the common good. Very little in these examples would exclude social liberal ideologies.

According to Berman (2003: 143) the former French Prime Minister Lionel Jospin voiced true or 'close' social democratic views in a 1999 Socialist International speech. He declared that 'the market is an instrument that is effective and important, but it is nothing more than an instrument.' As Berman holds, 'Jospin does not fully recognize, however, that times have changed and that achieving social democratic ends in the twenty-first century will require new means' (Berman 2003: 142). She concludes by adding that 'What exactly these means should be is beyond the scope of this essay' (Berman 2003: 142). Social democracy should prevent economic forces from becoming 'the final arbiter of societal developments' (Berman 2003: 142) but neither Berman nor social democracy really provide us with any more concreteness than that. The dilemma seems to be that some measures to keep the final arbitration within the hands of political authority threaten the fundamentals of the market economy. Social democracy does not appear willing to go that far. In that sense the social democratic parties accept the 'economic forces' to be 'the final arbiter of societal developments.'

Superficially it is easy to agree that social democracy applies the market as merely an instrument. The common good is by far the top goal. The market economy is an instrument. But as I have shown in this book, the market is not an instrument that can be abandoned in favour of another instrument. It is the very foundation upon which the welfare state rests and there is rock solid awareness about this inside social democracy as shown by the ideological trajectories of the Labour Party and the SAP. At least no social democratic leader has expressed any dissenting view over the last forty years. These things may have been different within the French Socialist Party and perhaps Labour and the SAP are deviant cases. The fact remains: Never does social democratic ideology, as it has been assessed here, express any true market-abolishing intentions. Even the most radical examples during the 1979–83 Labour Party radicalisation come far off the revolutionary mark. In the light of these results Berman's assurances that social democracy believes in 'the primacy of politics' is accurate only insofar as the market economy is not infringed upon.

It may have been that social democrats once 'accepted or tolerated the market because of its ability to provide the material basis upon which the good life can be built, but have been unwilling to accept the market's primacy in social life' (Berman 2003: 142). But the undeniable social democratic quest for some 'sort of shelter [to] be erected so that societies and individuals can weather the gales of economic, social, and political change that constantly howl around them' (Polanyi, 1944; quoted in Berman 2003: 142) seems to erect no shelter but the welfare state. If liberalism's only shelter against the market storms is the welfare state, then social democracy has become a liberal movement.

Occasionally both parties have tried to correct the market economy's 'direct economic forces in the service of the collective good' with a wider array of tools. Sometimes the list of measures has been less impressive but there is no doubt about the validity of the overarching goal: Work in the interest of the common good by directing economic forces; use the market as an indispensable means. The exact meaning of these goals can of course be disputed. In Nina Fishman's account of the Labour Party's history, the break with collectively expressed actions in the form of collective ways of life occurred during the Golden Age rather than with Blair's New Labour. In this sense Fishman's account corresponds to the overall results in this book. Individualist ideals less prepared than older generations to defer satisfaction have dominated the Party and she calls for new collective efforts. However, 'there is scarcely any form of collective expression left in British society ... [and] the destruction of our social fabric has been self-induced. It has been taking place in true British fashion, slowly, gradually but inexorably, from the 1960s' (Fishman 1996: 59–60). Fishman seems less prepared to acknowledge the possibility that the welfare state is a collective expression. While Fishman underlines the fact that 'the belief that socialism can only be constructed gradually by modifying elements of capitalism, has never been more relevant' (Fishman 1996: 52) she abstains from defining 'socialism' in much the same way as the Party has failed to use the term. 'Collectivist ideals' such as they materialise in 'people's plans, dreams, ambitions and behaviour' (Fishman 1996: 59) are offered in place of a more hard-core traditional version like an alternative economic system.

The ideological origins of social democracy included a dream that there was indeed a revisionist road to a social-economic system without the market. Social democratic roots included a theme about the devastating, dehumanising effects of capitalism. Capitalism had to be fought back and finally replaced by a more gentle and human system. That dream had been discarded long before the Golden Age of Social Democracy. In its place has come a perception that there is a way to a better life inside the rough terms set by the market economy.

Changing stability

In order to keep the ideological goal stable in a changing environment, there have had to be several formal policy changes. Both parties now fight inflation and unemployment in new forms, including the decision to give the National Banks independence. The defence of currency credibility has taken on new shapes as has positioning for trade competitiveness. Public sector incomes have to rely less on tax incomes and more on economic surplus. Taxes are based less on incomes and more on indirect sales taxes (Lindvall 2004; Sinclair 2001).

Public-sector deliveries have entered new territories with various public–private partnership solutions. The most obvious example of this trend in the UK is the increasingly applied 'Public Finance Initiatives' whereby 'the public sector contracts to purchase services on a long-term basis from the private sector, which provides finance and accepts some of the venture's risks in return for an operator's licence to provide specified service. . . . [Private providers] finance, design, build, maintain and operate new hospital facilities, which they then lease to the NHS, usually for periods of 25 to 35 years' (Shaw 2003: 2).

'Free' schools and day-care centres in Sweden prove that the same ideas as in the UK have taken root in the Swedish Social Democratic Party. Originally introduced by the 1991–94 non-socialist Government, the free schools were finally tolerated by the SAP. While the number of pre-school children in non-municipal establishments was negligible in 1985, the 2004 percentage of children in various forms of non-municipal establishments (including parent-run cooperatives) is about seventeen per cent and the trend continues (Skolverket 2004: 20). Similar developments have taken place in the nine-year compulsory school and sixth form grammar (high-school) school systems (1985: negligible, 2003: 6.2 and 10 per cent respectively; Skolverket 2004: 79, 139). The Swedish 'free schools' (*friskolor*) are a mixture of private and public as regards their classification. Very few are entirely 'private', many are trust-based. They are all (with very few exceptions) maintained financially by the Government (central and local) and allocated the same amount of resources per child as the old – still remaining and dominating – council schools. No parental fees are levied. The same system exists in the nursery school sector as well. Parental fees there (very generous fee ceilings apply) are the same regardless of type of establishment. Thus the reason for the introduction of free schools has not, so far, been to create a system where parents pay their way into good education, but rather to offer parents a school system where educational alternatives are provided. Acceptance into schools is based on various types of waiting lists and/or screening procedures. An element of competition has therefore entered the system with league tables etc. being used. In the longer run these novelties may of course lead to increased segregation.

In some instances, social policies have become less interfering with people's private lives, e.g. choice of school for children. In other instances policies have become more interfering, e.g. welfare-to-work programmes and, as in the Swedish case, certain paid parental-leave months earmarked for the mother and father respectively (out of a total of thirteen paid parental months, one month are earmarked for the father and one month for the mother. Should the parents decide not to use their right, the earmarked months cannot be transferred to the other parent). The mix of public sector policies has changed tremendously. For instance, reductions in the levels of State-pension may be compared with increases in the number of day-care places, child allowance levels and parental-leave days. Tougher criteria for unemployed may be compared with NHS resource increases (for an overview of policies, see Coates and Lawler 2000; Driver and Martell 2003; Ludlam and Smith 2004; Savage and Atkinson 2001; Seldon 2001).

Whether all these formal policy changes are to be considered small, medium or extensive is an important issue. The exact operationalisation of these changes is outside the scope of the present study. However, let us agree that over the time period under study, 1965–2002, they are more than small. This means there has been evident change on the environmental dimension as well as on the formal policy dimension and we are able to establish some kind of basic relationship between the two.

However, the overarching question for us would be whether changing formal policies on a day-to-day-level – below that of general ideology – could in fact contribute to keeping a party's ideology stable. The Labour Party's and the SAP's market ideologies have remained remarkably stable over the years. Both Parties have met the changing times with a multitude of new day-to-day policies, but which are still within the same overall ideological framework.

The point made here is that these changes, frequent and far ranging as they may have been, do not add up to an overall change in the basic character of the Parties' social policies. Rather the Parties have replaced some of the old tools with new ones. Thus, changing stability is a more apt description of the Parties' policies than either clear-cut stability or change. Surprising as these results may appear, they are less astonishing when we remind ourselves of the basic element of an ideology as a belief system. Ideologies are not changed with the frequency of changing shirts. In fact, it appears to take more than the odd currency crisis to shake a party's ideology from its foundations.

Whether the recent public–private partnership (PPP) Solutions amount to a further indication of the parties' acceptance or non-acceptance of the market economy is a moot point. Whereas some would argue the PPP offer new ways of securing traditional ideological goals (Bevir and O'Brien 2001; 'Labour's reforms to the NHS and education are far less dependent on market models of governance than were those of the Conservatives. And Labour modernizers are less ideological and more pragmatic about such reforms' Driver and Martell 2003: 167). Others would emphasise the changing ideological foundations behind the new solutions (Shaw 2003; 'But what Labour modernizers have embraced are private-sector techniques and private-sector actors ("partnership") in the management and delivery of public services' Driver and Martell 2003: 167).

As Shaw (2003: 14) indicates, 'it would be wrong to infer that the Blair Government has abandoned traditional Labour values. [It is still] committed to a welfare state in which core services are freely provided and financed by taxation [and it] seeks to promote greater social justice and social cohesion', At the same time, Shaw (2003: 16) convincingly shows that 'the large public sector [is] increasingly permeated by market arrangements and a more commercial ethos.' Whether this apparent acceptance of the market principle by the Labour Party as a way of handling the public sector, is any greater than the degree of market acceptance during the Golden Age of Social Democracy is unclear. As I have shown, the level of market-influences in social democratic thinking was always substantial. Past Labour governments never took planning very seriously, nor did they ever provide any distinct statements to show they believed other than that the key mechanism for co-ordinating economic life should be the market.

Still, New Labour's (more so than 'new' SAP's) ideology appears to be decidedly more optimistic about the market's merits in the early years of the twenty-first century than forty years before. Perhaps one could say that old Labour accepted the market more grudgingly. An interesting problem, though, relating to Shaw's conclusions is how the new market-based thoughts could find their way into Labour and SAP so relatively smoothly. According to Shaw the intra-Labour transformation process from hostility to outright praise took about five years (1995–2000). The SAP was a touch slower. About 1984 the Swedish Party cautiously began discussing 'alternatives' within the public sector. While rejecting PPP solutions the party still accepted the need for individual choice (Hinnfors 1992: 168 ff.). Ten years later the incoming SAP Government kept the legal framework, which had rendered possible the new free schools and day-care centres. Why, then, did the reforms not meet with greater resistance? Apart from voter considerations and the perhaps naïve hope that PPP arrangements would offer better bargains, one obvious reason for the change would be that the strong acceptance of the market economy already held the door ajar for similar approaches within the public sector. Or perhaps the door was more than ajar. In many ways it was wide open.

If everyone openly or tacitly favoured market solutions in the economy why not in the end try it on the public sector? To some extent one could claim that during the Golden Age the Parties supported the market economy with market-corrections, but the support was filtered through a clear element of planning rhetoric. Today, the Parties support the same market economy with market-corrections. Only today the Parties use market rhetoric.

One important reason for the willingness to use the market economy was always the conviction that the market economy would prove to be more efficient than any known alternative. With efficient companies the economy would boom and there would be a handsome surplus from which new resources could be extracted and directed to the welfare state. And a robust welfare state appears always to have been regarded as the most solid foundation for a society with ambitions to reduce poverty. It must have been extremely tempting for any politician to use the same kind of logic and apply it on the public sector. Especially given the rather bleak economic conditions of the 1990s, which invited some kind of rethinking. The soil was fertile; it had in fact been ploughed for at least four decades.

There was also the added cause that the public sector didn't always correspond to the rosy picture that public sector hospitals and schools did lead to better value service, delivered more flexibly and to a higher standard. Nor did public sector services have a super-record of adapting to changing requirements and expectations. Under funding and a failure to put patients' needs before hierarchical needs added to the attraction of the market.

That the economic gains from PPP deals may be less than marginal or even negative is a question that might prove an ideological linchpin for the parties. UK PPPs appear to be rather questionable success-stories with negative externalities, increased bureaucracy and reduced flexibility attached to them (Shaw 2004). Should New Labour continue to favour PPP in their present form, in spite of the mounting drawbacks, it might be fair to agree that PPPs in themselves add up to a significant break with old social democratic ideology. However, this is for the future to prove. We are not there yet.

An even more sinister challenge to social democracy attached to the PPP version of public service is the risk that private investors, who take big economic risks by undertaking to build hospitals and schools, will eventually demand a strong voice on how these services are run. It might then only be felt as fair and natural to compensate the investors. In that case, the general idea that the government is the final source of legitimate influence on overarching goals as well as on more short-term decisions will evaporate (Shaw 2002: 14). This risk is real and something the parties will have to consider. Did they really envisage such a withdrawal from power when they embarked on the road of PPP agreements and can the risk be reduced? Certainly, the social democratic model would be gone if such a development were really to follow in the wake of the PPP experiments.

Moreover, a more worrying conclusion, and something party ideologues appear to have shied away from during all those years, is the corresponding complex of problems about who is the final source of authoritative power concerning the whole market economy. If Shaw and others are correct that the private sector increasingly exerts more or less informal influence over the public sector as a consequence of PPP solutions and similar arrangements, how does the economy at large fare in comparison?

For decades now, old and New Labour and old and new SAP have in practice been in favour of market solutions for the economy. Swedish industrial giants have been able to be the best of friends with a string of social democratic governments, while British Labour governments have never seriously clashed with the City. Sometimes social democratic politicians have been more, sometimes less, eager to prod, regulate and stimulate the market, but they have never actually shown any real intention of countering it. If this is so, we have to conclude that Charles Lindblom's point about market actors indirectly being in charge would hold not only for the public sector but for the entire political sphere: 'Sometimes not even a word is needed; in an authority relation a docile person knows what is wanted of him and does it without being told' (Lindblom 1977: 18; Wickham-Jones 1995).

For those who fear the market as an entity with authoritative strength over a docile political system – and there might lie some truth in that fear – the PPP solutions might be yet another nail in the coffin. In that sense, New Labour may have taken distinct steps away from its ideological tradition. However, the real problem must then lie in the lack of genuine alternatives to the market economy as social democracy has never really offered a true belief in a socialist or planned economy. In that case, PPP arrangements and public sector market solutions generally are a symptom rather than a cause of how strong the market element in social democracy actually is and has been for several decades.

Compared to the vastly more important and overarching support in practice for the market economy as a whole, the fact that PPP arrangements as such are introduced must be rated as secondary. Private actors will perhaps eventually demand a strong voice on how the entire economy is run. This is a very important, and perhaps valid supposition but haven't private actors done so long ago? On the other hand, to the extent that private actors have been reluctant about market restraints in the form of taxes, workplace regulations etc., they have obviously had to accept quite a number of restrictions.

What we do find occasionally, however, is a decided opaqueness about the Parties' ideologies. From time to time, veils, mirages or smoke screens have flickered, seemingly in efforts to divert onlookers from the true character of the Parties' market ideologies. Whatever the reason, the ideologies have been incoherent. Occasionally, groups within the Parties have tried to move in a decidedly more radical direction, but the Party leaderships have held back. This is not to say that authors of manifestos, programmes etc. have been conspiratorial. Politics often consists of compromises and Party leaders have the difficult job of striking a balance, acceptable to sometimes hostile camps.

Especially during the 1980s radical parts of the Labour Party worked to lend Party manifestos a more planning-oriented character. The Party leaders accepted important parts of these more radical views to satisfy the far left wings within the Party as well as outside it. The far left wished for radical measures. The social democratic Party leaderships wanted more of an ideological status quo. During the conflict between these two broad groupings, the far left was offered at least phrases pointing in a radical direction. And in the event of a 1983 Labour victory some of those phrases had probably materialised into real policy.

The rhetoric reveals a constant acceptance of the market economy's efficiency. As stable as this acceptance is, so is the Parties' conviction that the efficiency of the market economy is socially and morally blind and therefore the market outcomes have to be corrected by far-reaching political measures.

Adjusting the rudder to reach the original destination

The relationship between State planning versus market capitalism as elements of social democratic ideology can take several forms. Stability could emerge in two ways. Either State planning was the most important part of social democratic ideology in 1965 and remains so, or market capitalism continuously holds the upper hand. As is often the case, the truth lies somewhere in the middle. Outright market capitalism was never the solution, nor was State planning. However, when forced to choose – and, in a way, that is what ideological positioning is all about – both Parties accepted market capitalism in 1965 as well as in 2002. Never did State planning appear to be a viable choice. Unerringly, market capitalism with a fair amount of corrections formed the basis of the ideologies.

Politics still has considerable room for action. Remember that market views are a different matter from real actions. We have concentrated on views rather than actions. But the data are so stable, and in many instances so concrete and tied to actual activities and real measures, that the parties are hardly able to err very far from what they formulate. The means may have changed but hardly the goals.

Obviously, stability and change can take on many faces. Let us for a moment go back to the metaphor, introduced in Chapter 1, of a ship's captain aiming for a certain port in an environment of rough and unstable weather. While the possible repercussions of environmental change have been hotly debated, the notion of major environmental changes in itself is widely accepted. This conclusion about a changing environment is based on a general understanding of the world economy and not the result of systematic measurement. Fully aware that the concept of 'environment' is somewhat nebulous, the present study has shown that, in spite of substantial environmental change, in comparison the variation at the ideological level is much lower. The sailor has remained on course for the destined port by constantly adjusting the rudder.

9
A dilemma

Generating fresh resources for constantly new market-correcting reforms seems to be of vital importance to social democratic ideology. As long as these correctives do not interfere with basic fundamentals of how the market operates new reforms can be introduced. Should the extraction of new resources from the private sector dwindle, the party leadership will finally have to decide whether it should cross the border to a distinctly State-providing economy or scrap enough reform plans or, even, scrap already existing programmes to keep the economy inside the market economy. Even by keeping welfare programmes stable in absolute figures will increase their relative share in a contracting economy. The ensuing policy junction has all the potential of becoming a true political dilemma.

Along the one route, i.e. scrapping popular programmes but keeping the party inside the market economy, the party will risk alienating wide circles of the electorate as well as core member groups. Taking this route has the strategically disturbing effect that by holding on to the party's principal market-positive ideological tenets the party leadership will make life worse for weak groups (by abandoning social programmes etc.) at the same time as big business justly can be described as being treated with silk gloves.

Along the other, alternative, State-oriented route the party will in a sense carry on with business as usual, directing new resources to market-weak groups but at the same time actually deserting its market-positive ideology. In a contracting or even stable economy there is a point where the market-positive ideology will actually be deserted. Important parts of the electorate and Party members will feel they have been let down. At the same time the Party leadership runs the risk of facing severe budget deficit problems, which might not always be easily handled. And the basic necessity of having to find new resources to fund the welfare programmes will not go away. Francois Mitterrand's 1981 French budget experiment might provide a *memento mori*. On the other hand some would argue that with the economy solidly in the hands of the State sector several of the problems caused by capitalism's inner logic would vanish.

So far, neither Labour nor the SAP has ever in actual ideological practice really questioned the market economy. In effect, this means that only an expanding

economy from which a stable (or increasing – but only to a certain extent) percentage of the growing resources available can be extracted for market-correcting
purposes will take the Party leaderships out of the dilemma.

With important nuances the answers to fundamental questions about the
market economy appear to have been fairly stable within social democracy. In that
respect the results presented here square well with some renderings of pre-Golden
Age social democracy. In his extensive *Planhushållningsdebatten* [The Debate on
Economic Planning] Leif Lewin (1967) concludes that during the early post-war
period (1945–66) SAP constantly hovered around the same stable overarching
goal: 'Liberal characteristics have been emphasised in SAP's policy for business and
enterprise, and the market forces have been accepted. With its socialist policies, the
governing party . . . seeks to return to the idea of harmony originally envisaged by
the economic liberals' (Lewin 1967: 519, see Kitschelt 1994: 268).

Lewin's conclusion is important in the sense that it suggests social democracy's
longstanding subscription to basic liberal economic tenets. Already in the 1920s
the SAP chose a decidedly reformist path (Berman 1998; Lewin 1967). '[B]oth
parties rejected orthodox Marxist socialism and arrived at essentially pragmatic,
doctrineless, and populist redistributive programs' (Kitschelt 1994: 268). In
Sweden 'The party's early doctrinal orthodoxy before World War I is easily over-
stated' (Kitschelt 1994: 268). The Labour Party was perhaps slower in its march
towards revisionism, but '[by] the summer of 1963 it was possible to argue that the
Labour Party is now definitely a revisionist party' (Minkin 1978: 325). This
conclusion holds true even though, as Minkin (1978: 325) emphasises, the
'Conferences of 1971 and 1972 were packed with proposed "shopping lists" of
industries for public ownership to an extent possibly unprecedented in Party
history, and the Conference decisions from 1971 to 1973 included a list of public
ownership commitments.' Individual unions went even further than shopping lists
and proposed to 'eliminate the capitalist system' (Minkin 1978: 325). However, as
is shown in this book, the authoritatively binding policy documents are still
basically market-oriented with distinct elements of State planning as a complement but especially various State-led corrections of the market's outcomes. Other
groups more sympathetic to the market economy balanced those who strove to
abolish capitalism. It appears today's Parties stand firmly on the shoulders of
their predecessors. In this sense the politics of Tony Crosland (Crosland 1956) and
Kjell-Olof Feldt (Feldt 1989) about social democracy as a force committed to
ameliorating the living conditions for ordinary people through welfare state
measures rather than public ownership (in the guise of nationalised industry or
wage-earners' funds) hold sway.

For the better part of last century the SAP showed reverence in practice towards
key principles of liberalism. The same is true for the British Labour Party. Even in
the midst of substantial nationalisation, the post-war Labour Government left the
liberal economy largely untouched (Gamble 1994: 137).

It is not surprising therefore that, as Gillian Peele holds, the Blair-led New
Labour which has 'come to terms with market-based reforms' has actually continued 'the revisionist project pursued by Gaitskell, Neil Kinnock and John Smith'

(Peele 1997: 91). Peele moves on to remark that 'Labour was by 1997 a free-market party, albeit one that believed market power and public purpose should be used together' (Peele 1997: 91). We are now able to hold that even Blair's predecessors were in charge of a free-market party; only they did not beat their drum for it to the extent that Blair and his fellow leaders do. At the same time it is obvious that the Swedish and British sibling parties are still revisionist in the sense that they don't accept the free play of market forces and that 'public expenditure and redistributory politics endangered liberty'. They still seem to believe that 'the good of the public could never be equated with that of self-interested market actors' (Shaw 1996: 56).

Donald Sassoon who underlines that West European socialism has aimed at a future non-capitalist society in its rhetoric only holds a similar view. In actual practice the social democrats have always ensured 'that the viability of capitalism was not seriously impaired' (Sassoon 1996: 734). Though Eric Shaw (1996) emphasises change in the Labour Party's policies since 1945 and that New Labour has modernised by 'a *detachment* from Labour's established values and objects and an *accommodation* with established institutions and modes of thought' (Shaw 1996: 218) he also, indirectly, acknowledges stability. The true test case, he claims, for the change thesis since 1945, would be the 1964–70 Labour Government, which was the only period Labour was in office during the Golden Age of Social Democracy (Shaw 1996: 212). Only during those six years could rhetoric transform into proper policies. Far from being true advocates of full employment, and distributional justice the '1964–1970 Wilson Government . . . gave preference to the defence of the pound and deflation, a choice which demolished hopes for a faster rate of growth and undermined its capacity to attain its social goals' (Shaw 1996: 212f.). With a record like that it seems a little premature to label the present-day Labour Party as more neo-liberal than its Golden Age ancestor.

However, emphasising the Labour Party's (and the SAP's) past apparent lack of delivering capacity when in office – which in itself is true – will somewhat block our views from the parties' core ideologies. Their inability to deliver was not so much founded in the clash with realities any party in cabinet position will encounter but at least as much in the realities of their ideologies. No doubt, the Parties' old rhetoric had 'produced hopes that could not be met when [they] took office' and the new leaderships, which took over in the 1990s understood that in the long run those unfulfilled expectations had proven strategically dangerous (Cronin 2004: 416f.). But, equally new in the Parties' packaging of their ideologies is the realisation among Party leaderships that they should call the various parts of their ideologies by their right name. There really weren't that many hard promises of alternative policies during the Golden Age. The abundance of visions were focused on a number of symbolically laden labels, which all hinted at 'socialism'. 'Plans', 'licences', 'public sector actions' were rife but the hard facts – as they were presented in the ideological documents meant to inform the general public of their overall intentions – usually absent even long before the Parties took office. People may not have seen or understood this and were consequently disappointed at their Parties' government record but, with a slightly more distanced attitude towards the

Parties' ideological statements and looking at what they actually had to propose to back up their visions the evidence was there for everyone to see. In the Swedish case, with a left-wing party on its flank, this is exactly what many of the SAP debates against the (reformed) communists came to deal with. As the Swedish Communists were so insignificant and the SAP so enormous and self confident generally contributed into making those debates rare and with extremely low saliency in the public eye. In the Labour Party most of the criticism for toothless policies has had to come from inside the Party but, as has been shown here, even here the majority of proposals have been surprisingly faithful to the core characteristics of the liberal market economy. Their market-correcting proposals have been ambitious, far-reaching and uncompromising but have left the 'system' intact.

The social democratic leaders appear to have decided that to call a plan a plan they need a plan and they have come to the conclusion that the market-correcting measures they more or less always suggested fail to add up to any plan. Instead they have gone a long way towards relabelling their versions of the liberal market economy and accept that it is just that: Liberal market capitalism. Within this framework there will be endless types of public sector involvement. The size of the public sector will vary from very limited to huge undertakings and so will the character of the public-sector policies.

Perhaps our rendering of the party's 1960's record as more 'planning' than 'market' is indirectly infiltrated by the fact that the Labour Party during a much earlier period, that of the immediate post-war era managed to implement a welfare state after World War II, though the Beveridge plan was as much a liberal project as a social democratic.

David Robertson's (1976: 98) classical mapping of 1924–66 British general election manifestos indicates short-time policy changes but over the years these changes are easily described as mere oscillations around highly stable trends. Klingemann, Hofferbert and Budge (1994: 60 ff. 160 ff.) demonstrate roughly the same stability for Labour and SAP in their 1945–87 overview of European party programmes. While drifting to the right since 1945, Labour's overall ideological position is surprisingly stable in a similar mapping by Budge (1999). However, Klingemann's and Budge's studies are based on a wider array of variables, some of which in the present study are deemed less relevant to social democratic ideology.

A social democrat's nightmare

In the 1950s Swedish SAP leaders found themselves on the brink of a nightmare. This is usually not the image we have of the social democratic 'harvesting years' during the 1950. A probably deeper crisis than any currency speculator could trigger off loomed when the SAP leadership came to a two-pronged conclusion. First, surprising as it may seem given later steep tax increases, the party strategists felt that taxes had hit the ceiling (Elvander 1972: 67ff., 73, 77f., 107ff.; Lewin 1967; 404f.; SOU 1951 No. 51: 96ff.). 'To be sure, welfare state programmes were part of the basic compromise between labor, capital and the state in Sweden – just as they were in every other advanced capitalist nation. But in the first several decades in which this decision-making model was in effect Sweden did not have a particularly heavy tax burden' (Steinmo 2003: 33). With the coffers empty they would have to content themselves with defending what was already achieved or possibly scrap some programmes. New reforms would be extremely difficult to carry through.

Second, and even worse, in the wake of SAP's *Post-War Programme* (1944) and following the 1947–56 sweeping reforms which included new health, pension and family support programmes, several leading SAP representatives felt the party's goals had actually been met. All major proposals, which had been formulated during the 1930s and 1940s, had been implemented under the catchword 'The People's Home'. Coined in the troubled 1930s 'The people's home' as a picture of the kind of society SAP wanted to create, was the legendary Social Democratic slogan, picked up from influential early twentieth century Swedish debaters, politicised and put forward by the increasingly extremely popular Prime Minister Per-Albin Hansson (see Lagergren 1999). In the 1950s, with post-war reforms behind them, a forlorn sense of emptiness suddenly emerged (Lewin 1967: 404f.). The people's home had been built. Only the upkeep remained.

The leadership soon realised that to declare that now, they had done it all, was a highly difficult strategic position unlikely either to attract voters or enthuse party activists. The position of admitting that the party's ideology had reached the end of the road seemed equally self-defeating. Apart from the rather dull character of such a position it also dawned upon the leadership that voters might think differently. Not only did various reports soon show there were still substantial pockets of poverty left, especially among blue-collar families with small children. It was also felt that an emerging discontent among the general public based on continuously rising expectations had to be handled. Tage Erlander, PM, formulated the dilemma as 'a discontent of a wholly different kind, . . . which I would like to characterise as the discontent of great expectations' (*Riksdag* minutes FK 2 1956: 23 ff., Erlander). Erlander's Finance Minister, Sträng, later modified the catchphrase to 'the discontent of unrealised expectations' (SAP 1964a: 278, Sträng). People's hopes were fuelled by the very fact that some of the Party's promises were actually met. The Party had to formulate new promises and increase its ambition.

But not until the 1960 VAT 'reinvention' (it had been used as an extraordinary measure during World War II) was there new scope for reform. Revamping the VAT was a formal solution, which hardly changed the overall character of the Party's ideology. After all taxes were believed to provide the means for welfare commitments but the VAT solved the dilemma of raising taxes without using income taxes (later the Party leadership shrugged off its inhibitions about higher income taxes). Nor did it alter the basic conditions of the demand for new resources facing the Party leadership.

The 'home' remained the same but there was, after all, temporary leeway for adding a few more improvements to it by using the VAT resort. The nightmare faded away. What the leadership did was in fact keeping up stability – a continuous expansion of the welfare state – by changing its attitude towards public incomes (Elvander 1972; Steinmo 1993; Steinmo 2003). Fittingly the 1964 election manifesto was titled 'Towards Brave New Goals'. The real reform spree came in the 1970s, particularly in the family support sector (Hinnfors 1999). Most of these new reforms were largely implemented by 1980. At that time taxes were once again perceived by public opinion and policy-makers alike to be at or near the ceiling (Hadenius 1981; Pontusson 1992: 105; Steinmo 1993; Steinmo 2003: 36ff.). Once again social democratic leaders faced the risk of rosy dreams turning into nightmares. Obviously a tax ceiling is not a given structure once and for all but depends on several parameters such as trust in government, extent of public services provided etc. Tax revolts may occur in countries with low taxes when important parts of the general public feel they are insufficiently rewarded by the system's distributive measures but still have to pay considerable taxes. High-tax payers on the other hand will often accept the tax burden as long as they get something back from the system (see Rothstein 1993). Swedish citizens are overwhelmingly in favour of keeping high taxes to safeguard public services. Indeed for most areas of the welfare state such as health care, support for the elderly, housing support, schools and employment robust majorities would rather increase public expenditures (Svallfors 1999: 16). As for the UK, 'the British public is generally in favour of the welfare state and its institutions. British social attitudes have resisted the ideological confrontation presented by the anti-welfare ideology of the New Right. One can find that the beliefs about the proper role of the state remained relatively stable even in the face of the powerful attacks of the anti-collectivists' (Mau 2003: 190).

A similar sense of lack of purpose took hold of the Labour Party after the Party had been returned to power after the end of World War II. According to Richard Crossman, leader of the House of Commons and given responsibility by Harold Wilson to coordinate relations between the Government and the extra-parliamentary party, there was a tendency for Labour governments 'to run out of radical drive because it ran out of intellectual ammunition' (Minkin 1978: 294). According to Crossman, '[w]e had nearly finished the job we had been sent to do in those first five years, without finding time to look ahead and plan the job for the next five years. And as a result our sense of direction began to go, and a radical reforming Labour Government without a clear sense of direction is sunk' (Crossman 1972, Lecture 3, quoted in Minkin 1978: 294). Without a constant focus on the formulation of future policies there is little left for activists and voters to be enthusiastic about.

A paradox of politics appears to be that political parties aim to fulfil certain goals while at the same time actually 'finishing the job' (e.g. creating the 'people's home') could prove lethal to the parties and something which they have to find a cure against. A sinister question for social democracy is whether the range of market-corrections can go on forever. Is there a point beyond which no more reforms will be fruitful? A similar situation as was felt in the 1950s might easily come back. What then would happen to the social democratic project? Can social democracy survive without the aid of grand projects? Will managing the status quo be enough to keep the magic alive? The temporary panic in SAP during the early 1950s indicates that there might be such a point, at least in the minds of the leading policy-makers and that the leaders try and avoid it at all cost. The ideological development over the last forty years should be seen in this light. After having tried the old model to the full, social democratic leaders are once more facing the dilemma of insufficient resources. Contrary to the 1950s situation there does not seem to be any sense of having achieved everything. Quite to the contrary, both the SAP and Labour leaderships dedicate a lot of energy and time to highlighting the need for improvements. In his speech to the 2004 Spring Party Conference Gordon Brown, the UK Chancellor elaborated on this topic:

> I believe we can enter the next stage of public sector reform in education and health; so that as people's aspirations grow and as the technology develops to meet them we also use public provision to offer people not just the minimum standards of the past but the maximum possible range of services which fit their requirements – collective provision tailored to personal needs and opinions. (Brown 2004)

Brown's echoing of Swedish Prime Minister Tage Erlander's speech forty-five years earlier, about rising expectations, indicates the grave strategic plight of the Labour Party, which is strikingly similar to the SAP's. The 1950s leaderships may have been too myopic in their narrow interpretation of goal fulfilment but when they realised that new goals were necessary – based on a dawning feeling that all was not well after all – they at least could come up with new resources. With an understanding that poverty, inequality and under-utilised skills are still unpleasant aspects of society the lack of resources available to present-day politicians is even more frustrating. The fundamental ideological tenets of caring for the less well off are still intact and the ideological discussion over the last couple of decades has been about finding new ways for the State to help the market achieve the goals.

And let us once again remind ourselves about the content of the 'New Brave Goals': Welfare state expansion. Only occasionally was the policy crisis perceived to be possible to solve through State-ownership expansion. A Swedish State-operated investment bank was indeed set up in 1968 but its duties were limited. Wage-earners' funds were decided on and implemented in 1982 but with derisory small powers.

A new political economy

In a sense one could claim that hitting the tax ceiling was equivalent to the introduction of a new Swedish political economy. While the earlier political economy was seemingly based on the primacy of the welfare state, the latter is based on the primacy of the economy. In plain English this would mean that the social democrats used to regard welfare state goals as beyond questioning. Once a certain welfare state reform was decided on, the economy had to adjust – within certain limits of course – to the new situation as it were. Often the adjustment involved raising taxes or introducing new taxes.

A prime example of how the taxes were handled is given by Gunnar Sträng's statement in 1964 that '[t]he proposal will mean a clear-cut activity towards more family-friendly tax policies. Consequently, it sums up to a request for increased child allowances from 700 to 1,200 *kronor* per child per annum. But all these things will have to be financed and how will that come about? Should an improved family policy be desired . . . the Swedish people would have to foot the bill itself through tougher indirect taxes' (SAP 1964a: 78, Sträng). Sträng was no friend of under-balancing the State budget.

As long as the tax ceiling was perceived to be distant these adjustments posed no ideological or strategic problem. Taxes could still be raised without interfering with the Party's basic understanding of the international capitalist economy. Business was left to operate freely (inside certain rules of course) and the budget could be kept in healthy balance (in spite of alleged Keynesianism). At the same time – and this is something which has been emphasised over and again in the present study – the conditions set by the liberal view on the capitalist economy were not to be threatened beyond certain distinct limits.

With the economy playing the leading role the estimations are reversed. Even though basic welfare goals are still firmly embedded in social democracy (and they are), the means to achieve them have been questioned. First the economy should be in balance. This is stated overtly to an extent that was rare in the 1960s and 1970s. Only when that goal is met, is there room for elaborating on the surplus available for welfare reforms. Economic balance was by no means downplayed in the former model, only the means were different. New revenues – tax incomes – would properly pay for a costly reform. The contradiction between the two models is partly exaggerated. The economy was always treated with prudence but the changed taxing ability has changed the contexts profoundly.

As from 1981 a distinctly new theme was heard. Alternative routes were now discussed as to how to deal with the fact that public incomes might not be sufficient to keep up the present level of support obligations. When public finances were no problem generally such themes were of course less pressing. In the new situation the Party leadership came to the conclusion that whatever happened the public sector had to be defended anyway – at least its absolute level – but there would be no major tax hikes. More likely than not there would instead be tax reductions. So in order to protect the public sector it was absolutely necessary the market economy generally, and the industrial sector in particular, generated handsome surpluses. These overall conclusions by the Party leadership came at a time when they were hard pressed by parts of the Labour movement, particularly the blue-collar LO, to move ahead in the direction of State planning. That no more than mere token wage-earners' funds were launched and the fact that the leadership was so clear about the relationship between a safe foundation for the public sector and a smoothly-operating market economy shows us that 'enabling' capitalism is no news to the SAP. It may be news to the Labour Party, at least the rhetoric about enabling the capitalist economy, but the close relationship with traditional SAP ideology is apparent.

Taxes remain continuously extremely important but increasing revenues can (more or less) only be attained through an expanding economy. There is still room for tax adjustments of course and several taxes have other reasons than providing budget surpluses. Inheritance tax, wealth and capital gains tax are based on redistribution and fairness goals rather than redistribution. So-called green taxes provide incentives to reduce pollution; inner-city congestion fees prevent over-crowding of streets and provide means to improve transport networks etc. An explanation as to why both the Swedish and the British Parties have been able to adjust so smoothly to this new political economy (which in its central characteristics applies to the UK as much as to Sweden) is the fact that they already subscribed to a market-economy friendly ideology. This is not to say that the Parties have had no strategic problems in shedding some of their earlier State-oriented rhetoric but the changing rhetoric has been made easier because the ideology was already there to support the new day-to-day policies. The character of 'smoothness' may not be entirely clear, but the fact is that both parties constantly attract between 35 and 45 per cent of the electorate. They have been in Government since 1994 (the SAP) and 1997 (Labour) respectively with fairly decent results as regards unemployment, economic growth etc. However, that the Rose Garden is still in need of tender cultivation to blossom is witnessed by research reports such as *Fattigdom i välfärdsstaten* [Poverty in the Welfare State] (FAS 2002).

To create handsome surpluses is sometimes easier said than done as the crisis years during the first half of the 1990s harshly revealed. The crisis years show us two – partly conflicting – things. In the new political economy the social democratic ideology is indeed vulnerable. There was simply no room for business as usual and welfare state support levels had to be worsened as the budget was subjected to pressure when unemployment went from about two per cent to twelve per cent over just a couple of years. The colossal economic problems (enormous budget deficits, massive speculation against the Swedish *krona*, devastating levels of interest) made the earlier unemployment goals impossible to keep (Lindvall 2004).

On the other hand the fact that support levels were actually kept within roughly the same interval as before, and that they were increased again as soon as possible and with generous family policy improvements thrown in plus the fact that the Government officially once again set up ambitious goals for employment show the ideological strength. Had the ideology been mere patina the crisis years would have presented a golden opportunity to shed it all overboard. Why not swallow the neo-liberal bait head, tail and all. It was certainly easily accessible through think tanks, newspaper articles and by political opponents. This was the time when radical (in the Thatcher sense) reforms could be implemented. Instead the opposite became true. Social democratic ideology may have endured a shaky period and proved to be vulnerable but is definitely still around.

Interestingly, about ten years later than the SAP the British Labour Party faced a somewhat similar crisis as the Swedish Party did in the 1950s. While perhaps not in shortage of reform ideas, Labour's 'real problem lay with an economic perform-ance which failed to deliver additional resources. . . . The viability of Labour's project rested heavily on a faster rate of economic growth, for it was growth which set the pace at which it could' (Shaw 1996: 93) 'build the fair and just society we want to see' (*Labour Party Economic Measures*, 1966, quoted in Beckerman 1972a: 44, quoted in Shaw 1996: 93). Owing to the British pound's position as an inter-national currency, the UK was among the first countries to feel the effects of expanding financial markets.

Already in the 1960s 'attacks' from international currency 'speculators' were part of the Labour Party leaders' vocabulary (Wilson 1971: 31, quoted in Shaw 1996: 94). Without proper appeasement of the financial market actors there would be no resources left to distribute, the leadership reasoned. As was mentioned above the Labour leadership came to this conclusion long before new economic ideas became the order of the day in the media and academic circles, an indicator of the Party's basic preparedness to accept the role of markets.

Though definitely aware of limits set by markets a similar conclusion inside the SAP about how close those limits were, was still about fifteen years in waiting. Again, what we see is the Labour leadership trying to do the same as the Swedish did in the 1950s, keeping stability – doing what they could to save the welfare state – by changing policies. However, as later developments would show, and in some contrast to the Swedish case the nightmare was less easy to shrug off for Labour's leaders.

On the other hand Labour's apparent post-2001 reform offensive proves that there might indeed be some manoeuvring room before the British tax ceiling has been hit. With taxes well below Sweden's the point where public opinion will deny further tax increases may still be some distance away as long as policy-makers are able to deliver improved and extended public services. High taxes appear to be readily accepted by the general public to the extent that most groups feel they actually get something back from the State and that their money is handled efficiently. 'Most non-Swedes find it surprising that Swedes did not revolt against their tax burden long before it reached 60 per cent of GDP. Few non-Swedes can understand how and why a people could tolerate paying over half of their income to the tax authorities. But what we (non-Swedes) fail to understand is that most Swedes clearly believe they get a lot for the high taxes they pay' (Steinmo 2003: 41). There is nothing to say that the same sense of return for your offerings could not be felt in the UK, which in fact employs fairly high taxes already.

Statements by Tony Blair as well as Gordon Brown towards the end of the research period indicate that the Labour leadership strongly contemplates a development where increased taxes may very well form an inevitable part. They now seem determined to upgrade central elements of the public services even though the improvements will require tax rises. The Labour Government's measures seem to be in harmony with research on attitudes towards the welfare state and taxation. In spite of cutbacks in the UK during the 1980s and in Sweden during the 1990s the welfare state is popular with the general public. Rich and poor support public spending. As long as taxes are perceived to result in welfare state improvements taxes are accepted (Mau 2003: 21ff.).

The Government's conviction to defend the welfare state becomes more and more apparent as Gordon Brown, the UK Chancellor of the Exchequer, shows determination to contemplate taxes to ensure the National Health Service is properly funded for the future (*Financial Times* 5 February 2002). In conjunction with Tony Blair's frequent speeches along communitarian lines, such efforts in favour of upgrading the public sector to become a safe haven for everyone, might even be reminiscent of the SAP's much-used catchword the 'people's home' of the Golden

Age. Then, as well as later, there was certainly no shortage of poverty and malaise within society. The people's 'home' was partly about real reforms, partly about setting a moral standard of inclusiveness and a feeling that society belonged to everyone. Against such a moral backdrop, real reforms could be laid out.

Wanted: a constant flow of new resources

Labour's and the SAP's post-war crises teach us several lessons. There is a case to claim that social democracy is not tied up to a certain mix between market and State planning *per se* but rather to a constant flow of new resources to the welfare state. This phenomenon is not new to the Parties. In fact it has set the ideological limits for the better part of last century. To some extent the Parties were able to increase the tax-flow during the Golden Age. This seems to be less possible later, but the main resource increase always came through the market economy. With the wheels of the economy running fast the same levels of tax will produce increasing resources, which could be tapped into the welfare state.

Sometimes the limits have been rather flexible, sometimes tighter. Limits they have always been and the parties have indeed developed market-ideologies to square with the limits. With dwindling or even stable resources, the social democratic project risks grinding to a halt with the nightmare lurking behind the corner. Deliver or die.

As the observant reader may have noticed, the author comes to the conclusion that the two Parties actually have been able to deliver and have, temporarily at least, managed to slip out of the nightmare scenario. An exception to this rule was perhaps the SAP's position during the middle of the 1990s. At that time all efforts were concentrated on coming to grips with the disastrous economy with giant budget deficits. Only towards the end of the decade did SAP manage to deliver once more what could be described as 'old' welfare state policies.

Although Labour began its first term in office 1997 with ambitious goals for the health and education sectors other parts of the social security system were squeezed down as a result of scarce funding. Only in the second term were new tax-based resources providing the system with a fresh start. These observations about the possibilities to deliver may put the present book in some opposition to earlier research. A far gloomier account would hold that social democracy generally, including Labour and the SAP, have failed completely on several counts. It has been suggested (Thomson 2000: 154ff.) that the Parties have failed to implement the 'classic' aims of social democracy; failed to fulfil the expectations of the electorate and promote confidence in the future; failed to build a stable electoral coalition. Based on the economically extremely turbulent first part of the 1990s such a conclusion seems reasonably correct. However, it is doubtful whether a short time period is particularly fruitful to study. As later developments have shown, the parties have indeed managed to do better than in the aftermath of the economic crisis. Caution is preferable. 1990s retrenchment was for real but I would like to emphasise the importance of a long time perspective when dealing with problematics concerning ideological change and stability.

Given that quite a few parties in the European party systems are more or less close to some kind of social liberalism the dilemma is further aggravated. With so many challengers fighting on the same field with much about the same means, social democrats have to make sure they deliver even more than their competitors. As long as the so-called 'bourgeois' (non-socialist) parties in the party systems stubbornly keep on reducing taxes while at the same time keeping up the main features of the welfare state the race may still not be so difficult for social democracy.

Apparently tax-reduction is a craving for most non-socialist governments. They seem to 'produce higher deficits and debt than left-wing governments. On the other hand, bourgeois governments favor lower taxes, which is best explained by the political tax-smoothing hypothesis ... the core constituency of bourgeois parties belongs to wealthier strata' (Wagschal 1998: 75, Chapter 4). At the same time most non-socialist parties usually want to protect important elements of the welfare state, sometimes even expanding and improving parts of it. Reducing taxes without slimming down the welfare state might backfire, as there are obvious budget-problem risks involved. Non-socialist governments therefore face the discrediting threat of being seen as second-rate economic managers.

Ideologically informed welfare cut-downs appear not to be a realistic vote-getting strategy. Nor is the prospect of huge budget deficits, which in the end will force the Government into austerity packages anyway. Should the non-socialist parties instead opt for keeping up taxes, some of their rhetoric will sound a touch hollow. Still this will probably be the only viable road and one, which in the long run will pose a danger to social democracy.

Tentatively we might discern three broad areas in which the social democratic leadership will have to consider questions of change and stability. First, the scope of the resources extracted: How much is available for particular reform pro-grammes? Can resources be increased or will reductions have to be made? Second, the character of the mix between market and State/planning forces will have to be considered: Is there room for further market-corrections or will the State have to be rolled back? Third, the character and number of particular programmes come to the forefront: Should certain programmes be kept, adjusted, scrapped or introduced?

The Party leaderships seem to be extremely unwilling to change their basic market-economy friendly ideology. When the dust has settled the liberal market economy seems to be a *sine qua non* of their policies and deeply embedded in social democratic thinking. At the same time the Parties' determination to deliver a wide range of market-correcting measures appears to be cut in stone. Over the entire period, the Parties have never failed to point to the international capitalist market economy's unfair distributive effects. The only way to deal with these effects is to provide some kind of service or support to those who can't make it on the market's terms. Whether the services should be State operated or only State controlled is a moot point. Increasingly New Labour has favoured public–private partnership solutions with the State as the final guarantor and financier (Shaw 2003). Conse-quently, with taxes at or near their ceiling, satisfactory economic performance is essential, but even that might be insufficient if the prospects for future economic performance are bleak – and if the voters' expectations about social reforms exceed the parties' ability to deliver.

A critical juncture for SAP and Labour policy-making would be when resources are perceived not to square with actual programmes. Then, a profound choice has to be made as to which means are available in the extraction of economic surplus. As a consequence fundamental questions on how to regard the market economy become inevitable. As always social democrats will then have to fight a two-front battle. To the left (inside the party as with several Labour Party groups, or mostly outside the party as with the Left Party in Sweden) parties and groups will always claim they form more trustworthy guardians of the market-correcting ideology (in the case of the Left Party the market-correction proposals are sometimes spiced-up with the same kind of planning rhetoric we found in Labour and the SAP twenty years earlier around 1980; the same can be said of the Labour left). To the right other actors will claim they are custodians of economic freedom and the liberal democracy without which there would be no surplus to distribute in the first place. Whatever happens, social democrats do not appear to be willing to play the socialist card in the sense that a true alternative economic system is provided. Up until the mid-1980s the socialist card seemed to be easier to play in the sense that some of the socialist terminology remained. Later even the rhetoric about socialism is out of bounds.

Socialism, social democracy, liberalism, social liberalism, socialist liberalism?

A subtle problem for the Parties will be how to convince voters, members and competing parties exactly what distinguishes social democracy from social liberalism or other related 'social' projects like Christian democracy (Huntington and Bale 2002). In both cases subscription to the market economy in conjunction with a wide collection of market-correcting policies is perceived to be vital parts of the ideologies.

There is a vast array of parties with more or less market-correcting measures on their programmes. Many parties propose social services, active labour-market policies, industrial legislation etc. In Sweden most parties actually would fit these criteria.[1] In the UK party system Labour as well as the Liberal Party are obvious candidates for being included in the wide social liberal fold. Although outside the immediate scope of the present study, the demarcation line between the two entities is important. Without any longer being able to make unequivocal references to some kind of socialism, social democrats will have a tougher time justifying their very existence. At the same time non-socialist parties with a social liberal outlook will find it decidedly more difficult to threaten the voters with the socialist ghost.

The point has been made elsewhere (Glyn and Wood 2001: 11)[2] about New Labour's present ideological record that the policies 'have little in common with those classically identified with social democracy.' At the same time the authors refer to the fact that New Labour has indeed continued to prioritise old Labour macroeconomic stability. Moreover New Labour has addressed poverty, disadvantage and social exclusion built on the overall idea that people should be helped back into the labour market. These factors sit rather comfortably with classical social democracy.

So there is no dearth of State activity. However, as Glyn and Wood emphasise, the character of State activity has changed. Rather than increasing equality between the various social strata in society the strategy has been to increase the standard of living for the poor at the same time as high incomes are accepted or even encouraged. The policies show a 'concern for improving the position of the most disadvantaged [coexisting] with . . . a tolerance for . . . the most advantaged.' While the quest for eliminating poverty is still strong, the means have no doubt changed considerably – to the disappointment of 'many on the left' (Glyn and Wood, 2001: 11). Still, even the Glyn and Wood list of measures provides an ambitious amount of State activity aimed at correcting the outcomes of the market. It is also questionable whether minimum wage, maternity leave, child tax credit etc. – which form the core of New Labour's post-1997 reform in the social policy field – do not after all amount to 'redistribution' in the old sense. But, as with Sweden, we seem to encounter arguments, which show something of a blind eye to the family support sector.

In comparison with the Swedish SAP, the verdict on Labour's policies are a bit bewildering. No doubt, the gap between rich and poor was diminished substantially until the late 1980s and still remains smaller than in most countries. In this sense the old Swedish social democratic policies showed less of concern with the advantaged groups and more with the more unfortunate sections of society. High taxes contributed to this effect. At the same time it is a fact that the SAP's welfare state policies increasingly aimed at including the better off income groups already as far back as in the 1950s. Income-related welfare support (a certain, fixed, per cent of income received in sick leave support etc. regardless of income level) per definition keeps income differentials at their original level.

Another element which points in the direction of old social democratic policies is the 2002 Labour decision to increase taxes (implemented in 2003) – although this was done after much hesitancy and only after using the almost pettifogging method of raising national insurance contributions rather than the tax system proper. Of course very few would find the view that New Labour was a high-tax party very convincing (apart from the more sensitive quarters of Toryism and certainly not as compared to the Swedish levels). Old tax-and-spend policies are probably gone for the foreseeable future. The early years after 1997 saw more talk than delivery on the issue of upgrading the public sector (Mullard 2001). Given that insight, the 2002 tax increase is still a step in the direction of the 1992 election manifesto's pledge to raise top income tax from 40 per cent to 50 per cent which would be close to the Swedish level.

The somewhat belated British tax increase gives us cause to rest for a moment on the differing contexts in the Swedish and British cases. SAP came back to power in 1994 after only three years of non-socialist Government. At that point the non-socialist parties had been in office for a mere nine out of the fifty years after World War II. Moreover, the 1991–94 non-socialist Government as well as its only predecessors (various non-socialist coalition governments between 1976–82) came to power offering no more than mildly different ideological alternatives to the Social Democrats. In many ways the non-socialist parties were as eager as the Social Democrats to 'produce welfare reforms of a certain kind' which had become 'what a Swedish ruler was expected to do' (Garme 2001: 135). However, recent developments may have seen the end to this hegemony of social democratic ideology.

As the 2002 Swedish election campaign proved, the non-socialist parties are trying to carve out a section along the left-right continuum, which is more of an alternative to social democracy than a diluted version of social democracy. In the end it might be the case that the only true remaining social liberal party in the Swedish party system will be the Social Democratic Party – a perhaps somewhat paradoxical outcome of ideological positioning since the Golden Age of Social Democracy. Naturally this is speculation. Distinct differences inside the non-socialist bloc are still evident especially as regards the extent to which tax cuts could be implemented. The Moderate Party takes the tax-cutting proposals much further than the other three non-socialist sibling parties.

In the UK, New Labour came back in 1997 after eighteen years of continuous Tory rule and with a Tory party, which, at least occasionally, provided the voters with a truly alternative ideological choice. Between 1945 and 1997 the Tories spent thirty-three years in office, Labour only eighteen years.

Being a party with reformist roots, the Labour Party may have found it awkward to start undoing everything overnight. Things take time. Nor had they perhaps the intention to undoing everything overnight as the 1997 Labour pledge to keep the national budget within the same spending limits as the Conservative Government had envisaged. All the same the 2002 decision to raise taxes shows that the initial post-1997 policy of distinctly increasing health and education budgets by denting into spending on other fields of social security in order to find available resources, had reached a limit. Further squeezing of social security funding would have led to a situation where no one had been able to claim that social security measures were still part of the Labour Party's policy package. Apparently social security as a means to achieving safeguards against marginalisation is still part of New Labour's policy even though the final verdict might still be too early to return (Taylor 2001b). Indirectly we have reason to conclude that though perhaps shaken, the ideology remains stable.

The much-debated 'Welfare-to-work' programme whereby unemployed on benefit should be encouraged, not to say forced, to leave social security and enter the labour market is yet another point where new policies are partially related to old Labour ideas and where comparison with the Labour Party's Swedish sibling party is particularly helpful. While the actual effects of the programme have been questioned and criticised for ruthlessness vis-à-vis people who suffer from unemployment, the programme's overall status and ideological character could be interpreted just in the opposite. The policy's underlying aim is strikingly and interestingly reminiscent of the SAP's 1970 perhaps underestimated decision about welfare and work. Until then the Party leadership had actively contemplated introducing a new system of family policy benefits (the 'home care allowance') aimed at raising the standard of living among families with small children. Social security benefits were well in line with the party's general ideology, which emphasised the need for an active welfare state to secure the well-being of the population.

What happened around 1970 was that the Party leadership suddenly panicked over the scheduled costs of the new system. In order to provide true economic security for all families the proposed benefits would have had to reach levels, which the Finance Minister felt were totally irresponsible. In a very short period of time the party leadership made a complete policy U-turn.

The only viable economic security for the working-class, the leadership now reasoned, especially for those with small children, had to be based on gainful employment rather than on social benefits and two salaries were then preferable to one. The logical consequence of this overall conclusion was to start planning for a society where both men and women were equally active on the labour market. The 'two-earner family' became active policy.

In a sense the SAP's welfare-to-work policy was then formed before rather than after the benefits were introduced. In a way one might say that the Party leadership abolished some of the proposed welfare benefits before they had even been introduced. The extra 'home care allowance' (in every respect but the name an additional child allowance) which was vehemently discussed during the 1960s and backed up by the Party was never implemented. A major contributing factor behind the decision was that the party leadership came to the conclusion that the proposed benefits would be too costly for the Government's budget. There were simply no economic resources available for that kind of benefit. The welfare budget has been regarded as a means to clear up temporary problems for people, not as a continuous source of incomes for wide groups of the general public. Instead people had to be encouraged to enter the labour market – helped along via a vast number of labour market measures (Hinnfors 1999) and a number of other welfare measures, most notably paid parental leave and day-care centres. Whether women actually left homework as a result of changed Government policy or whether the policies came as a consequence of women's new work life ideals is not entirely clear. Anyway, the number of women entering the workforce far exceeded all forecasts. Only later did policy makers realise that the increased number of women in the labour force almost exclusively went to the public sector, which – as a result of other considerations – expanded to unprecedented levels. The increase had the later, unpredicted, effect that the budget costs for paid parental leave and day-care centres multiplied (Hinnfors 1999).

The present UK context is different to what happened in Sweden around 1970 in the sense that Labour's welfare-to-work programme is launched as a way of getting people out of benefit reliance; benefits which they already receive. The contextual difference means people in the UK and Sweden face different feelings of hardship (and different feelings of relief) when they try to adapt to the new systems. At the same time many ideological statements in the Swedish case as compared to the British case are remarkably similar as well as the practical consequences for affected citizens. New Labour's efforts obviously put tremendous demands on certain individuals who risk facing double pressure from a tough labour market and simultaneous loss of social security. Similar hardships were caused by the SAP's unwillingness to provide necessary funding to the day-care centres during the 1970s, 1980s and early 1990s. Literally hundreds of thousand families were left desperate in their relations with an unpredictably operating queuing-system bureaucracy. Those who did not make it in the 'day-care lottery' had the unpalatable choice of either losing a job because there was no child-care available or taking the job and accepting that the child was not taken care of properly.

The other clear instance of the SAP's early attachment to the notion of welfare-to-work is the Rehn–Meidner Model and the fundamental acceptance, or rather promotion of industrial competitiveness at the expense of people's possibilities to get a job locally. The extremely rapid transfer of workers from remoter parts of the country to more centrally located industries (and public sector bureaucracies) in the major cities during the 1950s to 1970s were nothing less than full-blown welfare-to-work programmes. Welfare state programmes at a scale to keep people at an acceptable standard of living was impossible in the sectors and parts of the country where capitalism had changed the industrial landscape and made people redundant. The SAP's solution was to provide the jobless with tickets south and removals subsidies. All in order to make people stay away from welfare and to be gainfully employed.

The methodological question we have to pose is whether we should interpret the aims differently or whether the Swedish case should count as more true to the social democratic project than the New Labour experiment thirty years later. My point has been to indicate that the attitude towards poor people's sense of bereavement and the character and quantity of State activities display a number of parallels as regards distance from the ideal social democracy. The over-arching ideological aims may not be entirely different. The ideological flaws in Labour's and SAP's ideologies have certainly been different, but flaws all the same throughout the period (if measured against some idealised version of social democracy).

With some earlier allusions to socialism having been more or less rhetoric only, several voters may have found some ideological phrases a little hollow, with no concrete measures to underpin them. Getting rid of the planning-burden from their market ideologies might therefore prove beneficial to the parties. Instead of playing the socialist card today, the parties may want to paint the image of being the only true protectors of the welfare state. Voters with an interest in welfare state services might find social democrats the more credible alternative. Welfare-state protection always took centre stage. It may even be the case that the earlier formulations about planning and socialism were in fact the social democrats' way of getting the message across to the voters that social democrats were the true protectors of the welfare state.

The Parties might even be able to benefit from abandoning the more planning-oriented overtones in that welfare-state protection will stand a chance of becoming more the focus-field with no need to fight battles about ideas on State ownership, planning etc. in which the party leaderships had lost interest long ago anyway. Of course there is always a risk of opening up the left-wing flank. As the success of the Swedish Left Party has shown, a more radical version of social democracy can be attractive to segments of the voters. But as soon as the social democrats manage to get across the message to the voters that the policies are in tune with the basic fundamentals of the old welfare state, success at the polls is possible. The SAP's return as a 40 per cent party in 2002 proves this point. The election campaign juxtaposed two ideological alternatives. The Social Democrats (with the help of the Left Party and the Greens) hammered in the importance of a robust public sector supported by sufficient taxes whereas the non-socialist parties emphasised the need for extensive tax-cuts. In their propaganda, these tax-cuts were not necessarily the same as proposing welfare state limitations. A popular theme was focused on the supposedly 'dynamic' effects of tax-cuts. By cutting taxes people would be willing to take on more work, would be able to make ends meet without any help from social security etc. In the end the Government budget would even benefit from receiving less tax incomes. In comparison, the SAP in many ways appeared as a party willing to fight for 'old' ideals. Whether these ideals will receive sufficient backing as regards concrete means is something for which we will have to look to the future.

Part of the voter-drift to the Left Party is explained by EU-resistance, feminism and green politics. Even in the case of the Left Party important elements of the old planning rhetoric has vanished from the Party's ideology and technically the Party has indeed shared responsibility with the SAP for economic policies during the 1998–2002 period. Though outside the Cabinet, the Left Party and the Green Party cooperated formally with the SAP in a kind of Lib-Lab equivalent, on economic matters during the lifetime of the 1998–2002 Parliament. The agreement continued after the 2002 elections albeit after a few political pirouettes by the Green Party. In reality the Swedish party system now consists of two distinct political blocs where the left bloc is composed of the Greens plus two more or less similar parties with a social democratic outlook.

The UK party system lacks a viable alternative to the left of the Labour Party (though the Holyrood Scottish multiparty systems offers an interesting comparison as to what could have happened UK-wide after electoral reform, with its Scottish Socialist Party clearly to the left of Scottish Labour plus the Green Party) with the effect that the Liberal Party sometimes is lured into taking at least as social-liberal positions as Labour, which could function in much the same 'corrective' way as the Swedish Left Party.

To the extent that the notion of planning the economy in the socialist sense has been thrown overboard, the future for social democracy might be to revitalise its emphasis on solidarity. The whole idea behind solidarity is about the 'haves' giving to the 'have-nots'. The realisation of this worldview does not necessarily require that the 'haves' be made extinct. Solidarity taking the place over State-ownership in the parties' rhetoric is made the easier since – as has been shown here – welfare state redistribution – or safeguards against marginalisation – always took centre stage anyway.

The change in emphasis has rendered the Parties' ideologies more clear-cut. In the old days, what were in essence market-accepting parties risked confusing some of the voters by sometimes using phrases and expressions belonging to State-planning parties. Only in a few cases were more hard-core socialist measures brought forward in proposals, such as nationalisation of banks and credit institutions. The exceptions are few, and almost uniquely found in the middle period party programmes.

Mostly the references to public ownership were vague and accompanied with elaborations on how to make the market function in a desired manner. Those voters who never took to reading the Party programmes almost never encountered even the word 'socialism.' As was shown earlier not a single 1968–2002 SAP election manifesto contained this word. Labour manifestos were only slightly more elaborate. Today the ideologies, and the Parties, are more easily placed on the left-right scale. The problem is that the ensuing left-right position is closer to the 'middle' than to the 'left.'

In shedding some of the earlier rhetoric both Parties made it more difficult for them to appeal to the left-of-middle voters. The role of left voters, or at least working-class voters had been downplayed for some time anyway, and this applies to most social democratic parties. Somehow the development towards shedding the socialist rhetoric in favour of more unequivocal acceptance of the welfare state as such was triggered off by the trends towards less reliance on the working class in favour of the middle classes or 'the whole society'. Examples of this trend abound.

After its brief drift towards Soviet socialism during the 1920s, the Norwegian Labour Party decided it was a party for 'poor' people rather than for 'workers' (Karvonen 1991). In the 1959 Bad Godesberg programme the German Social Democrats opted for being a party for the entire population rather than for the workers. In Sweden no leading SAP representative has been caught out using the word 'working-class' in any major speech since at least World War II. Some of the old symbols are still there to be sure, and the SAP has not gone as far as New Labour which dropped singing 'The Red Flag' at Conference and similar gatherings. 'The Red Flag' never was part of the SAP's culture but 'The International' was and still is. Though some members join in the sing-along a bit less enthusiastically these days 'The International' is still heard towards the end of major party gatherings. 1 May is still held as a public holiday with marches organised by social democrats and socialists.

In order to widen the tax base from which resources aimed at the welfare state could be extracted groups outside the working class were necessary supporters. A wider following was gradually becoming necessary not least because the working class actually began to dwindle in numbers. Without changing class composition of the voters social democrats were doomed to diminishing minority status. To the extent that this new strategy was launched the old class rhetoric had to go. Offering them a welfare state on which they could benefit to some extent could attract the middle classes (Svensson 1994). The more politically correct term, these days, is 'wage-earner' which subtly includes almost every adult citizen in the population. No one seems to be excluded.

The real steps away from a true socialist position were taken before rather than after World War II and right-of-middle voters who felt deterred by the earlier socialist planning-speak will now feel less inhibited to vote for SAP/Labour. So without actually becoming more 'catch-all', the Parties' strategies might prove successful in the voter arena. Rhetorically they have moved to unequivocal middle ground, a ground they occupied in practice before but which has now taken the upper hand also in most spheres of rhetoric. In a sense the strategically necessary emphasis on the welfare state which materialised sometime after World War II held the seed which has now come to bloom: Social democracy is about the welfare state rather than about socialism. It is about protecting weak groups in society rather than about a certain economic system.

Efficiency, full employment and equality. The core defining characteristics of social democracy look clear enough. However, as Per Selle (1991: 140) has remarked, the full meaning of these concepts is never really clarified. What exactly is meant by 'equality?' Do we refer to equality in chances or equality in outcome? Are any types of income differentials acceptable? When is employment 'full'? Zero per cent unemployed or 5 per cent? And what is the criterion of 'efficient?'

Selle's account emphasises the fact that rather than being tied to 'redistribution' (another vague concept) *per se* social democracy has been in favour of developing 'institutions and regulations which are to prevent any form of *marginalization* [italics in original] of ordinary folk. So far, full employment has been the principal means of preventing marginalization' (Selle 1991: 144).

To the extent that full employment becomes important, an efficient economy takes centre stage as the strategic means. This version of social democracy, which Selle identifies as the middle-of-the road version post-World War II is by no means distant to either the current SAP or New Labour to the extent that '[e]conomic efficiency and full employment have been far more important than redistribution and equality' (Selle 1991: 144). Even though the top 20 per cent in the UK get richer and richer the bottom twenty per cent have seen their standard of living rise too. The Government has not managed to decrease the income gap but raised the floor for the poorest. This might mean the policies fall short of preventing wide groups from being marginalised, but the case is not clear. A substantial number of people have actually come off benefits and yet others have seen their daily lives improving somewhat although equality has not increased (measured as degree of income differentials). In that respect Blair's Labour party squares well with social democracy's roots of fighting marginalisation.

However, the quest for a decent society in which no group is marginalised is still not very unique to social democracy. Indeed there are several similarities to Christian democratic ideals, even though Labour's secular political culture as such is remote from Christian democracy (Crouch 2000; Huntington and Bale 2002). Apparently social democracy has for a long time now opted for promoting equal rights rather than equal outcomes (Selle 1991: 150). In this sense nothing separates social democracy from liberalism. Equal rights are a fundamental liberal value and to that extent 'social democracy as we know it' is liberal.

The strange phenomenon – given a belief in profound differences between socialism/social democracy and liberalism – is the blurred distinction between these two ideological worlds. Taken as a whole there is nothing in Labour's and the SAP's ideological views about the capitalist market economy that presupposes socialism nor closes the door to liberalism. In the earlier stages there remained traces of socialist phrases. Perhaps those traces, and long before the Golden Age more concrete socialist proposals, were necessary to build up the energy and fervour needed to mobilise the masses in support for the market economy as we know it: Solid acceptance of the capitalist market economy with an equally solid awareness about the needs to correct the outcomes by funnelling back some of the surplus to those in need. But apart from those traces there is no socialism. Nor are there any signs of illiberalism.

That liberalism should prevail at the formal State-level and, at a somewhat lower ideological level, for welfare state policies, which have been formed by social democrats as well as by non-socialist parties, is slightly less surprising. Welfare states as we know them are the result of measures taken by different parties over a long period of years. Labour's and the SAP's influence is reduced correspondingly (less so in Sweden, more so in the UK). Hicks and Kenworthy (2003: 40) emphasise the fact that present-day 'progressive liberal' welfare state regimes neither presuppose socialist nor 'illiberal' policies. 'They are neither socialist nor illiberal in the sense that the defining regime characteristics – universalistic public social insurance, large public sectors, and both male and female empowerment . . . do not require one to go beyond capitalism and liberal democracy for rationales and precedents.' However, this reduced distinction between socialism and liberalism still leaves room for a distinctly different welfare state category, conservatism.

Once again we are left with extremely vague notions of what actually constitutes social democracy. If the defining qualitative set of criteria is identical to that of (social) liberalism we will instead have to provide some kind of quantitative indicators by which to separate the two siblings. How many people could be marginalised before social democracy is no longer social democracy? Is there an income distribution ceiling above which uneven distribution becomes unacceptable no matter how generously the bottom groups are saved from marginalisation? And is there an unemployment figure above which social democracy becomes a hollow concept void of any meaning? Supposing we actually had robust indicators of marginalisation we will also have to presume that liberalism would accept greater numbers of marginalised or unemployed people than social democracy. There is little empirical evidence to suggest that social liberal parties on the middle range of the left-right scale in any way correspond to such a version of 'tough' liberalism. Selle (1991) makes an effort to separate social democracy from one of the other main 'social' movements, Catholicism. Selle claims that the 'social democratic view of welfare [is different] from the "Catholic" view [by having] a far less fatalistic outlook on the individual and thus on society, a view which says that we do not always need to have large numbers of marginalised and poverty-stricken people among us. It is possible to intervene to manage social developments.' However, not even Selle appears to be convinced when he adds that these views separate 'or separated' [italics mine] the two ideological approaches. Nor does Selle offer any real differences between social liberalism and social democracy.

As the socialist rhetoric fades away from the parties' policy thinking, a growing problem will be that there is precious little to safeguard the welfare state in times of budget deficits or ideological attacks from the right. There is nothing left to question the validity of the international capitalist market economy. At least since the 1920s (Sweden) or early 1960s (UK) the market economy has been taken for granted. This book has shown the depth with which it has been embraced. Lacking such ideological safeguards there is little to prevent the parties from drifting in a more liberal direction. We could very well envisage the 'socialist façade' as a robust obstacle against which attacks from the right had to fight. Socialism worked as a kind of first defence line. The line was rather easy to cross – after all very few seem to have really believed in the possibility of replacing the marker capitalism, that is what this book has emphasised – but having done that the second line: The welfare state's function as market-correction – was less easy to cut into. Those who nurtured dreams about socialism could at least regard the welfare state as a tool, albeit a toothless and inefficient tool, for stemming the capitalist tide. With some kind of ideas about a future society the welfare state took on a character of not only correcting today's market outcomes but of the first step towards something else.

In austere times all the focus is directly on the welfare state. There is no barrier to cross before the eyes are turned to its costs and character. Its status is that of corrective rather than any step towards a new society. The size and character of concrete measures and policies then become matters of prudence, convenience and appropriateness. In the end all policies will then be open for discussion. In austere times there will always be the case to hold that prudence calls for cutbacks. In the end there will be few, if any, protections against drifts in a neo-liberal direction.

The end of ideology?

On a more overarching level one may raise the question of Herbert Tingsten's thesis about the end of ideologies. Tingsten, the Swedish 1930s social democrat later turned social liberal ideologue, newspaperman and political scientist, published his works on the diminishing ideological distance between the socialist and non-socialist parties in modern democracies. 'Democracy' itself became the non-contested goal, which everyone accepted and which set the limits for the ensuing political debate. With socialism finally thrown overboard all parties are united in the defence of liberal democracy and of the liberal market economy. In a way, Tingsten's observation would be more correct today than in his own days. Tingsten's point was that ideological zeal was normally put in the closet. Only on solemn occasions like the 1 May were Sunday suits donned and the old phrases more or less reluctantly brought to use. Normally party politics was instead characterised by pragmatic approaches towards most issues. No more than minor differences between the parties prevailed (Tingsten 1966).

As we have seen, rhetoric about planning and other market-steering measures were still an important part of SAP and Labour market ideology in the 1960s. So to some extent one could say that Tingsten's analysis was in fact incorrect during the Golden Age of Social Democracy. Elements of 'socialism' found their way into central, authoritatively binding documents even though few may actually have believed there was a reformist path to socialism or that socialism actually formed the goal in the first place. In a vague way socialism apparently was regarded as a goal to fight for or at least something which could enthuse voters and members in their strive for a better society.

At the same time one is struck by the apparent lack of concrete measures to back up the notion of socialism. Socialism 'today' is always left defined in a way, which is bewilderingly close to any version of social liberalism, perhaps with a touch more ambitious reforms attached to 'socialism'. Socialism 'yesterday' is invariably defined in ways, which come closer to pure forms of socialism. Socialism 'tomorrow' is always left undefined or defined in a way that looks suspiciously close to a kind of market capitalism with a number of State-controlled corrections via the welfare state, regional policies, labour market policies etc. This last point is perhaps the most surprising of our findings. Please observe that the findings here are not in any way based on the presumption that 'socialism' should by necessity presuppose 'revolutionary' action and a drastic upheaval of society. On the contrary, it is one thing to accept that social democracy has always been a movement which has accepted democratic means and that the road to socialism had to be reformist with step-by-step actions. But reformism needs a goal. Step-by-step actions are indeed possible to describe as being reformist but even when it's 'reform not revolution' (Fishman 1996: 44; Hodgson 1981: 196 f., 216ff.) the end result must be about an altogether different society. This is not the position taken by the core echelons of SAP and Labour. 'Revisionist socialism' has had more to do with full employment, tax-based welfare state and social justice (Shaw 1996: 54f.; see Crosland 1956) than with needs-based, state-enforced allocation of values. It has been described as 'a puzzle' why 'remarkably talented' thinkers, such as Crossman, Foot, Mikardo, Castle, Wilson and Bevan 'signally failed to provide any sustained fresh political thinking and mount a serious ideological challenge to revisionism' (Shaw 1996: 58). The answer to the puzzle may simply be that to confront revisionism would have challenged the very heart of social democratic thinking. Full employment etc. amount to measures that all are within the liberal capitalist market economy. Not then the neo-liberal version of that economy but a more socially conscious variety. To challenge these economic foundations would be to enter into completely new ideological territory and 'very few' linked even 'socialism' to 'the notion of a revolutionary break' and more to an overall 'ethic' of equity (Cronin 2004: 29, Hinnfors and Shaw 2004: 7). The problem is that, failing such challenge, the meaning of revisionism loses its cutting edge.

'Revisionist' became more or less synonymous with 'modernising', with optimistic views about the possibilities to boost the quality of society through technological and scientific advances (Cronin 2004: 88 f.). As part of the modernising drive came the view that the ineffective industries, be they old nationalised or private, could in fact be turned into competitive exemplars (Cronin 2004 88ff.). The paradox was that notions of competition became associated with public enterprise and the major yardstick with which to define efficiency and competitiveness the international market.

Party leaders are surprisingly unwilling to dwell for very long on the topic of what a future society is going to look like. With socialism firmly in the background there is precious little left. However, in a rare moment of reutilising the old battered concept, even new leaders venture into elaborations on the concept. Tony Blair referred to socialism in the following way in his 2003 Conference speech:

> That's the reason for change. Not to level down but to level up. Not to privatise but to revitalise a public service we all depend on.
>
> I don't want the middle class fighting to get out of the state system. I want them fighting to get into it but on equal terms with working class patients and children. That's what the founders of socialism dreamt of. (Blair 2003)

Though not crafted in terms of class antagonism, Blair does in fact endeavour to use terms like 'working class' – something which his Swedish counterparts has shunned for decades. Swedish social democrat leaders swapped the much more bloodless 'working class' for 'wage earners' already in the 1940s. Blair's rendering of socialism is telling in several ways. Although they are very thinly stretched in the Labour Party's present version the roots back to the working class are still there. Moreover, this version of socialism has lost its meaning as an alternative economic system where the working class will enjoy all the fruits of its labour. Instead the inequalities between the social classes remain more or less untouched but with an important exception. There will be a substantial societal sphere in which the working class will play on equal terms with the middle class: the public sector. Socialism's founding fathers dreamt of class equality but they did not confine their dreams to the public service sector. In this sense the 2003 Labour Party is a far cry from the dreams of the founders of socialism but the break took place long before Tony Blair took the helm. On the other hand, it may also be fair to hold that the new party leadership dreams of a fair society in a more general sense than merely confined to the public sector. With the public sector as a tool the goal of providing people with equal chances can be extended to the whole society. Moving from one type of welfare state to another type of welfare state or from slightly less ambitious social care to more far reaching social care is not about reformism. Reformism has to lead to something new; it is not an end in itself.

An altogether different matter is to define what the abstract end product called socialism is all about. Socialism needs to be defined in terms of at least something like a distinctly non-market society based on people's needs rather than private profit and with a view on equality founded on equality in outcomes/results rather than equality in opportunities. The absolute lack of references to that kind of alternative society in the data indicate that social democracy is not reformist in the sense that it is set to enter socialism. It is definitely a reform-focused movement with a wide range of proposals of how to improve people's lives through various supporting policies and through policies for making the market's actors act in a way which is truer to the spirit of the market economy than had the actors been left to operate on their own. But all these efforts are very different from socialism.

Perhaps the Swedish Party was earlier than Labour in changing its overall rhetorical goal from being 'the socialist State' to being 'the welfare state'. The verdict depends on how we evaluate the wage-earners' funds, but their diluted character merits a conclusion that whatever they were, they were not meant to show the way to socialism. Even Labour's 1971–73 or 1979–83 leftward drifts can hardly be described as reformist versions of socialism (in the sense that reforms will lead to a distinctly new type of society with a new economic system). But rhetorically the Party leadership was at least able to hold out the image of a distant future society with a socialist lining. The leadership also managed to allow some of the grassroots and activist radicalism to play on the same field as the leadership for a few years. In the sense that 'Party' equals all the activists and branches taken together, social democracy was a more vital concept during those activist outbursts of leftwing energy than either before or after. The paradox remains that the Golden Age of Social Democracy was more of a leadership-led appeasement of the old tenets than was later to be seen among certain party groups. At the leadership level the ideological development has been far less tumultuous with more modest changes. Today most of the demands for public ownership seem to have left the rank and file as well. Left is the concern for the welfare state.

In this sense social democracy has travelled far. The promise of a future Eden is gone. What is left is a range of improvements to the existing structure. We have even shown that the Party leaderships most probably had their fingers crossed when socialism was on the agenda. What they really meant was a version of the old market economy with a few extra market-corrections added to it and perhaps the odd nationalisation. In most instances the rhetorical veil is surprisingly thin.

In 2006 no one would find a description of the two Parties as being in favour of a reformist path to socialism very convincing. It would be more credible to talk about something like a reformist path to the welfare state. At the same time, the end-of-ideology thesis might even hold more truth today when even the rhetoric is gone. There is scant material for speeches on solemn occasions. Rarely – or indeed never – do citizens face the challenge of revolution, nor even of reformism, be it from the right or the left. This means that politics has to be carried out within a sphere of mutual understanding as regards the general direction of society.

Some parties in the party systems emphasise the market's merits more than do the other parties. Yet again some parties are more elaborate than others on the need for market-correction. Perhaps social democracy is extra eager to stand up as the provider of a more tight-woven net of market-corrections than social liberalism, but increasingly managing skills rather than new radical versions of society have to be offered to the voters. So called 'valence issues', i.e. where parties claim they are best suited to reach a commonly agreed goal would then take the upper hand over so-called 'position issues', i.e. controversies about profoundly conflicting world-views.

But after second thoughts perhaps a slightly different picture emerges. With due respect to the fact that only social democratic parties were investigated here, we may surmise that the end-of-ideology thesis is somewhat misconceived. While many parties support wide arrays of market-correcting measures, the character of these measures may still contrast substantially between parties. Not only do they vary between major ideological groups. Differences also occur between parties within the same ideological group and, to some extent, in the same party over time. While differences between the parties as regards the size of the public sector has diminished, it is probably much premature to underestimate these other differences as vehicles for attracting voters and by providing them with distinct alternatives.

Family policy is a case in point. High quality low-fee public-sector day-care establishments and income-related parental leave make it easier for both men and women to enter the labour market. Massive commitments to increase child allowances (which are unrelated to gainful employment) will instead make it easier for those who want to stay home with their small children. In the first case, the ideology behind day-care is founded on the concept of the 'two-earner family' and that the State should help families realise this life-style by providing some kind of collectivised responsibility for the children. In the latter case, the ideology is based on the concept of the 'bread-winner/one-earner family'. Here the State should help families to make the one-earner concept viable. The State should then provide financial means to make individualised models of child minding possible.

In both cases we deal with far-reaching efforts of market-correction. The public sector is regarded as a legitimate entity and something on which society relies for its well-being. In both cases the government has to foot a hefty bill. Both cases can be characterised to fall within social liberalism. Still, the worldviews are extremely different and voters have a real choice between a selection of distinctly different concepts of society. So perhaps the end-of-ideology thesis is premature after all even though none of the competing ideologies has much to do with classic social democracy as such. A *memento mori* for us all about the presence of more unpleasant deep ideological cleavages of a new kind would also be the emergence of populist xenophobic parties. The effects on the political system of such parties gaining power should not be underestimated.

What is different to the voters, though, and something which bodes ill for the parties' ability to tie citizens to life-long loyal relationships with the parties, is the loss of the all-encompassing ideological concept. Though always extremely vague, and extremely disputed, the notion of 'socialism' provided a worldview where everything, in theory, was held together in a more or less coherent web of thought. In the new context everything is rendered more complex. Parties may share family policy views and social service views while at the same time remaining bitter opponents as regards economic policy, environmental policy or housing policy. Complication has replaced clear-cut answers.

Notes

1   The reverse of this dilemma is, of course, a fate shared with many liberal parties (Smith 1988). For readers less familiar with the Swedish party system the parties unfold like this on a left-right continuum – by far the most salient dimension in Swedish politics

(Esaiasson and Holmberg, 1996): The Left Party, until 1967 Sweden's Communist Party and the Left Party-Communists until 1990, has drifted from Soviet communism via Euro communism to a version of social democracy. The party's voting share has hovered around the 4 per cent *Riksdag* hurdle although 1998 and 2002 elections saw the party's share rise to around 10 per cent. With seemingly bedrock stability the Social Democratic Labour Party usually receives around 40 to 45 per cent of the vote, and held cabinet incumbency 1960–76, 1982–90 and 1994–; most were minority cabinets. Two parties compete in the ideological mid-field: the People's Party-the Liberals is a middle-size and contracting party with a social liberal middle-class outlook (usually between five–fifteen per cent of the votes). The Centre Party is a farmers' party with ambitions to catch the 'urban green vote'. This strategy was extremely successful in the mid-1970s when the party peaked at 25 per cent of the voters, but by 1998 its support fell to 5 per cent. On the 'Conservative' right flank the Moderate Party (before 1969: the Right Party) occupies a position between social conservatism and liberalism. Over the years the Conservatives have tried to emerge as the major challenger to Social Democratic hegemony – with varying success (voting share 1960: 16 per cent, 1970: 11 per cent, 1998: 23 per cent, 2002: 15 per cent). In the 1988 election the new Environmental Party-the Greens entered Parliament with 5 per cent of the vote (2002: 5 per cent) to politicise green issues. Founded in 1964, the Christian Democratic Party did not pass the 4 per cent *Riksdag* hurdle until 1991 (7 per cent, 1998: 12 per cent, 2002: 9 per cent). Originally of a rather sectarian character the party leadership deliberately moved into more middle-of-the-road non-socialist ground in the 1980s. Between 1976 and 1982 various non-socialist constellations were in cabinet position.

2   Please note that page references emanate from electronic version.

10

The ubiquitous market

Why would supposedly neo-liberal parties still busy themselves trying to keep unemployment down? Why would they try and defend the welfare state? Why not just throw it all over board and finally getting rid of the old public sector? Do we actually face two neo-liberal parties in the British Labour Party and the Swedish Social Democratic Party? Such were the puzzled questions formulated nine chapters ago. As for the explanatory model, I suggested a relationship between day-to-day policies (child care benefits levels, NHS public support etc.) and overall ideological position, in this case about the international capitalist market economy.

The general answer to the puzzled questions has been that conclusions about neo-liberalism were premature. We had reason to question the neo-liberal content in day-to-day policies and it turned out we are able to formulate grave objections against the claim about neo-liberalism in the more deep-rooted ideologies as well.

Within a changing framework of new issues, new organisational patterns and new leadership styles the Parties have been guided by surprisingly stable ideologies as regards the relationship between State and market. The best way of describing these ideologies is to use the phrase 'market corrected by the State'. This overall result may not be altogether new to the world. Perhaps some of the readers will claim that this is something they knew all the time. But as I have indicated before, there seems to be a bias in earlier research in favour of the change thesis.

I do not purport to say that ideas on international relations such as bombing or not bombing Iraq are uninteresting or peripheral. Nor are ideas on whether women should be given a fairer share of power or whether pollution should be halted. International issues, feminism and green politics are extremely important and in some respects social democratic parties have taken major leaps along these issue dimensions over the past forty years; leaps in several, sometimes contradictory, directions. Nor do I claim that the structure of the Parties have remained intact, that the part played by unions, members and activists should be the same in 2006 as it was in the 1960s, 1970 or 1980s. My claim is more modest. I would simply point to the fact – or to remind us all about the fact – that amid all this change there is an important element of stability. This element is at the core of social democracy and is best described as adherence to the liberal market economy. This stability is not negligible and it gives us reason to reinterpret social democracy.

At least in the Swedish case, acceptance of market principles is perhaps less surprising given the position of what Peter Katzenstein labelled *Small States in World Markets* (Katzenstein 1985; see Esping-Andersen 1996). Obviously trade dependency has created a sense among all political camps that the market is a mighty force putting Swedish industry in the position of the price taker rather than the price maker.

The idea that the country could in any way isolate itself from the outside world has never occurred to the Parties. Or maybe the thought has occurred, certainly among some Party members and among some groups inside the Parties, but the Party leaderships always rejected it. The surrounding markets are there whether we like them or not and one has to do the best one can to survive. This seems to have been the preferred solution among most politicians who almost invariably have been willing to focus on the positive effects of the market economy.

Indeed distinct aspects of the Swedish model (with world market competition guiding wage levels, investments and labour market mobility etc.) were always totally geared towards the firm belief that politics had to accept market laws rather than changing them. By enabling private enterprise to function well on competitive markets, a handsome sufficient surplus could even be generated for the welfare state. The SAP and Labour still occupy the very same general position. Several concrete measures have been changed but those in place serve much the same object of creating taxable surpluses. That was what distinguished social democracy from its competitors in the Golden Age of Social Democracy. With communism thrown over board and with several non-socialists parties deeply committed to various kinds of welfare programmes, the differences become less and less clear.

Perhaps the UK has been somewhat less of a price taker, though it is questionable whether British industry has ever had any real price-making capacity. At least since 1945, 'the principles and perspectives of liberal political economy ... governed Britain's external policy' (Gamble 1994: 137). For long the Labour leadership has 'continued to hold liberal conceptions of Britain's external policy and world role, and shared the belief in free trade and cosmopolitanism which it proclaimed' (Gamble 1994: 169).

Sterling's position within the global monetary system with a status as an international currency exposed Britain to pressures from the money market long before economic deregulation in the 1970s and 1980s (Shaw 1996: 95; Strange 1971). Social democracy enabled 'capitalists to accumulate further capital; meanwhile, socialists would protect workers, extend welfare, redistribute access to education, expand health care' etc. (Sassoon 1996: 734). Viewed from this angle it is less surprising that several of the post-1992 crisis Labour Party policy twists had been tried on before. In this sense stability is as accurate a description of Labour's policies as change.

The globalisation literature wants us to believe that the global markets set exceedingly narrow limits on what governments can do or even desire to do

(Kapstein 2000; Martin and Schumann 1996; Moses 1994; Scholte 2000). The SAP's and Labour's ideological developments tell a somewhat different story. There is simply no obvious relation between the Parties' market views and globalising economic markets (rough as these indicators are). Nor is there any relationship over time within the same country/Party or when the two countries/ Parties are compared.

If anything, new global market conditions hit the UK earlier than Sweden. The British pound always had the status of an international exchange currency. Speculation and attacks on the pound from international currency traders were part of the picture already in the 1960s (Richardson 1982; Shaw 1996: 94).

The drift towards a mild version of a less market-correcting view in favour of a slightly higher State ownership role in the UK occurs in 1974 as well as in 1983 with seemingly no joint relation to external market developments. In Sweden the SAP's only moderately negative general opinion-drifts towards the market occur in 1983 as well as in 1995, i.e. before and after strong market developments. In 1995 freed financial markets would perhaps have led us to expect a more market-economy friendly attitude – given a belief that market forces had indeed grown stronger and that this development somehow is related to State–market ideologies. It did not materialise.

The years 1983 and 1995 are interesting points for comparison since they cover periods before and after the alleged increase in market forces (and in Sweden before and after some of the financial market deregulations as well; a similar comparison in the UK would be between the comparatively radical 1974 – before UK financial deregulation – and 1995 – after UK deregulation). Since the market–State ideologies remained relatively stable between these years there is apparently no obvious relationship between degree of market forces and character of the Parties' State–market ideologies. Evidently it takes more far-reaching societal changes to make the parties react by changing their ideologies.

During the heydays of the 1960s we would instead have expected a decidedly more market-sceptic stance. With the internationally accepted and implemented restraints on financial markets and currency movements, State-planning views should have had much easier to make themselves heard. Lacking such data, the argument about a drift from State planning to neo-liberalism becomes a touch weak. Very little was in fact heard from real-life social democracy.

Generally the fluctuations between certain years are small and haven't really been jerkier in the UK than in Sweden. The broader picture is much the same in 1965 as in 2002 regardless of the various changes in market behaviour. These overall relationships (or lack of relationships) tell us two things. First, even though there might be subtler and indirect links between market characteristics and politics there is still scope for wide policy manoeuvres. Second, we have reason to believe the Parties have actually reached their market-accepting positions out of free will.

Some may find the conclusion about market-acceptance provocative. Why should not the visions about a better society still brought forward in the 1980s be valid today as indicators about a sincere conviction among the leading Party officials that a profoundly different world based on a new economic system was not only possible but indeed desirable? Why should not the visions about social-ism be for real and how could I claim that there were no fundamental changes within the Parties when for instance references to socialism have been dropped?

On the rhetorical level the change is indisputable. The political language has changed. Several key words have left the Party documents; others have taken their place. We have seen 'socialism' vanish from the texts altogether. Behind the rhetoric there is less concrete change. Conclusions about social democracy's adherence to market principles was hinted at in Stinchcombe's (1979: 1) analysis of Norwegian social democracy. 'Norway has come a good deal farther in giving a good life to the poor than in reducing the power of capital.' If socialism is limited to issues about standard of living, its meaning is seriously watered down. Short of taking issue with the real power of capital, socialism is reduced to being a synonym with welfare state or something similar. Social democracy has managed to use 'socialism' and 'welfare state' more or less interchangeably. There is nothing inherently wrong in that as long as we keep the similarity in mind. One of the words has been kept alive, while one of them has been relegated to the history books. A linguistic difference indeed but there is less convincing evidence that it should signify real ideological change.

Britain and Sweden are no unique cases. Welfare statism rather than socialism is, and has been, social democracy's solution to society's problems. In this sense the visions are still there to encourage people to fight for a better world. There is still a profound readiness to correct the market's outcomes and to improve the lives of ordinary people. The focus on people's hardships and on solutions to bring about a better society for wide parts of the populations is still dominant in the leading Party documents. Whether the parties are still able to reach out to wide sections of society with the new formulations, with the new language is another question.

However, while the visions are there it is still undeniable that the ubiquitous market must have been felt to set the limits for the visions. Sometimes the cata-logue of corrections has been more ambitious sometimes less so but they have always been inside the confines of the market economy. This cannot be by chance. That the Parties should have left the 'correction-approach' in favour of either no correction (or very limited correction) or State-planned complements (with vari-ous 'complements' to the market) is hardly corroborated by our data. I suggest that these findings indicate deep-rooted and stable ideological ends rather than merely reflect day-to-day concrete measures pending more hard-core 'real' goals.

In order to have been able to speak about more intensively felt alternatives to the market economy we would have wanted at least two criteria to be fulfilled. First we would have wanted some kind of definition in the documents, which qualitatively separated the old (non-socialist) society from the desired new (socialist) society. Second we would have needed clearer examples of exactly how such desired changes were to have come about. That we have failed to detect such data over so long a time period gives us a firmer standing to draw the conclusion about ideological stability.

New ideas?

An obviously relevant contextual change here is the transformed character of international capitalism over the last forty years. While international trade has long been an important aspect of most Western economies (though by no means completely unchanging), international capital movements have risen sharply over the last decades (Kitschelt et al. 1999). Several authors seem to agree that the increased ability of international capital to move freely among countries, in conjunction with the sheer size of these movements, changes the environment in which nationally based policy makers have to operate.

Today 'democratic governments have to sell their policies not only to electorates, but to international investors, who are usually presumed to be leery of public sector growth' (Simmons 1999: 64; Moses 1994). Herbert Kitschelt (1999: 344) takes the argument as far as to claim that 'social democratic parties are doomed to extinction, if they are unable to respond to the new political-economic conditions of post-industrial capitalism after the golden age.' Be that as it may.

Despite misgivings like Kitschelt's, social democracy has been extremely successful in surviving under new conditions. Social democracy was able to co-opt important parts of the Vietnam movement, substantial elements of the environmental movement and essential parts of the feminist movement. As regards the market economy and turmoil in that sector of politics there have been tremendous changes. The whole industrial sector has suffered from repeated and extremely difficult structural change when whole industries of the old smokestack version literally died away during the 1960s. The change is not over yet. The communications industry has already been exposed to several deep recent transformations. Financial markets have developed enormously, including a number of collapses or near collapses (Black Wednesday 1992). The oil crisis hit the industrialised world in the 1970s. Crises seem to be the normal state. How could the Parties survive these market changes? The present study offers a guide to the answer why: Market-acceptance was always there. Sometimes it was out in the open sometimes it was dressed in a veil depicting a (perhaps distant) socialist future. But more or less it was always there. The road travelled to accepting the need for constant adaptation to realities outside the scope of one's own force has been comparatively short, because that is what the market economy is all about: Adaptation rather than planning.

More and more 'traders [are perceived to] act on *expectations* about the economy and government policy as much as they do on present-day policies or economic indicators' (McNamara 1998: 16, Woolley et al. 1989). And, in the 1978 words of Sir Douglas Wass, former British Permanent Secretary to the Treasury (Quoted in Hall 1992: 103): 'If markets take the view that policies pursued by a particular country are likely to damage assets held in that country or in that country's currency, they are likely to behave in ways which can actually enforce a policy change.' In a way we could argue that market behaviour has become interactive with the political elite as government actions generate immediate responses in the currency market. Every action taken by politicians can be gauged by the development of interest rates, exchange rates etc. (Hinnfors and Pierre 1998). As a token of this interaction Göran Persson's smiling, poisonous, remark during the 2002 election campaign that the non-socialist alternative economic manifesto proposals did not go down well with the international markets is a perhaps anecdotal but telling point.

Long into the post-war years the pace of market operation was comparatively slow and gave some leeway for politicians to act according to comparatively stable plans. The relatively wide scope for forward planning contributed to lend an air of force to the politicians. The daily fighting within the social liberal framework further strengthened voter legitimacy. This fighting allowed the parties to emphasise their ideological foundations and make party cleavages visible to the voters.

With money shuffled all around the globe at the touch of a button, the time for 'allocating time' is now down to a minimum (Bauer et al. 1973: 408ff; Bergström 1987) with simply no time for manoeuvring in the event of a crisis. Instead predictability and unequivocal postures will be necessary policy-making virtues.

A number of influential works emphasise the importance of new ideas as essential triggers of change in political behaviour. Many studies point to the fact that certain structural changes cause disillusionment among political leaders about how their policies work. Suddenly an expansionary policy does not yield the expected reduction in unemployment or an exchange rate adjustment fails to deliver currency stability and so on. When such disillusionment is linked to the availability of new ideas on the 'ideas market', policy change is likely to occur (for an excellent overview, see Berman 2000).

Two prime examples of this tradition are Peter Hall (1992) and Mark McGann Blyth (1999). However, while both authors provide ample data on a sudden outburst of new international ideas on economic policy making in the 1970s as produced by think-tanks, the media etc. we have difficulty explaining why the British Labour Government already in 1966–67 began to introduce decidedly non-Keynesian elements in its economic policy. The Government chose to introduce cut packages, postpone reform and do everything it could to restore confidence with international currency dealers (Shaw 1996: 94 ff.). What is more, the Labour Party definitely was in favour of the market economy, probably more so in the 1960s than in the 1980s. If anything it appears that new ideas came after the policies rather than the other way round.

As 'central to [the] popularization in Britain' of monetarist ideas, Peter Hall points to the media, which ferociously 'took up monetarist issues during the 1970s' (Hall 1992: 105). But we still cannot explain the fact that as early as in a 1975 speech to the National Union of Mineworkers, Prime Minister Harold Wilson verbalised the new route (which had been practised already in 1966–67) when he claimed that 'it is not a question to-day . . . of choosing between inflation and unemployment. Inflation is causing unemployment' (Wilson 1979: 267f., quoted in Thompson 1996: 236). This speech on the need for fundamental changes in economic policy was held before rather than after media attention rose. Next year, at the 1976 Labour Party Congress, the new Labour leader James Callaghan (Callaghan 1987: 426) was equally clear:

We used to think that you could spend your way out of a recession, and increase employment by cutting taxes and boosting government expenditure. I tell you in all candour that that option no longer exists, and in so far as it ever did exist, it only worked on each occasion since the war by injecting a bigger dose of inflation into the economy, followed by a higher level of unemployment as a next step.

Indirectly Callaghan actually opens up here for a view that even though certain market friendly elements may be part of the Labour Party's economic policy perhaps there was never an option to act differently. Let us also remind ourselves of the 1966 Labour Party election manifesto which echoes Wilson's and Callaghan's words: 'The weapon specially fashioned for this attack is the policy for productivity, prices and incomes, which forms an essential part of the National Plan. Without such a policy it is impossible either to keep exports competitive or to check rising prices at home. The alternative, in fact, is a return to the dreary cycle of inflation followed by deflation and unemployment' (Labour 1966). Apart from the socialist-sounding term 'the National Plan', the manifesto is, in fact, putting forward a basic view about letting the market have its way. There is an international capitalist system out there and keeping 'exports competitive' entails nothing else than playing according to the rules of that system.

As for Sweden, in his study of Swedish Social Democracy (SAP), McGann Blyth presents an abundance of evidence that conservative think-tanks, business organisations, the media etc. flooded the Swedish ideas market with neo-liberal elements during the 1980s and 1990s. Again, timing becomes a problem. Already in 1982, just after the come-back SAP Government had devalued the *krona* and launched the highly disputed so called wage-earners' funds (albeit in a much diluted form compared to original blue prints; see Pontusson 1992: 186ff.), Finance Minister Kjell-Olof Feldt began the road to what had been done in the UK some eleven years before: Interest rate and currency deregulations (Hall 1992 101; Brodin 1995; Brodin 1996; Johansson 1996; McGann Blyth 1999: 444ff., 456ff.).

Even though McGann Blyth constantly refers to the SAP's adherence to basic tenets of the welfare state he fails to draw the conclusion that maybe in the end the ideas from organised and politicised business and right-wing think tanks were not as relentless and powerful as he pictures them to be. The Swedish confederation of employers (SAF) may have declared the Swedish model dead, dubbed itself 'the driving force in changing the system' and 'spelled out a detailed plan for the complete privatization of the welfare state by the turn of the century' (Pestoff 1992: 153) but it actually failed completely in this task. The SAP's ideological change was more limited than McGann Blyth wants us to believe.

Hall suggests that in the UK 'many Conservatives began to show interest in monetarism [towards the end of the 1970s] as a coherent standpoint from which to attack the Labour Government's lackluster economic policies. They faced strong institutional incentives to pick up and press the alternative economic doctrine.' This rendering may hold some truth, but it still leaves us in doubt over the theoretical implications of Hall's suggestion.

Since the Labour Party under both Harold Wilson and James Callaghan turned important elements of the Labour Party's economic policy in a decidedly monetarist direction as early as 1966–67 and even more so in 1975 one can hardly regard Conservative monetarism as a truly alternative doctrine to Labour monetarism. Hall's statement might be applicable to the Labour Party's 1979–83 U-turn back down the more familiar socialist planning lane, but we have difficulty explaining why Labour began the journey back to monetarism a few years later.

Commenting on the brief 1974–75 period of expansionary policies of the British Labour party, Peter Hall (1992: 100) claims that they 'were largely a response to the power of organized labor'. However, only a year later 'it was the power of finance capital, working through the financial markets, that rose dramatically' (Hall 1992: 100). Is such a collapse for the unions really plausible given what we know of the 1979 'winter of discontent' when labour unrest literally threw the Labour Government out of office?

Bo Rothstein explains the failure of the SAP to abandon the welfare state in the 1990s and enforce ever bigger cuts on the Government's budget as the result of voters' resistance (Rothstein 1992, see McGann Blyth 1999: 484.). But if free market ideas were so powerful it is strange that they should falter in front of the voters. Wouldn't an equally plausible conclusion be that the SAP's ideological change was not so far-reaching after all? For a dissenting view on the thrust of neo-liberalism within the SAP, see Steinmo (2003: 39) who claims that, '[a]t first it appeared that the Socialists had accepted the basic neoliberal logic as they [1994–] began cutting back several social welfare policies. But careful analysis of these policies suggests that, rather than slashing programmes wholesale, most of the reductions were in fact designed to make them more fiscally reasonable and remove some of the opportunities for abuse that had been created earlier by the stunning generosity of these policies.'

The new policy environment poses challenges to social democracy to the extent that some question even its status as a surviving species. Jonathon Moses' (1998: 125) view that 'the defining characteristic of social democratic governance . . . [is] defined by the relative immobility of capital. . . . [R]eferences to social democracy . . . should assume a condition of managed capital flows' is in essence tantamount to saying that social democracy does not exist any longer since capital is indeed freely mobile. Moses is, of course, entitled to express this point. However, the argument borders to the absurd when we consider earlier periods of the twentieth century when capital was almost as mobile as today (see Hirst and Thompson 1996: Chapters 1–3). Few have questioned the existence of social democracy during those days. On the other hand, if we really were to apply Moses's criterion we would indeed have approached the sensitive meaning of socialism. Power over the free flow of capital is beginning to sound like a version of socialism.

But whether capital was ever immobile even during the Golden Age is a moot point. As Notermans (2000: 219) points out, '[e]xchange regulations were never tight enough, however, to prevent large-scale financial flows like the ones that occurred at the time of the Swedish elections of 1982.' In such an interpretation the era of social democracy in Jonathon Moses's rendering of capital mobility is pushed even further backwards in history. Perhaps there is some common ground possible in the view that I have been offering in this book: Social democrats accept the market economy. Did an alternative view ever exist?

Perhaps national economic independence was never a real alternative. 'National autonomy in economic policy enjoyed by some States after 1945 was heavily dependent on the existence of a system of international economic institutions and politics underwritten by the most powerful, the USA' (Hirst 2000: 23). Other authors take the opposite stance by underlining that 'results call for a substantial scaling back and qualification of arguments about new domestic constraints imposed by globalisation' (Garrett 1997). Thus social democratic politics would still be possible, and indeed practiced, in many countries – at least social democratic policies in the more low-key version of focusing on the welfare state with goals about relieving some of the hardships for poor people and backed up by tax-based resources (see Swank 1997). Both arguments emphasise stability – the one stable dependency, the other stable independence.

The prospect that globalisation undermines democracy is grim indeed. However, with Gösta Esping-Andersen we may ask ourselves whether Keynesianism in one country was ever possible. Moreover, Scandinavia and Germany are among the most open economies in the world and still managed to develop the most advanced welfare states in the world. Less ambitious welfare states have instead tended to develop in more protected economies, such as the United States and Australia (Esping-Andersen 1996: 257).

Likewise, in a recent comparison of effects from globalisation on different countries, Kitschelt et al. (1999) show that while changes within the so-called 'Business-coordinated market economies' (CME; to which Sweden belongs) and 'Liberal market economies' (LME; to which Britain belongs) has occurred, the 'European CMEs as a group are extremely unlikely to converge on the Anglo-American LME pattern' (Kitschelt et al. 1999: 451). So ideology-conversion does not seem to be necessary and again conclusions on stability alongside change seem warranted.

While on any account it is still fair to claim that some environmental requirements for change have been present in both countries it remains an open question whether the two Parties have indeed made small, medium or extensive formal policy changes. At face value it appears they have been very different in their willingness to seize the opportunity to change. The Labour Party's policies have seemingly been very jerky, leaving and re-entering Keynesianism/planning more than once while their Swedish sibling Party's policies have proceeded more hesitantly.

Given a view that the degrees of freedom within the global economy have indeed not changed dramatically over the years it is less surprising that social democrats keep their market ideology stable. What counts, then, is not so much adapting to iron laws of surrounding, and changing, economic markets, as sheer political will.

The Parties have actually formulated something they desire. This assertion could of course be moulded somewhat differently. Although the global economy has not changed in a more relentlessly forceful direction it was always more or less around to set the terms for any country. So, if we sober up for a while it will be prudent to admit that in this case there might be less ideological manoeuvring room for the parties. The ubiquitous market is difficult for any party to get around. It always was and perhaps that is the reason why these Parties actually have decided to live with it rather than replacing it.

Ideologies do not come by the dozen. They are carefully developed, calculated and thought over. Day-to-day policies may change, sometimes dramatically, in order to fulfil ideological goals, but apparently ideologies themselves are kept more stable than is sometimes expected. The degree of stability that we have found for the SAP and Labour is of a magnitude that makes us believe that even though the market's conditions set very narrow limits for the Parties it would be premature to deduce that their ideologies were in any way forced upon them. There is of course an element of accepting the unavoidable but the stability tells a different story. That is if the market's position and way of functioning are unavoidable. The answer to that question is, no doubt, a highly disputed matter. I do not intend to force the reader to accept such a view; my intention is only to draw the attention to the fact that the Parties appear to have come to the conclusion that within certain limits the market economy as such is something, which has come to stay.

Apparently the Parties actually feel rather comfortable with their ideological positions. The real battle about the market economy was fought in the first decades of the twentieth century. The clash between Soviet communism and social democracy was not only about democracy. For a couple of decades there lingered the dream of a peaceful, reformist and democratic way to socialism in the sense that an alternative future economic system could at least be contemplated. Post-World War II most traces of that future alternative economic model were gone. The results of this book show that in 1965, the supposedly apex for the Golden Age of Social Democracy, two of the most traditionalist and well-organised social democratic parties in the world, the SAP and Labour, were deeply rooted in the market economy. In that respect the 2006 situation is not any different.

To the extent that we have detected change it is not from a less market-friendly position during the 1960s to a more friendly position today. Rather we have seen a development from a market-friendly stance in the 1960s to a somewhat less friendly position towards the early 1970s. Then back again in the late 1970s to a more clear-cut understanding of the market's requirements (a little less so in the SAP). In the early 1980s radicalisation erupted once more and then back again to the present more market-friendly position.

The radicalisation of the 1970s should neither be underestimated nor overrated. Both Parties did indeed start entertaining ideas about reforming society. Even though the reform proposals were never intended to embark upon the road to socialism they were playing with the thought of reforming democratic socialism. With the welfare state in place, more so in Sweden than in Britain but even there the Beveridge plan had forever changed the British political landscape with the promise to challenge the 'warfare states' with a 'welfare state', it was somehow natural to consider the character of the next step. Reformist parties have an inner drive for reform. They have to move on and on and on. Deliver or die.

The fact that in spite of the 'inner logic' to look for new brave solutions post-welfare state reforms, so few real ideological innovations emerged proves the point that the social democratic leaders actually felt they had something to defend. They had once taken the fight with communism and had carved out a section for themselves on the ideological left-right scale, which was unequivocally social democratic. At times the leaders allowed, endorsed even, debate about stretching the limits of what would be plausible inside the general confines of the ideology but as soon as the debate came perilously close to radical economic alternatives the leaders pulled the emergency brake. They really had something to defend and that was 'capitalism with a human face'. Whether such a dream can ever be fully realised is a moot point. Whether social democracy is a unique force in this quest is equally debatable, but in practice that is what social democracy has been fighting for.

If for a moment we recall the classifying tools introduced in Chapter 2 we may conclude that 'State only' was never even close to being represented in the documents studied. This observation includes the radical debate outside of the immediate leadership in Labour after the 1979 election defeat. The State as the only arbiter of how to distribute goods and services was never ever an option. More or less the same goes for the less strict category about 'State complemented by market'. To correspond to this category the ideology would have had to suggest that the very major part of the economy, and of social life generally, should rest in the hands of the State with only a few sectors left to the market economy. Nothing of the kind emerges from the party documents. Perhaps some radical parts of the Labour Party approached this category in 1974 and in 1983. Proposals about nationalising twenty-five leading sectors of the economy were ambitious but would probably still have let the brunt of the economy remain inside the market economy.

'State corrected by market', the third category in the State–market continuum, has been equally absent in the documents, at least when it comes to radical proposals. In a way, public–private partnerships would correspond to this category. In a sense that would mean a more 'leftist' way of dealing with the market than that implied by the next category ('market corrected by State'), and indeed claimed by the critics of the proposals. On the other hand the context of public–private partnership solutions has been that former public-sector arrangements have been transformed into PPP arrangements rather than former private arrangements having been transformed into PPP solutions. In that context PPP correspond to a reduction of State interference. In another context, where PPP had been introduced as a way of bringing already private hospitals (or other institutions) in the direction of State involvement, the PPPs would have corresponded to increased State interference over the economy. On these grounds it is fair to interpret the recent UK PPP experiments as a development in the direction of 'private' rather than 'State'.

The 'market corrected by State' category always takes centre stage in the documents with a wide selection of public sector measures designed to correct the market. During the radicalised periods a number of measures corresponding to the fifth category, 'market complemented by State', were pondered though they seldom left the blueprint stage. At no stage have we encountered the last category 'market only' (Bengtsson 1995: 32ff). Overall our conclusion is that of stability with a few deviations, sometimes in a slightly 'leftist' direction, sometimes in a more 'rightist' spirit.

Given the constant emphasis in the documents on programmes, proposals etc. which correspond to the 'market corrected by the State' category we have reason for some self-criticism. As it turned out this category proved to be too wide to be entirely satisfactory. A couple of sub-categories, which would have helped us to provide a more refined view of types of market-correction, would have been fruitful.

The constant unwillingness to address radical economic alternatives gives us reason to ponder for a moment the relationship between democracy and economic system. Apparently the social democratic worldview presupposes a close correlation between the two concepts. Although the Parties want to stay clear from both communism and capitalism it is obvious that they are closer to capitalism than communism. Capitalism in its pure form is of course far from social democratic ideology – and indeed far from several other major political movements. But capitalism is a wide concept. In a broader sense capitalism is a system where the preliminary allocation of values in society rests on the market principle but where the final allocation is corrected by political measures. Social democracy has been willing to accept quite a number of politically decided corrections but has always stood clear of eliminating the market's function as the preliminary value allocating agent.

Could it be that the results are mere artefacts due to unsuitable data material? This is a methodological point of major importance and something, which always has to be considered. Would alternative data point in an altogether different direction? Academic activity is about making choices. We cannot, and should not, feel obliged to take in everything. The real world is unfathomable and we have to make wise choices so that we do not get bogged down in the complex world. It is our job to provide a specific approach where we offer a view about reality. On the other hand we cannot hide behind the mantra that we have to choose. We must choose wisely.

In my case I have chosen data about standpoints, which the Party leadership is willing to endorse authoritatively. All my documents are central to the Parties' official ideologies – my central object of this study. Occasionally I have let the reader get a feeling of the continuing ideological struggle, which almost constantly rages on outside the official standpoints. Hardly a day passes by without challenging views about the future of the parties. The struggle is aiming at changing the Parties' ideological direction and can, from time to time, be cutting. Even so, it would have been a mistake to let the struggle as such function as evidence of official ideology. At times, and especially in the Labour Party, it might have been the case that the leadership's ideological position actually represented a minority of the 'Party' in a wider sense of the word. When opposing groups fight it out the leadership will have to reconcile the opposing camps.

The success of the never-ending reconciling process indicates a number of things. The first observation is that party leaderships probably enjoy rather powerful tools for keeping the Party ship on course. In spite of the fact that we have detected several deviating opinions about the Party ideology (and this is so even though we have primarily aimed at the leadership; the number of rebellions is probably far greater than those identified here) they have been unable to rock the boat. Under the surface of this stability must lay tactics and measures where the party leaderships have been forced to show their mettle rather than their talent for nice compromises. To some extent parties have to be governed from above especially when the ideological foundations of the party are concerned. There simply has to be some kind of continuity. Another version of this conclusion would be that party leaders actually have to be masters in the art of compromise. Every attempt at changing the fundamental tenets, which guide the party, will meet with opposition. The opposition inside the Labour Party during the left's 1979–83 attack is a telling example. Even though the Party leaders failed to keep the party together when several leading characters deserted the party to form the Social Democratic Labour Party the faithful who remained in the Party fold had to strike compromises. As the documents have revealed, the binding, authoritative Party documents never went as far as the radical wing would have preferred (and even the radical proposals were surprisingly vague on the role of the market). The same struggle between opposing camps is evident in the SAP. The wage-earners' funds were never loved by the whole Party. Most of the leaders dreaded the proposals. The final outcome was as clear-cut an example of a compromise as one could get.

The second observation is about the inherent conservatism, which characterises the Party ideologies. Apparently the old goals provide a tremendous preservative effect. There is an inherent bias in favour of keeping the ideological status quo. So many have invested so much effort.

The third observation is derived from the two first ones. One reason why the Party leaderships really seem to act as defenders of the old goals and why the ideologies are so stable would probably be because the ideologies actually tell us something about the inner soul of the Parties. They are not merely convenient labels, which can be used at one's leisure. They are the result of decades of debate and positioning and as such powerful symbols of the parties and powerful vehicles for the development of day-to-day political policies.

Fourthly we may conclude that ideologies are far from static and inflexible phenomena. Within the all-embracing framework of market capitalism acceptance combined with extensive catalogues of State/politics-determined corrections, there is wide scope for change. The face of correction is different compared with what was used during the Golden Age. Over the years a number of alterations have taken place and ideologies emerge as more pliable and less cut in stone than we might expect. But this variation is still superficial in the context of the more universal stability. Although the general framework is much the same these adjustments have probably repelled certain voters and attracted others.

Whether the changes are deep enough to merit conclusions about more profound changes is a question of interpretation. Academic work is always about providing tools for interpretation. In my view the core ideological goals have remained stable within SAP and Labour, but some of the means have changed.

A look through a set of partly different interpretative glasses might suggest that most of the means have indeed been roughly the same – public services, welfare state – but the goals have changed. Perhaps the 1960s Party ideologues really believed that in the end the welfare state would transform the society into a social-ist Eden. I feel we have every ground to claim they were wrong but if they were convinced it is still fair to accept that the Parties' goals have changed. In this, alter-native, version, the means have overtaken the goals in the sense that the Parties have adjusted their goals to a set of means, which everyone could agree about.

It is always extremely difficult to decide unequivocally which groups that should be included in the notion of 'Party' and different theoretical tasks will need differ-ent definitions. The leadership's task is to harmonise the various tendencies and I have thought it wise to be very clear on this point; in this book 'Party views' equals the leadership's views. Any other methodological stance would risk the concept of party changing meaning during the journey from the book's first to its last page.

A plausible explanation for the Labour/SAP differences could be differing political clout. One such account is suggested by Garrett (1993: 2) that 'only governments that are relatively secure in office ... can assume the longer-term time horizon necessary successfully to engage in the politics of structural change.' Superficially Garrett's view is not borne out by Labour and SAP actions as most changes took place when the parties were either in opposition (Labour) or in a weak government position (the SAP). Anyway, accepting the market as an actor with mighty political consequences is nothing new to the parties.

Some differences between the parties do exist in the sense that the Swedish Party appears to be much more confident about its strength as a governing party, which is rather paradoxical given the British political system's majority-style as opposed to the Swedish system, with its decidedly more consensus-minded political culture (Lijphart 1999). British governments almost invariably rule from a position, which formally gives them the confidence of stable parliamentary majorities. Even so the Swedish Social Democrats have been in office a stunning 85 per cent of the time since World War II, while Labour's time-share has only been about 40 per cent.

The view about government security works two ways. When in office Labour is formally secure by means of seat-majorities. But perhaps Labour has felt less con-fident about the Party's governing future than has been the case with the SAP. The SAP always has to count on the infidelity of coalition and cooperation partners but appears to have mastered that type of basic insecurity to the extent that the Party is confident it will be able to rule forever. Over the years the SAP have become masters of strategies for causing rifts in the non-socialist camp. Repeated resort to different jumping majorities where the SAP strikes deals with first one of the non-socialist parties, then with a second, then with a third has become a standard ingredient in the relationship between the parties (Särlvik 1983; Särlvik 2002). Through the fact that the Swedish Party encounters a non-socialist group of oppo-nents who is deeply split along several ideological dimensions, such confidence of a well-organised major party is easy to understand. The Labour Party has to fight a far more hard-boiled opponent, which can concentrate its efforts on criticising the Labour Party without at the same time having to deal with competing non-socialist parties. Most would probably agree to this description without being disrespectful of the British Liberal Party.

The differences in confidence may contribute to explain why the Swedish Party has been following a slightly more stable ideological trajectory than the British sibling party. There appears to have been less need for wild experimentation neither in a left nor in a right direction. Stop-go politics as a part of ideological orientation has been rare.

Paradoxically, the market – in the sense of flesh and blood political actors – is much less present today in Swedish organised political networks. The once so firm corporatist structures have largely been abandoned as of the 1990s, though informal arrangements reminiscent of the old formalised system still linger on (Uhrwing 2001). Thus the Swedish model has changed. Not so long ago it actually included economic actors within the political structures. That is what traditional corporatism is all about. In a sense the market was an institutionalised political actor invited to the authoritative decision-making by the social democrats. On the other hand it was possible to keep an eye on at least some of the market actors while they were sitting around the same table. That potential is now gone and the market actors are symbolically left outside of formal politics.

The same retreat from corporatism is found in New Labour, though perhaps much more outspokenly so than in Sweden. To the extent that there was ever a true corporatist relationship between government, employers and employees in the UK it is now ended. In September 1999, Tony Blair asserted that 'in many ways we have a better, clearer relationship than ever before between trade unions and Labour . . . You run the unions. We run the government. We will never confuse the two again' (Address to the TUC Annual Congress, quoted in Glyn and Wood 2001: 6). Apparently New Labour does not want to engage in setting wage bargaining restraints (a view shared by the SAP, which has left bargaining to unions and employers' organisations). Apart from pious admonitions to employers and unions to show restraint and responsibility no real coordination takes place between the 'social partners.' On the other hand, the experiences from 'the winter of discontent' do not necessarily strengthen the position of those who demand tighter coordination. The reactions to the Callaghan Government's modest suggestion that wage increases were to stay below 5 per cent were not exactly framed in an understanding, corporatist atmosphere. The fact is that a stable pattern of give and take controlled through formalised continuous negotiations, between employer and employee organisations 'failed to evolve' (Shaw 2002: 10). How difficult this failure was to predict becomes clear in Lewis Minkin's 'Epilogue' to his 1978 *The Labour Party Conference*. Even though Minkin is very cautious and emphasises that 'the distribution of power and authority within the Party . . . [is] so complex and the future contours of factional and institutional alignment so uncertain' (Minkin 1978: 350) he appears confident in the prospects of reconciling unions and Party. James Callaghan, Minkin claims, 'understands the trade union connection, is on good terms with the union leaders and also has a good relationship with the General Secretary, the National Agent's Department and the Conference Arrangements Committee' (Minkin 1978: 350). Less than a year later the Labour

Government was thrown out of office as a consequence of one of the worst Labour movement infightings since the War.

Once again we will also have to remember the differing Swedish and British contexts. More or less centralised wage bargaining was always a distinctive characteristic of the Swedish model (Kjellberg 2002) but this part of the corporatist process never included the government. The government has always been extremely clear about the division of labour. Wages are not set by politicians but through negotiations between employers and employees via their organisations. The Swedish Government was as unable to cap the record wage increases in the middle of the 1970s as the UK Government was. Swedish unions and employers are vastly better organised with far higher membership rates than the UK equivalents and this is a fact, which goes back in history long before New Labour. New Labour appears to be happy about the arrangements, which might be a novelty. The rest of the British labour movement apparently took this independent position long ago. It might prove fatal to the social democratic project but this independency is something for which other forces than the present Party and union leaderships ought to take responsibility.

The overall repercussions from the market's renewed formal freedom to affect politicians are still somewhat opaque. In the public mind its influence is certainly felt to be illegitimately high.[11] Occasionally politicians themselves express despair after seemingly hostile market actions. During the darker days of Swedish budgets in the red, Mr Persson, the present Swedish Prime Minister repeatedly emphasised that those in debt are not free (Persson 1997). The market's status as an authoritatively binding actor was driven home by the *Financial Times* when commenting that 'the financial markets are likely to approve the choice of Mr. Persson [for Prime Minister] who has won their confidence' (*Financial Times*, 6 December 1995).

However, whether playing together with the politicians actually served as a bridle against anti-social policies by market actors is hard to prove. The politicians certainly hoped corporatism would lead to moderation and the decorporatisation has provided political rhetoric at least with a new context.

The market as a political actor is hardly any news – rather the political presence has become less institutionalised. What is new is the character of the acting. Social democracy has always invited the market but the terms have changed. With Charles Lindblom (1977: 8), we may claim that 'much of politics is economics, and most of economics is also politics'. Bewildering as the globalisation literature is we are able to make one general conclusion. Market and politics were always entangled. To claim that market influence over politics is a new phenomenon would be jumping to conclusions. As far as industrialisation goes back, British and Swedish economies have been exposed to stern international conditions (Gamble 1994; Hansson 1990; Pilkington 1998). Rather than ring the knell for political manoeuvrability it would be more to the point to claim that political elites now operate in changing decision-making contexts.

This view tacitly presupposes that 'market influence on domestic political decision making is more contextual and contingent on a fortuitous (from the point of view of market actors) state of circumstances, some of which appear to be reasonably easily manipulated by domestic political institutions' (Hinnfors and Pierre 1997: 115). Market influence is contingent on several political and economic circumstances rather than fixed. Certain configurations of such circumstances create potential for speculation while other configurations don't. To some degree the nation-State can control these factors, by exercising strict fiscal and budgetary policies, by creating institutional preconditions for stable political leadership, by yielding autonomy to institutions with key positions in the economy from elected officials and by unambiguously and with determination follow through economic policy (Hinnfors and Pierre: 115).

Forcing the market into submission was never really even a remote desire. The political consequences of such a policy would have been unforeseeable and the parties seem to readily accept this for a fact. Such acceptance does not mean anti-market rhetoric has been absent. On the contrary, but rather than pointing in the direction of abolishing the market economy or denying its positive effects, the rhetoric appears to have been a means to emphasising the need for a constant flow of politically induced and implemented corrections to the market economy's outcomes. At the same time the market economy has been regarded as the only safe provider of means to the welfare state.

Both parties have stood for reaping the harvests produced by the market economy's apparently superior efficiency while at the same time never forgetting about capitalism's inner drive to cause misery to those who won't make it in the competitive race. Market-correction appears to be as vivid an element in the parties' ideologies as always. Some of the means have changed but given the general research definitions about what constitutes social democracy these means have always staid within fairly narrow limits. This is not to say that crises would never shake the politicians' ability to achieve anything. However, '[w]ithout over-interpreting the data, it appears as if the political elite interpreted the economic recovery as so stable and sustained that renewed party conflict would not jeopardise the economy. Put slightly differently, the political parties seem to be confident that there is now some latitude for the nation-State, i.e. that more than one economic policy is conceivable and that the consensus, which was integral to the crisis management choked political debate. Thus the nation-State perspective holds at least as much true as the globalisation perspective' (Hinnfors and Pierre 1997: 114f.).

Whichever their position has been, the claim here is that the SAP's and Labour's solution to the dilemma of balancing market and State power has been through keeping the acceptance of the market economy stable while changing some of the means of correcting the market. In short, they have been pragmatic.

Note

1   Swedish public opinion in 1997 on the actual and legitimate extent of 'the market's influence over the Swedish society' was on average 7.3 (actual influence on a scale measured from 0 'very limited' – 10 'very extensive'; 1995/1996: 7.3/7.3) and 4.6 (legitimate influence on a scale measured from 0 'very limited' – 10 'very extensive'; 1995/1996: 4.4/4.5; Hinnfors 1997: 213).

References

Adler-Karlsson, G. (1967) *Funktionssocialism: ett alternativ till konmmunism och kapitalism* [Functional Socialism. An Alternative to Communism and Capitalism]. Stockholm: Prisma.

Ahlqvist, B. and L. Engqvist (1984) *Samtal med Feldt* [Talks With Feldt]. Stockholm: Tiden.

Alcock, P. (1992) 'The Labour Party and the welfare state', in Smith, M. J. and J. Spear (eds) *The Changing Labour Party*. London: Routledge.

Alsterdal, A. (1967) *Samtal med Tage Erlander mellan två val* [Talks with Tage Erlander Between Two Elections]. Stockholm: Tiden.

Annesley, C. and A. Gamble (2004) 'Economic and welfare policy', in Ludlam, S. and M. J. Smith (eds) *Governing as New Labour. Policy and Politics under Blair*. Houndmills: Palgrave.

Bauer, A. R., de Sola Poole, I. and L. A. Dexter, (1973) *American Business and Public Policy. The Politics of Foreign Trade*. Chicago: Aldine, Atherton, Inc.

Beckerman, W. (1972a) 'Industrial policy', in W. Beckerman (ed.) *The Labour Government's Economic Record: 1964–1970*. London: Duckworth.

Beckerman, W. (ed.) (1972b) *The Labour Government's Economic Record: 1964–1970*. London: Duckworth.

Bengtsson, B. (1995) *Bostaden – Välfärdsstatens marknadsvara* [Housing – Market Commodity of the Welfare state]. Uppsala: Acta Universitatis Upsaliensis.

Bennett, L. and E. Åsard (1997) *Democracy and the Marketplace of Ideas: Communication and Government in Sweden and the United States*. Cambridge: Cambridge University Press.

Bergström, H. (1987) *Rivstart* [Flying Start]. Stockholm: Tiden.

Berman, S. (1998) *The Social Democratic Moment. Ideas and Politics in the Making of Interwar Europe*. Cambridge, MA and London: Harvard University Press.

Berman, S. (2000) 'Ideas, norms and culture in political analysis', Department of Political Science, Göteborg University, mimeo version.

Berman, S. (2003) The roots and rationale of social democracy, *Social Philosophy and Policy Foundation*.

Bevir, M. and D. O'Brien (2001) 'New Labour and the public sector in Britain', *Public Administration Review*, Vol. 61 No. 5.

Blair, T. (1997) Speech 2 June 1997, at the Aylesbury Estate, Southwark, London.

Blair, T. (1999) Labour Party Conference speech, Bournemouth, 28 September 1999, http://labour.org.uk/lp/new/labour/labour.wwv_main.main?p_language=usandp_cornerid=1200.

Blair, T. (2000) Labour Party Conference speech, Brighton, 26 September 2000, http://labour.org.uk/.

Blair, T. (2001) Speech 16 June 2001, http://number-10.gov.uk/news.asp?NewsId= 2305andSectionId=32.

Blair, T. (2003) Labour Party Conference speech, Bournemouth, 30 September 2003, http://politics.guardian.co.uk/labour2003/story/0,13803,1052843,00.html.

Blomqvist, P. and B. Rothstein (2000) *Välfärdsstatens nya ansikte. Demokrati och marknadsreformer inom den offentliga sektorn* [The New Face of the Welfare state. Democracy and Market Reform in the Public Sector]. Stockholm: Agora.

Blyth, M. (2002) *Great Transformations. Economic Ideas and Institutional Change in The Twentieth Century.* Cambridge: Cambridge University Press.

Boréus, K. (1994) *Högervåg. Nyliberalism och kampen om språket i svensk offentlig debatt 1969–1989* [Tide from the Right. Neo-Liberalism and the Battle for the Discourse in 1969–1989 Swedish Public Debate]. Stockholm: Tiden.

Braybrooke, D. and C. Lindblom (1970) *A Strategy of Decision.* Glencoe, Illinois: The Free Press.

Brewer, M., Goodman, A., Mack, M., Shaw, J. and A. Shepherd (2002) *Poverty and Inequality in Britain: 2004.* Institute of Fiscal Studies.

Brodin, S. (1995) 'Valutamarknaden avregleras. En illustration av interaktionen mellan politik och ekonomi utifrån en makroteoretisk systemmodell' [Deregulating the Currency Market. An Illustration of the Interaction Between Politics and Economics through a Macro Theory System Model], Department of Political Science, Göteborg University, mimeo version.

Brodin, S. (1996) 'Valutareglering eller inte? En fallstudie av intresseorganisationers intresseartikulering vid avregleringen av valutamarknaden' [Currency Deregulation Or Not? A Case Study on Interest Organisations' Interest Articulation Concerning the Deregulation of the Currency Market], Department of Political Science, Göteborg University, mimeo version.

Brown, G. (1999) Labour Party Conference speech, Bournemouth, 27 September 1999, http://labour.org.uk/lp/new/labour/labour.wwv_main.main?p_language=usandp_ cornerid =1200.

Brown, G. (2000) Speech at the London School of Economics, 8 May 2000.

Brown, G. (2004) Labour Party spring conference speech, Manchester, 12 March 2004.

Budge, I. (1999) 'Party policy and ideology: Reversing the 1950s?' in Evans, G. and P. Norris (eds) *Critical Elections. British Parties and Voters in Long-Term Perspective.* London: Sage Publications.

Callaghan, J. (1987) *Time and Chance.* London: Collins.

Castles, F. (1978) *The Social Democratic Image of Society.* London: Routledge and Kegan Paul.

Coates, D. (1980) *Labour in Power. A Study of the Labour Government 1974–1979.* London: Longman.

Coates, D. (2000) 'New Labour's industrial and employment policy', in Coates, D. and P. Lawler (eds) *New Labour in Power.* Manchester: Manchester University Press.

Coates, D. (2001) 'Capitalist models and social democracy: The case of New Labour', *British Journal of Politics and International Relations*, Vol. 3 No. 3.

Coates, D. and P. Lawler (eds) (2000) *New Labour in Power.* Manchester: Manchester University Press.

Cortell, A. P. and S. Peterson (1999) 'Altered states: Explaining domestic institutional change', *British Journal of Political Science*, Vol. 29 No. 1.

Cronin, J. A. (2004) *New Labour's Pasts. The Labour Party and its Discontents*. Harlow: Pearson.

Crosland, A. (1956) *The Future of Socialism*. London: Jonathan Cape.

Crossman, R. (1972) Inside view: The Godkin Lectures at Harvard University. London: Jonathan Cape.

Crouch, C. (2000) 'The quiet continent: Religion and politics in Europe', in Marquand, D. and R. L. Nettler (eds) *Religion and Democracy*. Oxford: Blackwell.

DEA (Department of Economic Affairs) (1969) *The Task Ahead*. London: H.M.S.O.

Demker, M. (1997) 'Changing party ideology: Gaullist parties facing voters, leaders and competitors', *Party Politics*, Vol. 3 No. 3.

Douglas, R. D. (2004) 'Confrontational comrades: The British and Irish Labour Parties 1918–1951', Paper presented at the American Political Science Association, Chicago 2–5 September 2004.

Driver, S. and L. Martell (1998) *New Labour. Politics After Thatcherism*. Cambridge: Polity Press.

Driver, M. and L. Martell (2003) *Blair's Britain*. Cambridge: Polity.

Dunleavy, P. (1997) 'Introduction: "New times" in British politics', in Dunleavy, P. et al. (eds) *Developments in British Politics*. London: Macmillan Press.

Durant, R. and P. Diehl (1989) 'Agendas, alternatives, and public policy: Lessons from the U.S. foreign policy arena', *Journal of Public Policy*, Vol. 9 No. 3.

Easton, D. (1979) *A Framework for Political Analysis*. Chicago: The University of Chicago Press.

Eduards, M. (2002) *Förbjuden handling: om kvinnors organisering och feministisk teori* [Forbidden Acts: On Female Organising and Feminist Theory]. Malmö: Liber Ekonomi.

Elvander, N. (1972) *Svensk skattepolitik 1945–1970* [Swedish Tax Politics 1945–1970]. Uppsala: Rabén and Sjögren.

Elvander, N. (1980) *Skandinavisk arbetarrörelse* [Scandinavian Labour Movement]. Vällingby: Publica.

Esping-Andersen, G. (1990) *The Three Worlds of Welfare Capitalism*. Cambridge: Polity Press.

Esping-Andersen, G. (1996) 'After the Golden Age? Welfare state dilemmas in a global economy', in Esping-Andersen, G. (ed.) *Welfare States in Transition. National Adaptations in Global Economies*. London: Sage.

Evans, G. , Heath, A. and C. Payne (1999) 'Class: Labour as a catch-all party?' in Evans, G. and P. Norris (eds) *Critical Elections. British Parties and Voters in Long-Term Perspective*. London: Sage Publications.

FAS (2002) *Fattigdom i välfärdsstaten* [Poverty in the Welfare state]. Stockholm: Alfa Print.

Feldt, K.-O. (1982) *Ett handfast och konkret program* [A Hands-On Concrete Programme]. Borås: Sjuhäradsbygdens tryckeri AB.

Feldt, K.-O. (1989) 'Vad skall vi göra med kapitalismen?' [What Shall we do with Capitalism?], *Tiden* Vol. 1 No 2.

Feldt, K.-O. (1991) *Alla dessa dagar* [All These Days]. Stockholm: Tiden.

Financial Times, 16 July 2001.

Financial Times, 24 September 2001.

Financial Times, 28 March 2002.

Financial Times, 18 April 2002.

Financial Times, 30 August 2003.

Fishman, N. (1996) 'Modernisation, moderation and the Labour tradition', in Perryman, M. (ed.) *The Blair Agenda*. London: Lawrence and Wishart.

Franklin, B. (2004) 'A Damascene conversion? New Labour and media relations', in Ludlam, S. and M. J. Smith (eds) *Governing as New Labour. Policy and Politics under Blair.* Houndmills, Palgrave.

Gamble, A (1992) 'The Labour Party and economic management', in Smith, M. J. and J. Spear (eds) *The Changing Labour Party.* London: Routledge.

Gamble, A. (1994) *Britain in Decline. Economic Policy, Political Strategy and the British State.* London: Macmillan Press.

Garme, C. (2001) *Newcomers to Power. How to Sit on Someone Else's Throne.* Uppsala: Acta Universitatis Upsaliensis.

Garrett, G. (1993) 'The politics of structural change', *Comparative Political Studies*, Vol. 25 No. 4, Internet version: http://ehostweb6.epnet.c...diesandfuzzyTerm=#FullText.

Garrett, G. (1997) *Partisan Politics in a Global Economy.* Cambridge University Press, mimeo version.

Geyer, R. (1997) 'Globalisation and the (non-) defence of the welfare state', *West European Politics*, Vol. 21 No. 3.

Geyer, R., Ingebritsen, C. and J. Moses (eds) (2000) *Globalization, Europeanization and the End of Scandinavian Social democracy?* London: Macmillan Press.

Giddens, A. (1998) *The Third Way. The Renewal of Social Democracy.* Cambridge: Polity Press.

Glennerster, H. (2001) 'Social policy', in Seldon, A. (ed.) *The Blair Effect. The Blair Government 1997–2001.* London: Little, Brown and Company.

Glyn, A. and S. Wood (2001) 'Economic policy under New Labour: How social democratic is the Blair Government?' *Political Quarterly*, Vol. 72 No. 1.

Goldstein, J. and R. O. Keohane (eds) (1993) *Ideas and Foreign Policy. Beliefs, Institutions, and Political Change.* Ithaca and London: Cornell University Press.

Goodhart (1965) PRO: EW24/93 Goodhart to MacDougall, 6 September 1965.

Gould, A. (1993) *Capitalist Welfare States.* New York: Longman.

Gould, A. (1996) 'Sweden: The last bastion of social democracy', in George, V. and P. Taylor-Gooby (eds) *European Welfare Policy. Squaring the Circle.* New York: St Martin's Press.

Gourevitch, P. (1986) *Politics in Hard Times. Comparative Responses to International Economic Crises.* Ithaca and London: Cornell University Press.

Gray, J. (1996) *After Social Democracy.* London: Demos.

Hadenius, A. (1981) *Spelet om skatten* [The Tax Game]. Lund: P A Norstedt & söners förlag.

Hadenius, A. (1983) 'The verification of motives', *Scandinavian Political Studies*, Vol. 6, New Series, No. 2.

Hall, P. (1984) *Governing the Economy. The Politics of State Intervention in Britain and France.* Cambridge: Polity Press.

Hall, P. (ed.) (1989) *The Political Power of Economic Ideas. Keynesianism across Nations.* Princeton: Princeton University Press.

Hall, P. A. (1992) 'The movement from Keynesianism to monetarism: Institutional analysis and British economic policy in the 1970s', in Steinmo, S. et al. (eds) *Structuring Politics. Historical Institutionalism in Comparative Analysis.* Cambridge: Cambridge University Press.

Hall, S. (2003) 'Labour's double-shuffle', *Soundings*, Vol. 24 No 3.

Harmel, R. and K. Janda (1994) 'An integrated theory of party goals and party change', *Journal of Theoretical Politics*, Vol. 6 No. 3.

Haseler, S. (1969) *The Gaitskellites.* London: Macmillan Press.

Hatfield, M. (1978) *The House the Left Built. Inside Labour Policy-Making, 1970–1975.* London: Victor Gollancz Ltd.

Hay, C. (1999) *The Political Economy of New Labour. Labouring Under False Pretences?* Manchester: Manchester University Press.

Hay, C. (2002) 'Globalisation, "EU-isation" and the space for social democratic alternatives: Pessimism of the intellect: A reply to Coates', *British Journal of Politics and International Relations,* Vol. 3 No. 3.

Heclo, H. and H. Madsen (1987) *Policy and Politics in Sweden. Principled Pragmatism.* Phildelphia: Temple University Press.

Hedborg, A. and R. Meidner (1984) *Folkhemsmodellen* [The People's Home Model]. Borås: Rabén & Sjögren, Tema Nova.

Heffernan, R. (2000) *New Labour and Thatcherism. Political Change in Britain.* London: Macmillan Press.

Herman, E. S. (1999) The threat of globalization', *New Politics,* Vol. 7 No. 2 (new series), Winter 1999.

Hibbs, D. (1987) *The Political Economy of Industrial Democracies.* Cambridge MA: Harvard University Press.

Hicks, A. and L. Kenworthy (2003) 'Varieties of welfare capitalism', *Socio-Economic Review,* Vol. 1 No 1.

Hinnfors, J. (1992) *Familjepolitik. Samhällsförändringar och partistrategier 1960–1990* [Family Politics. 1960–1990 Societal Changes and Party Strategies]. Stockholm: Almqwist & Wiksell International.

Hinnfors, J. (1995) 'Book review: Bostaden – välfärdsstatens marknadsvara' (Housing – Market Commodity of the Welfare state). Uppsala: Acta Universitatis Upsaliensis, 1995 Author, Bengtsson, B., *Scandinavian Housing and Planning Research,* Vol. 12 No. 3.

Hinnfors, J. (1997) 'EMU: Marknadens politik?' [EMU: Politics by the Market?], in Holmberg, S. and L. Weibull (eds), *Opinionssamhället* [The Opinion Society]. Göteborg: SOM-rapport 20, 1998.

Hinnfors, J. (1999) 'Stability through change: The pervasiveness of political ideas', *Journal of Public Policy,* Vol. 19 No. 3.

Hinnfors, J. and J. Pierre (1998) 'The politics of currency crises in Sweden: Policy choice in a globalised economy', *West European Politics,* Vol. 21 No. 3.

Hinnfors, J and E. Shaw (2004) 'New Labour Britain, SAP Sweden and the two dimensions of social democracy', Paper presented at the American Political Science Association, Chicago, 2–5 September 2004.

Hirdman, Y. (2002) 'The Importance of gender in the Swedish labour movement, or: A Swedish dilemma', Paper delivered for the Conference on The International Labour Movement on the Threshold of Two Centuries, Stockholm, 24–25 October 2002.

Hirst, P. and G. Thompson (1996) *Globalization in Question. The International Economy and the Possibility of Governance.* Cambridge: Polity Press.

Hirst, P. (2000) 'Democracy and governance', in Pierre, J. (ed.) *Debating Governance.* Oxford: Oxford University Press.

Hodgson, G. (1981) *Labour at the Crossroads.* Oxford: Martin Robertson.

Holland, S. (1975) *The Socialist Challenge.* London: Quartet Books.

Holmberg, S. and H. Oscarsson (2004) *Väljare. Svenskt väljarbeteende under 50 år* [Voters. Swedish Voting Behaviour During Fifty Years]. Stockholm: Norstedts Juridik.

Howell, C. (2000) 'Is there a third way for the party-union relationship? The industrial relations project of New Labour, 2000', Paper delivered for the Political Studies Association Conference 2000.

Huber, E. and J. D. Stephens (1998) 'Internationalization and the Social Democratic Model: Crisis and future prospects', *Comparative Political Studies,* Vol. 13 No. 3.

Huntington, N. and T. Bale (2002) 'New Labour: New Christian democracy?' *Political Quarterly*, Vol. 73 No. 1.

Ingebritsen, C. (2000) 'Europeanization and the Scandinavian model: Securing borders and defending monopolies', in Geyer, R. et al. (eds) *Globalization, Europeanization and the End of Scandinavian Social Democracy?* London: Macmillan Press.

Johansson, F. (1996) 'SAP avreglerar marknadsrekonomin' [SAP deregulating the Market Economy], Department of Political Science, Göteborg University, mimeo version.

Kapstein, E. (2000) 'Winners and losers in the global economy', *International Organization*, Vol. 54 No. 2.

Karlsson, B. (2001) Att handla neutralt. Sverige och den ekonomiska integrationen i Västeuropa 1948–1972 [Trading Neutrally. Sweden and the 1948–1972 Western Europe Economic Integration]. Göteborg: Kompendiet.

Karvonen, L. (1991) '"A nation of workers and peasants". Ideology and compromise in the interwar years', in Karvonen, L. and J. Sundberg (eds) *Social Democracy in Transition*. Aldershot: Dartmouth.

Karvonen, L. and J. Sundberg (1991) 'Introduction: Social democracy old and new', in Karvonen, L. and J. Sundberg (eds) *Social Democracy in Transition*. Aldershot: Dartmouth.

Katzenstein, P. J. (1985) *Small States in World Markets. Industrial Policy in Europe*. Ithaca: Cornell University Press.

Keegan, W. (2003) *The Prudence of Mr Gordon Brown*. Chichester: John Wiley and Sons.

King, A. (ed.) (2002) *Britain at the Polls 2001*.

Kingdon, J. (1984) *Agendas, Alternatives, and Public Policies*. Boston: Little, Brown and Company.

Kitschelt, H. (1994) *The Transformation of European Social Democracy*. Cambridge: Cambridge University Press.

Kitschelt, H. (1999) 'European social democracy between political economy and electoral competition', in Kitschelt, H. et al. (eds) *Continuity and Change in Contemporary Capitalism*. Cambridge: Cambridge University Press.

Kitschelt, H., Lange, P., Marks, G. and J. D. Stephens (1999) 'Convergence and divergence in advanced capitalist democracies', in Kitschelt, H. et al. (eds) *Continuity and Change in Contemporary Capitalism*. Cambridge: Cambridge University Press.

Kjellberg, A. (2002) 'Nordic trade unions from an international perspective', Paper delivered for the Conference on the International Labour Movement on the Threshold of Two Centuries, Stockholm 24–25 October 2002.

Klingemann, H.-D., Hofferbert, H. I. and I. Budge (1994) *Parties, Policies, and Democracy*. Boulder, San Francisco, Oxford: Westview Press.

Krasner, S. D. (1984) 'Approaches to the State. Alternative conceptions and historical dynamics', *Comparative Politics*, Vol. 16 No. 2.

Labour (1964) *The New Britain*. Election Manifesto (electronic version).

Labour (1966) *Time for Decision*. Election Manifesto (electronic version).

Labour (1970) *Now Britain's Strong – Let's Make it Great to Live in*. Election Manifesto (electronic version).

Labour (1973) *Labour's Programme 1973*. London: Labour Party.

Labour (1974a) *Let us Work Together – Labour's Way out of the Crisis*. Election Manifesto (electronic version).

Labour (1974b) *Britain Will Win With Labour*. Election Manifesto (electronic version).

Labour (1979) *The Labour Way is the Better Way*. Election Manifesto (electronic version).

Labour (1982) *Labour's Programme*. London: Labour Party.

Labour (1983) *The New Hope for Britain.* Election Manifesto.

Labour (1985a) *Jobs and Industry. Investing in Britain.* London: Labour Party.

Labour (1985b) *Jobs and Industry. Working Together for Britain.* London: Labour Party.

Labour (1987) *Britain Will Win With Labour.* Election Manifesto (electronic version).

Labour (1989) *Meet the Challenge, Make the Change.* London: Labour Party.

Labour (1990) *Looking to the Future.* London: Labour Party.

Labour (1992) *It's Time to get Britain Working Again.* Election Manifesto (electronic version).

Labour (1997) *Britain Will be Better With New Labour.* Election Manifesto (electronic version).

Labour (2001) *Labour's Manifesto 2001.* Surrey: HH Associates.

Labour, NEC (1981) *The Socialist Alternative.* London: Labour Party.

Labour, NEC (1984) *A Future that Works.* London: Labour Party.

Labour , NEC (1985) *A New Partnership. A New Britain.* Statements to Conference by The National Executive Committee 1985. London: Labour Party.

Labour, TUC-NEC (1987) *Work to Win.* London: TUC.

Lagergren, F. (1999) *På andra sidan välfärdsstaten* [On the Other Side of the Welfare State]. Stockholm: Symposion.

Laver, M. (1989) 'Party competition and party system change. The interaction of coalition bargaining and electoral competition', *Journal of Theoretical Politics,* Vol. 1 No. 3.

Lewin, L. (1967) *Planhushållningsdebatten* [The Debate on Economic Planning]. Stockholm: Almqvist and Wiksell.

Lewin, L. (1988) *Ideology and Strategy. A Century of Swedish Politics.* Cambridge: Cambridge University Press.

Lijphart, A. (1999) *Patterns of Democracy.* Yale: Yale University Press.

Lindblom, C. (1977) *Politics and Markets. The World's Political-Economic Systems.* New York: Basic Books Inc., Publishers.

Lindbom, A. (2001) '"Dismantling the social democratic welfare model?" Has the Swedish welfare state lost its defining characteristics?' *Scandinavian Political Studies,* Vol. 24 No. 3.

Lindvall, J. (2004) *The Politics of Purpose.* Department of Political Science, Göteborg University, Grafikerna Livréna AB. Kungälv.

Lindvall, J. and B. Rothstein (2004) 'The fall of the strong state', Paper presented at the American Political Science Association Annual Meeting, Chicago 2—5 September 2004.

Lipset, S. M. and S. Rokkan (1967) 'Cleavage Structures, Party Systems and Voter Alignment', in Lipset S. M. and S. Rokkan (eds) *Party Systems and Voter Alignments. Cross National Perspectives.* New York: New York Free Press.

LO (1953) *Trade Unions and Full Employment.* Malmö: Framtiden.

Löwdin, P. (1998) *Det dukade bordet* [The Set Table]. Stockholm: Gotab.

Ludlam, S. (2004) 'New Labour "vested Interests" and the union link', in Ludlam, S. and M. J. Smith (eds) *Governing as New Labour. Policy and Politics under Blair.* Houndmills: Palgrave.

Ludlam, S. and M. J. Smith (eds) (2004) *Governing as New Labour. Policy and Politics under Blair.* Houndmills: Palgrave.

Lundqvist, L. (1988) 'Privatization: Towards a concept for comparative policy analysis', *Journal of Public Policy,* Vol. 8 No. 1.

Lundqvist, L. J. (2000) 'Capacity-building or social construction? Explaining Sweden's shift towards ecological modernisation', *Geoforum,* Vol. 31 No. 1.

McGann Blyth, M. (1999) 'Great Transformations: Economic Ideas and Political Change in the Twentieth Century', mimeo version.

McKay, S. (2001) 'Between flexibility and regulation: Rights, equality and protection at work', *British Journal of Industrial Relations*, Vol. 39 No. 2.

McNamara, K. R. (1998) *The Currency of Ideas. Monetary Politics in the European Union.* Ithaca and London: Cornell University Press.

Martin, H.-P. and H. Schumann (1996) *Globaliseringsfällan* [The Globalisation Trap]. Stockholm: Symposion.

Mau, S. (2003) *The Moral Economy of Welfare States. Britain and Germany Compared.* London: Routledge.

Meidner, R. (1975) *Löntagarfonder* [Wage-Earners' Funds]. Stockholm: Tiden.

Michels, R. (1925) Zur Soziologie des Parteiwesens in der modernen Demokratie. Leipzig: Alfred Kröner Verlag.

Middlemas, K. (1990) *Power, Competition and the State*. Volume 2: *Threats to the Postwar Settlement Britain, 1961–74.* London: Macmillan.

Miles, L. (2000) 'Making peace with the union? The Swedish Social Democratic Party and European integration', in Geyer, R. et al. (eds) *Globalization, Europeanization and the End of Scandinavian Social Democracy?* London: Macmillan Press.

Miller, D. (1989) 'In what sense must socialism be communitarian?' *Social Philosophy and Policy*, Vol. 6 No. 2.

Minkin. L. (1978) *The Labour Party Conference. A Study in the Politics of Intra-Party Democracy.* London: Allen Lane.

Morgan, K. O. (2001) '"New Labour" in historical perspective', in Seldon, A. (ed.) *The Blair Effect. The Blair Government 1997–2001.* London: Little, Brown and Company.

Moses, J. (1994) 'Abdication from national policy autonomy: What's left to leave?' *Politics and Society*, Vol. 22 No. 2.

Moses, J. (1995a) 'The social democratic predicament in the emerging European Union: A capital dilemma', *Journal of European Public Policy*, Vol. 23.

Moses, J. (1995b) 'The fiscal constraints on social democracy', *Nordic Journal of Political Economy*, Vol. 22.

Moses, J. (1998) 'The social democratic predicament and global economic integration', in Coleman, W. D. and G. R. D. Underhill (eds) *Regionalism and Global Economic Integration. Europe, Asia and the Americas.* London: Routledge.

Moses, J. (2000) 'Floating fortunes: Scandinavian full employment in the tumultuous 1970s-1980s', in Geyer, R. et al. (eds) *Globalization, Europeanization and the End of Scandinavian Social Democracy?* London: Macmillan Press.

Mullard, M. (2001) 'New Labour, new public expenditure: The case of cake tomorrow', *Political Quarterly*, Vol. 72. No. 3.

Müller, W. (1997) 'Inside the black box: A confrontation of party executive behaviour and theories of party organizational change', *Party Politics*, Vol. 3 No. 3.

Myrdal, A. (1968) Speech held at the 1968 SAP Party conference. Conference minutes.

Notermans, T. (2000) *Money, Markets, and the State. Social Democratic Economic Policies Since 1918.* Cambridge: Cambridge University Press.

Öberg, P.-O. (1994) *Särintresse och allmänintresse: Korporatismens ansikten* [Particular and Public Interest: The Faces of Corporatism]. Stockholm: Almqwist & Wiksell International.

Olsson, U. (2000) *Att förvalta sitt pund. Marcus Wallenberg 1899–1982.* [Taking Good Care of One's Assets. Marcus Wallenberg 1899–1982]. Ekerlids Förlag.

Opposition Green Paper (1980) *The National Enterprise Board. Labour's State Holding Company.* Report of a Labour Party Study Group. London: Labour Party.

Palme, O. (1976) *Tillsammans kan vi göra ett bra land bättre* [Together We Will Make a Good Country Even Better]. Borås: Tiden.

Palme, O. (1982) *Vår väg ur krisen* [Our Way Out of the Crisis]. Sundbyberg: Scangraf.

Panitch, L and C. Leys (1997) *The End of Parliamentary Socialism. From New Left to New Labour.* London: Verso.

Paterson, W. E. and A. H. Thomas (1986) *The Future of Social Democracy.* Oxford: Clarendon Press.

Peck, J. (2001) 'Neoliberalizing states: Thin policies/hard outcomes', *Progress in Human Geography*, Vol. 25 No. 3.

Peele, G. (1997) 'Political parties', in P. Dunleavy et al. (eds) (1997) *Developments in British Politics.* London: Macmillan Press.

Pennings, P. (1999) 'European social democracy between planning and market: A comparative exploration of trends and variations', *Journal of European Public Policy*, Vol. 6 No. 5.

Persson, G. (1997) *Den som är satt i skuld är inte fri* [He Who is in Debt is not Free]. (Stockholm: Atlas).

Persson, G. (1999) Labour Party Conference speech, Bournemouth, 30 September 1999, http://labour.org.uk/lp/new/labour/labour.wwv_main.main?p_language=usandp_cornerid=1200.

Pestoff, V. A. (1992) *Towards a New Swedish Model: From Neo-Corporatist to Neo-Liberal Priorities for the Welfare state.* Cracow: Cracow Academy of Economics.

Petersson, H. F. (1964) *Power and International Order.* Lund: C W K Gleerup.

Pierre, J. (1986) *Partikongresser och regeringspolitik* [Party Congresses and Government Politics]. Lund: Kommunfakta förlag.

Pierre, J. (1999) *Marknaden som politisk aktör* [The Market as a Political Actor] SOU 1999: 131.

Pierson, P. (1994) *Dismantling the Welfare State? Reagan, Thatcher, and the Politics of Retrenchment.* Cambridge: Cambridge University Press.

Pilkington, C. (1998) *Issues in British Politics.* London: Macmillan Press.

Pontusson, J. (1992a) *The Limits of Social Democracy. Investment Politics in Sweden.* Ithaca and London: Cornell University Press.

Pontusson, J. (1992b) 'At the end of the third road: Swedish social democracy in crisis', *Politics and Society*, Vol. 20 No. 3.

Prabhakar, R. (2004) 'New Labour and the reform of public services', in Ludlam, S. and M. J. Smith (eds) (2004) *Governing as New Labour. Policy and Politics under Blair.* Houndmills: Palgrave.

Przeworski, A. (1987) *Capitalism and Social Democracy.* Cambridge: Cambridge University Press.

Radice, G. (2002) *Friends and Rivals.* Boston: Little, Brown and Company.

Rhen, G. (1957) 'Hata inflationen' [Hate Inflation], *Tiden*, Vol. 49 No. 2.

Rhodes, M. (1998) '"Subversive liberalism." Market integration, globalization and West European welfare states', in Coleman, W. D. and G. R. D. Underhill (eds) *Regionalism and Global Economic Integration. Europe, Asia and the Americas.* London: Routledge.

Rhodes, M. (2000) 'Desperately seeking a solution: Social democracy, Thatcherism and the "third way" in British welfare', *West European Politics*, Vol. 23 No. 2.

Richardson, J. J. (ed.) (1982) *Policy Styles in Western Europe.* London: George Allen and Unwin.

Riksdag [Parliament] minutes of the Swedish Riksdag.

Robertson, D. (1976) *A Theory of Party Competition.* London: John Wiley and Sons.

Rose, R. (1993) *Lesson-Drawing in Public Policy. A Guide to Learning Across Time and Space.* Chatham, New Jersey: Chatham House Publishers, Inc.

Rose, R. and P. L. Davies (1994) *Inheritance in Public Policy. Change Without Choice in Britain*. New Haven and London: Yale University Press.

Ross, F. (2000) 'Interests and choice in the "Not Quite so New" politics of welfare', *West European Politics*, Vol. 23 No. 2.

Rothstein, B. (1992) 'Explaining Swedish corporatism: The formative moment', *Scandinavian Political Studies*, Vol. 15 No. 3.

Rothstein, B. (1993) 'The crisis of the Swedish Social Democrats and the future of the universal welfare state', *Governance*, Vol. 6 No. 4.

Rothstein, B. (1996) 'Political institutions: An overview', in Goodin, R. E. and H-D. Klingemann (eds) *A New Handbook of Political Science*. Oxford: Oxford University Press.

Sainsbury, D. (1996) *Gender, Equality and Welfare states*. Cambridge: Cambridge University Press.

SAP (1964a) Party Congress minutes.

SAP (1964b) *Resultat och reformer, riktlinjer för socialdemokratisk politik* [Results and Reforms, Guidelines for Social Democratic Politics]. Stockholm.

SAP (1968a) Party Congress minutes.

SAP (1968b) *1968 Election Manifesto*, electronic version provided by the *Swedish Social Science Data Service*, Gothenburg University.

SAP (1970) *1970 Election Manifesto*, electronic version provided by *Swedish Social Science Data Service*, Gothenburg University.

SAP (1973) *1973 Election Manifesto*, electronic version provided by *Swedish Social Science Data Service*, Gothenburg University.

SAP (1974) Party Programme Draft.

SAP (1975) *Party programme*, electronic version provided by *Swedish Social Science Data Service*, Gothenburg University.

SAP (1976) *1976 Election Manifesto*, electronic version provided by *Swedish Social Science Data Service*, Gothenburg University.

SAP (1979) *1979 Election Manifesto*, electronic version provided by *Swedish Social Science Data Service*, Gothenburg University.

SAP (1981) *Framtid för Sverige* [Future for Sweden]. Jönköping: SAP/Tiden.

SAP (1982) *1982 Election Manifesto*, electronic version provided by *Swedish Social Science Data Service*, Gothenburg University.

SAP (1985) *1985 Election Manifesto*, electronic version provided by *Swedish Social Science Data Service*, Gothenburg University.

SAP (1988) *1988 Election Manifesto*, electronic version provided by *Swedish Social Science Data Service*, Gothenburg University.

SAP (1990) *90–talsprogrammet* [The 90s Programme], electronic version provided by *Swedish Social Science Data Service*, Gothenburg University.

SAP (1991) *1991 Election Manifesto*, electronic version provided by *Swedish Social Science Data Service*, Gothenburg University.

SAP (1994) *1994 Election Manifesto*, electronic version provided by *Swedish Social Science Data Service*, Gothenburg University.

SAP (1998) *1998 Election Manifesto*, electronic version provided by *Swedish Social Science Data Service*, Gothenburg University.

SAP (2000) Party Programme Draft.

SAP (2001) *Party Programme*, electronic version provided by *Swedish Social Science Data Service*, Gothenburg University.

SAP (2002) *2002 Election Manifesto*, electronic version provided by *Swedish Social Science Data Service*, Gothenburg University.

SAP and LO (1968) *Program för aktiv näringspolitik* [Programme for an Active Industrial and Enterprise Policy]. Stockholm.

SAP and LO (1969) *Jämlikhet* [Equality]. Stockholm.

SAP and LO (1972) *Jämlikhet* [Equality]. Stockholm: Prisma.

SAP and LO (1974) *Välfärd och arbete åt alla, riktlinjer för sysselsättningspolitiken* [Welfare and Employment for All, Guidelines for Employment Policy].

Särlvik, B. (1983) 'Coalition politics and policy output in Scandinavia: Sweden, Denmark and Norway', in Bogdanor, V. (ed.) *Coalition Government in Western Europe*. Guildford: Heinemann Educational Books.

Särlvik, B. (2002) 'Party and electoral system in Sweden', in Grofman, B. and A. Lijphart (eds) *The Evolution of Electoral and Party Systems in the Nordic Countries*. New York: Agathon Press.

Sassoon, D. (1996) *One Hundred Years of Socialism. The West European Left in the Twentieth Century*. London, New York: I. B. Tauris Publishers.

Savage, S. P. and R. Atkinson (eds) (2001) *Public Policy under Blair*. Houndmills: Palgrave.

Scase, R. (1977) *Social Democracy in Capitalist Society*. London: Croom Helm.

Schlytter, A. (1993) *Om rättvisa i barnomsorgen: den kommunala barnomsorgens fördelningsregler ur ett vardagsperspektiv* [On Fairness in the Child Care System: The Municipal Child Care Allocation Rules from an Every-Day Perspective]. Stockholm: Centrum för kvinnoforskning vid Stockholms universitet.

Scholte, J. A. (2000) *Globalization. A Critical Introduction*. Basingstoke: Macmillan.

Seldon, A. (ed.) (2001) *The Blair Effect. The Blair Government 1997–2001*. London: Little, Brown and Company.

Seliger, M. (1976) *Ideology and Politics*. London: Allen and Unwin.

Selle, P. (1991) 'The idea of equality and security in Nordic social democracy', in Karvonen, L. and J. Sundberg (eds) *Social Democracy in Transition*. Aldershot: Dartmouth.

Shaw, E. (1993) 'Toward renewal? The British Labour Party's policy review', *West European Politics*, Vol. 16 No. 1.

Shaw, E. (1994) *The Labour Party Since 1979. Crisis and Transformation*. London and New York: Routledge.

Shaw, E. (1996) *The Labour Party Since 1945*. Oxford: Blackwell Publishers.

Shaw, E. (2002) 'The role of the British Labour Party a century on', Paper delivered for the Conference on the International Labour Movement on the Threshold of Two Centuries, Stockholm 24–25 October 2002.

Shaw, E. (2003) 'What matters is what works: The third way and the case of the private finance initiative', in Leggett, W. et al. (eds) *The Third Way and Beyond: Criticisms, Futures and Alternatives*. Manchester: Manchester University Press.

Shaw, E. (2004) 'The control freaks? New Labour and the party', in Ludlam, S. and M. J. Smith (eds) (2004) *Governing as New Labour. Policy and Politics under Blair*. Houndmills: Palgrave.

Shonfield, A. (1965) *Modern Capitalism*. Oxford and New York: Oxford University Press.

Simmons, B. (1999) 'The internationalization of capital', in Kitschelt, H. et al. (eds) *Continuity and Change in Contemporary Capitalism*. Cambridge: Cambridge University Press.

Simon, H. A. (1966) *Administrative Behavior*. New York: The Free Press.

Sinclair, P. (2001) 'The financial sector: Delegation, unification and optimism', in Seldon, A. (ed.) (2001) *The Blair Effect. The Blair Government 1997–2001*. London: Little, Brown and Company.

Sjöblom, G. (1968) *Party Strategies in a Multiparty System*. Lund: Studentlitteratur.

Skinner, Q. (1974) 'Some problems in the analysis of political thought and action', *Political*

Theory, Vol. 2 No. 3.

Skinner, Q. (1978) *The Foundation of Modern Political Thought. Volume One, The Renaissance.* Cambridge: Cambridge University Press.

Skoglund, R. (2000) 'Synen på marknaden. En undersökning av socialdemokratiska regeringars syn på marknaden mellan 1965 och 1995' [Market Views. A Study of Social Democratic Governments' 1965–1995 Market Views], Department of Political Science, Göteborg University, Göteborg, mimeo version.

Skolverket (2004a) *Beskrivande data 2004* [Descriptive Data 2004]. Rapport 248.

Skolverket (2004b) Pressmeddelande (Press Release), 22 December. http://skolverket.se/publicerat/press/press2004/press041222.shtml.

Smith, G. (1988) 'Between left and right: the ambivalence of European liberalism', in Kirchner, E. J. (ed.) (1988) *Liberal Parties in Western Europe.* Cambridge: Cambridge University Press.

Smith, M. (1994) 'Understanding the politics of "catch-up": The modernization of the Labour Party', *Political Studies,* Vol. 42 No. 4.

Smith, M. J. (1992) 'Continuity and change in Labour Party policy', in Smith, M. J. and J. Spear (eds) *The Changing Labour Party.* London: Routledge.

SOU 1951 No. 51 [The 1951 Royal Parliamentary Investigation Committee Report No. 51] *Den direkta statliga beskattningen* [The Direct State Taxation].

SOU 1967 No. 52 [The 1967 Royal Parliamentary Investigation Committee Report No. 52] *Barnbidrag och familjetillägg* [Child and Family Allowances].

SOU 1972 No. 34 [The 1972 Royal Parliamentary Investigation Committee Report No. 34] *Familjestöd* [Family Support].

SOU 1983 No. 14 [The 1983 Royal Parliamentary Investigation Committee Report # 14] *Barn kostar. . .* [Children Cost. . .].

Smith, M. J. and J. Spear (eds) (1992) *The Changing Labour Party.* London: Routledge.

Steinmo, S. (1993) *Taxation and Democracy: Swedish, British and American Approaches to Financing the Modern State.* Yale University Press.

Steinmo, S. (2003) 'Bucking the trend? The welfare state and the global economy: The Swedish case up close', *New Political Economy,* Vol. 8 No. 1.

Steinmo, S., Thelen, K. and F. Longstreth (eds) (1992) *Structuring Politics. Historical Institutionalism in Comparative Analysis.* Cambridge: Cambridge University Press.

Stephens, J. D., Huber, E. and L. Ray (1999) 'The welfare state in hard times', in Kitschelt, H. et al. (eds) *Continuity and Change in Contemporary Capitalism.* Cambridge: Cambridge University Press.

Stephens, P. (2001) 'The Treasury under Labour', in Seldon, A. (ed.) *The Blair Effect. The Blair Government 1997–2001.* London: Little, Brown and Company.

Stewart, M. (1977) *The Jekyll and Hyde Years. Politics and Economic Policy since 1964.* London: J. M. Dent and Sons Ltd.

Stiglitz, J. (1997) *Economics.* New York: W. W. Norton and Co.

Stinchcombe, A. L. (1979) *On Norwegian Social Democracy: An Introduction for Non-Norwegians.* Bergen: Industriøkonomisk institutt.

Strange, S. (1971) *Sterling and British Policy.* Oxford: Oxford University Press.

Svallfors, S. (1999) Mellan risk och tilltro: Opinionsstödet för kollektiv välfärdspolitik [Between Risk and Confidence: Opinion Support for Collective Welfare Policy]. Umeå Universitet.

Svensson, T. (1994) *Socialdemokratins dominans. En studie av den svenska socialdemokratins partistrategi* [The Dominance of Social Democracy. A Study of the Swedish Social Democracy's Party Strategy]. 1994 Uppsala: Acta Universitatis Upsaliensis

Svensson, T. (2001) *Marknadsanpassningens politik. Den svenska modellens förändring 1980–2000* [The Politics of Market Adaptation. The 1980–2000 Swedish Model Change]. Uppsala, Acta Universitatis Upsaliensis.

Swank, D. (1997) 'Social democratic welfare states in a global economy: Scandinavia in comparative perspective', Paper prepared for presentation at the 1997 Annual Meetings for the American Political Science Association.

Swank, D. (2000) 'Social democratic welfare states in a global economy: Scandinavia in comparative perspective', in Geyer, R. et al. (eds) *Globalization, Europeanization and the End of Scandinavian Social Democracy?* London: Macmillan Press.

Swenson, P. (1989) *Fair Shares. Unions, Pay, and Politics in Sweden and West Germany.* Ithaca and London: Cornell University Press.

Taylor, R. (2001a) 'Employment relations policy', in Seldon, A. (ed.) *The Blair Effect: The Blair Government 1997–2001.* New York: Little Brown and Co.

Taylor, M. (2001b) 'Too early to say? New Labour's first term', *Political Quarterly,* Vol. 72 No. 1.

Thelen, K. and S. Steinmo (1992) 'Historical institutionalism in comparative politics', in Steinmo, S. et al. (eds) (1992) *Structuring Politics. Historical Institutionalism in Comparative Analysis.* Cambridge: Cambridge University Press.

Thomas, R. (2001) 'UK economic policy: The Conservative legacy and New Labour's third way', in Savage, S. P. and R. Atkinson (eds) *Public Policy Under Blair.* Houndmills, Palgrave.

Thompson, N. (1996) *Political Economy and the Labour Party. The Economics of Democratic Socialism 1884–1995.* London: UCL Press.

Thomson, S. (2000) *The Social Democratic Dilemma. Ideology, Governance and Globalization.* London: Macmillan Press.

Tingsten, H. (1966) *Från idéer till idyll. Den lyckliga demokratien* [From Ideas to Idyll. The Happy Democracy]. Stockholm: Norstedts.

Tilton, T. (1990) *The Political Theory of Swedish Social Democracy.* Oxford: Clarendon Press.

Tilton, T. (1992) 'The role of ideology in social democratic politics', in Misgeld, K. et al. (eds) *Creating Social Democracy. A Century of the Social Democratic Labor Party in Sweden.* University Park, Pennsylvania: The Pennsylvania State University Press.

Tomasson, R. F. (1973) 'Introduction', in Tingsten, H. (ed.) *The Swedish Social Democrats. Their Ideological Development.* New Jersey: Bedminster Press.

Uhrwing, M. (2001) *Tillträde till maktens rum* [Access to the Offices of Power]. Hedemora: Gidlunds Förlag.

UK National Statistics (2005) http://statistics.gov.uk/healthaccounts/international_comparison_total_health_expenditure.asp.

Undy, R. (1999) 'New Labour's 'industrial relations settlement', *Representation,* Vol. 37 No. 3/4.

Wagschal, U. (1998) 'Parties, party systems and policy effects', in Pennings, P. and J-E. Lane (eds) (1998) *Comparing Party System Change.* London and New York: Routledge.

Wainwright, H. (1987) *Labour. A Tale of Two Parties.* London: The Hogarth Press.

Walker, D. (1987) 'The first Wilson Governments 1964–1970', in Hennessy, P. and A. Seldon (eds) *Ruling Performance. British Governments from Attlee to Thatcher.* Oxford: Basil Blackwell.

Weiss, L. (1998) *The Myth of the Powerless State. Governing the Economy in a Global Era.* Cambridge: Polity Press.

Wickham-Jones, M. (1995) 'Anticipating social democracy, preempting anticipations: Economic policy-making in the British Labour Party, 1987–1992', *Politics and Society*, Vol. 23 No. 4.

Wickham-Jones, M. (2000) 'New Labour in the global economy: Partisan politics and the social democratic model', *British Journal of Politics and International Relations*, Vol. 2 No. 1.

Wickham-Jones, M. (2002) 'British Labour, European social democracy and the reformist trajectory: A reply to Coates', *British Journal of Politics and International Relations*, Vol. 4 No. 3.

Widfeldt, A. (1999) *Linking Parties With People? Party Membership in Sweden 1960–1997*. Aldershot: Ashgate.

Wilde, L. (1994) 'Swedish social democracy and the world market', in Palan, R. P. and B. Gills (eds) (1994) *Transcending the State-Global Divide. A Neostructuralist Agenda in International Relations*. Boulder and London: Lynne Rienner Publishers.

Wilson, H. (1979) *Final Term, the Labour Government 1974–76*. London: Weidenfeld and Nicolson and Michael Joseph.

Winberg, E. (1997) 'Sjukförsäkringen under 90–talet. De politiska turerna runt förändringen av den svenska sjukförsäkringen' [The Sick Leave Insurance During the 1990s. The Political Twists Concerning Changes in the Swedish Sick Leave Insurance], Department of Political Science, Göteborg University, Göteborg, mimeo version.

Woodward, N. (1993) 'Labour's economic performance 1964–70', in Coopey, R., Fielding, S. and N. Tiratsoo (eds) *The Wilson Governments 1964–1970*. London and New York: Pinter Publishers.

Index